SAMUEL L. JACKSON

COLD SPACE

ERIC CALDERON JEREMY ROCK

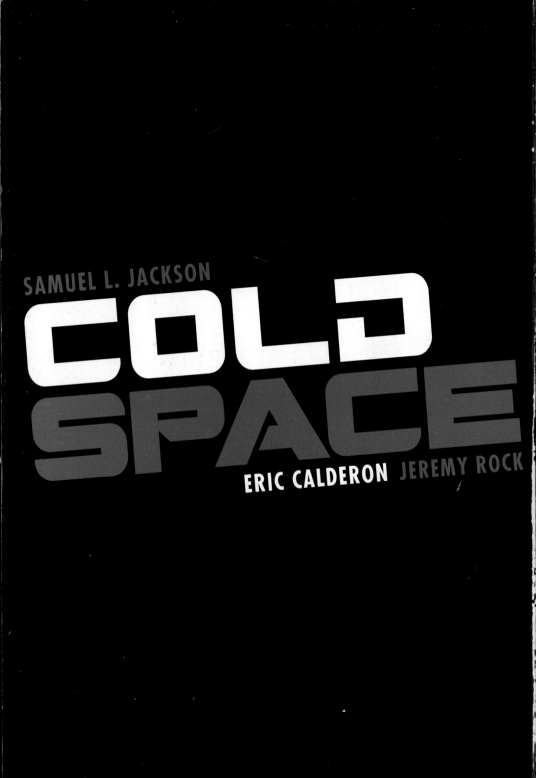

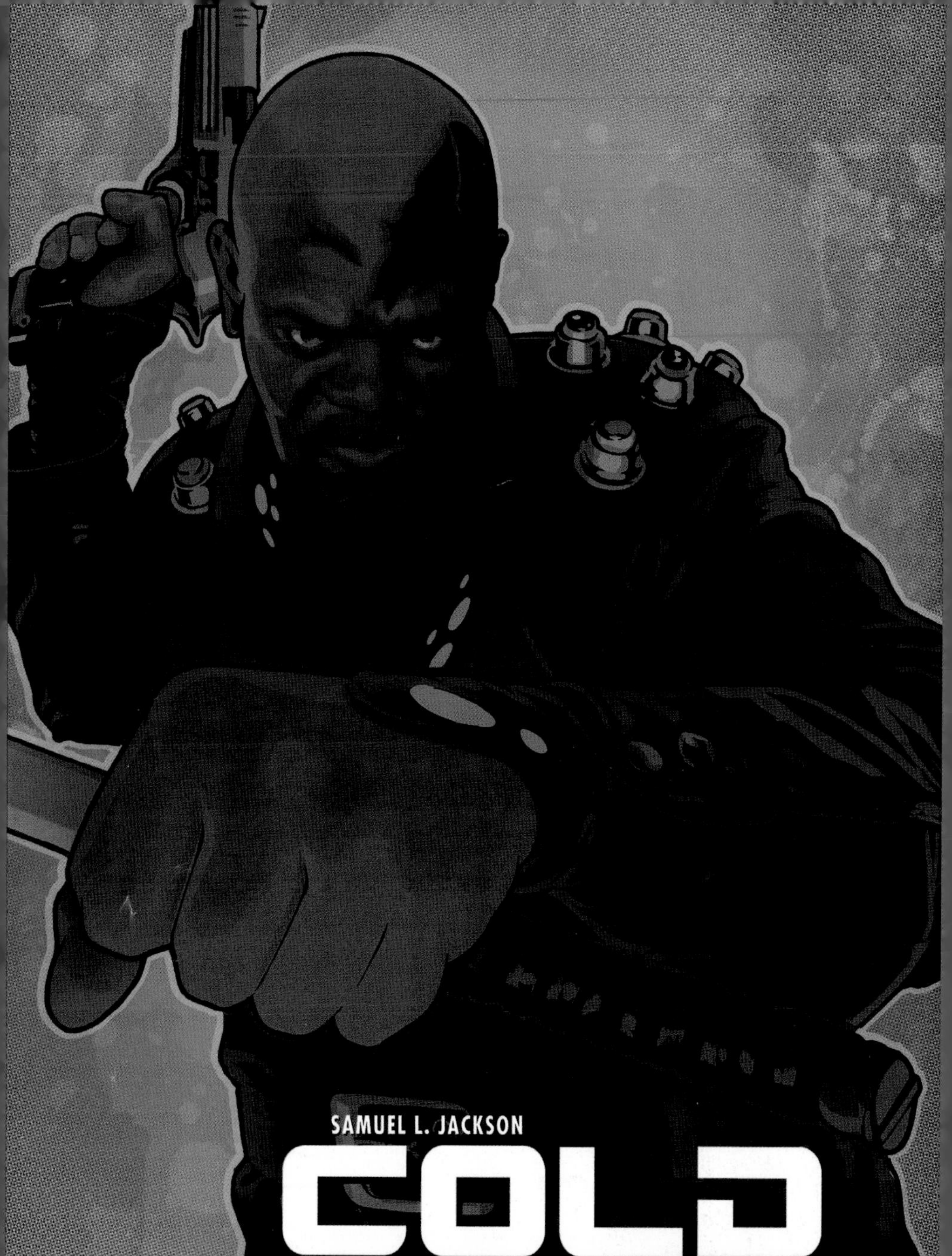
SAMUEL L. JACKSON
COLD
SPACE
ERIC CALDERON JEREMY ROCK

FREY SPOKES

SAMUEL L. JACKSON

COLD SPACE

ERIC CALDERON   JEREMY ROCK

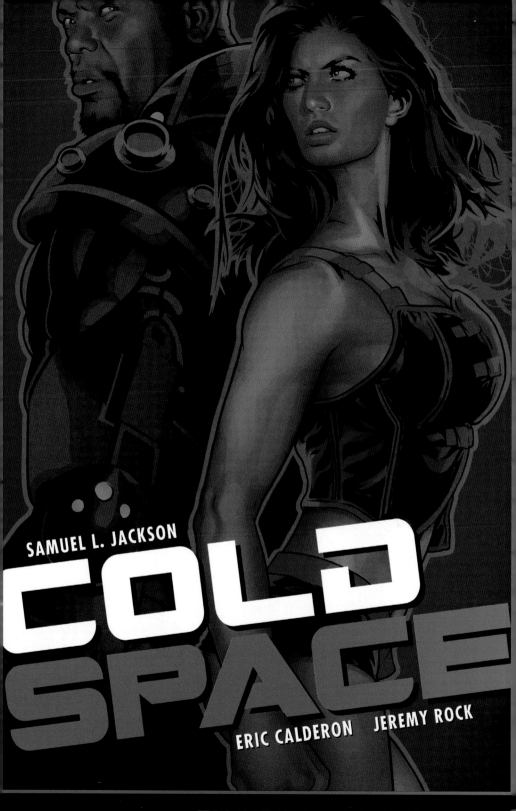

SAMUEL L. JACKSON

COLD SPACE

ERIC CALDERON   JEREMY ROCK

COVER 3B: JEFFREY SPOKES

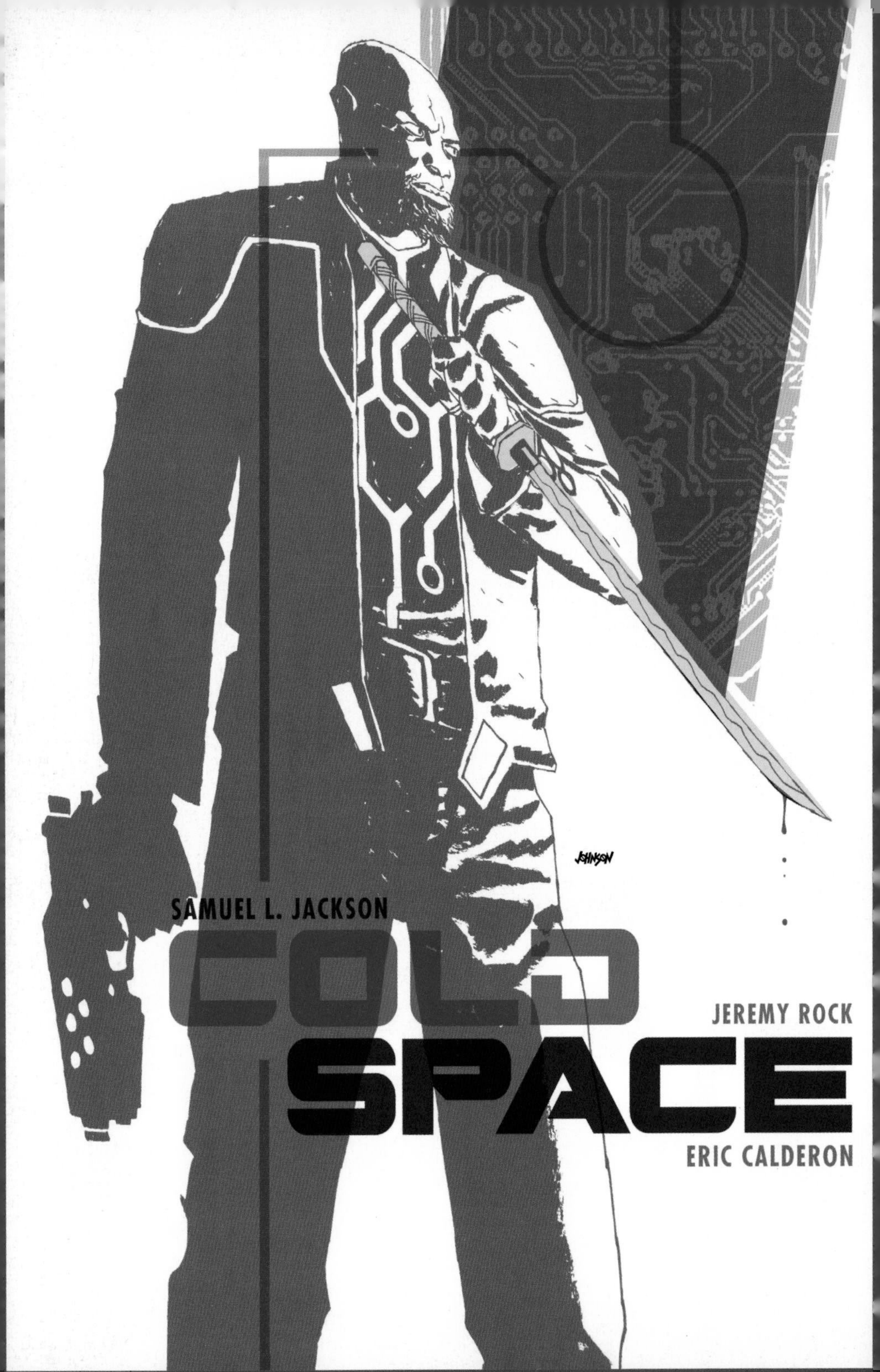
JOHNSON
SAMUEL L. JACKSON
COLD
JEREMY ROCK
SPACE
ERIC CALDERON

COVER 3A: DA

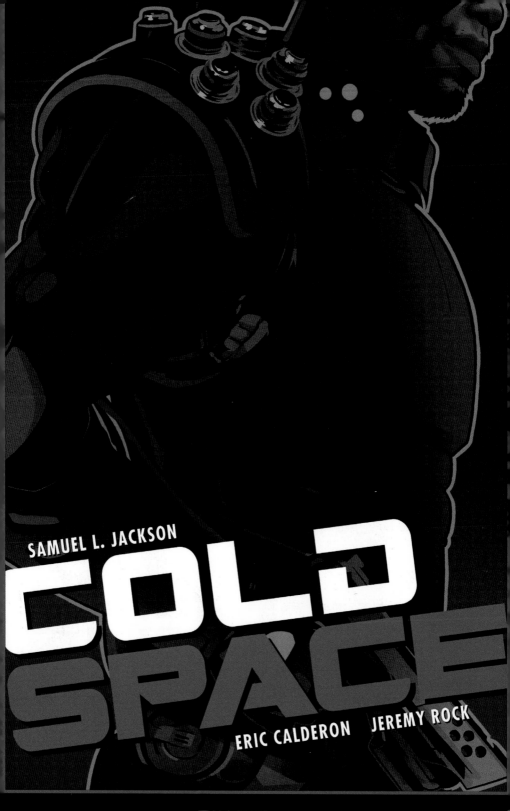

SAMUEL L. JACKSON

COLD SPACE

ERIC CALDERON   JEREMY ROCK

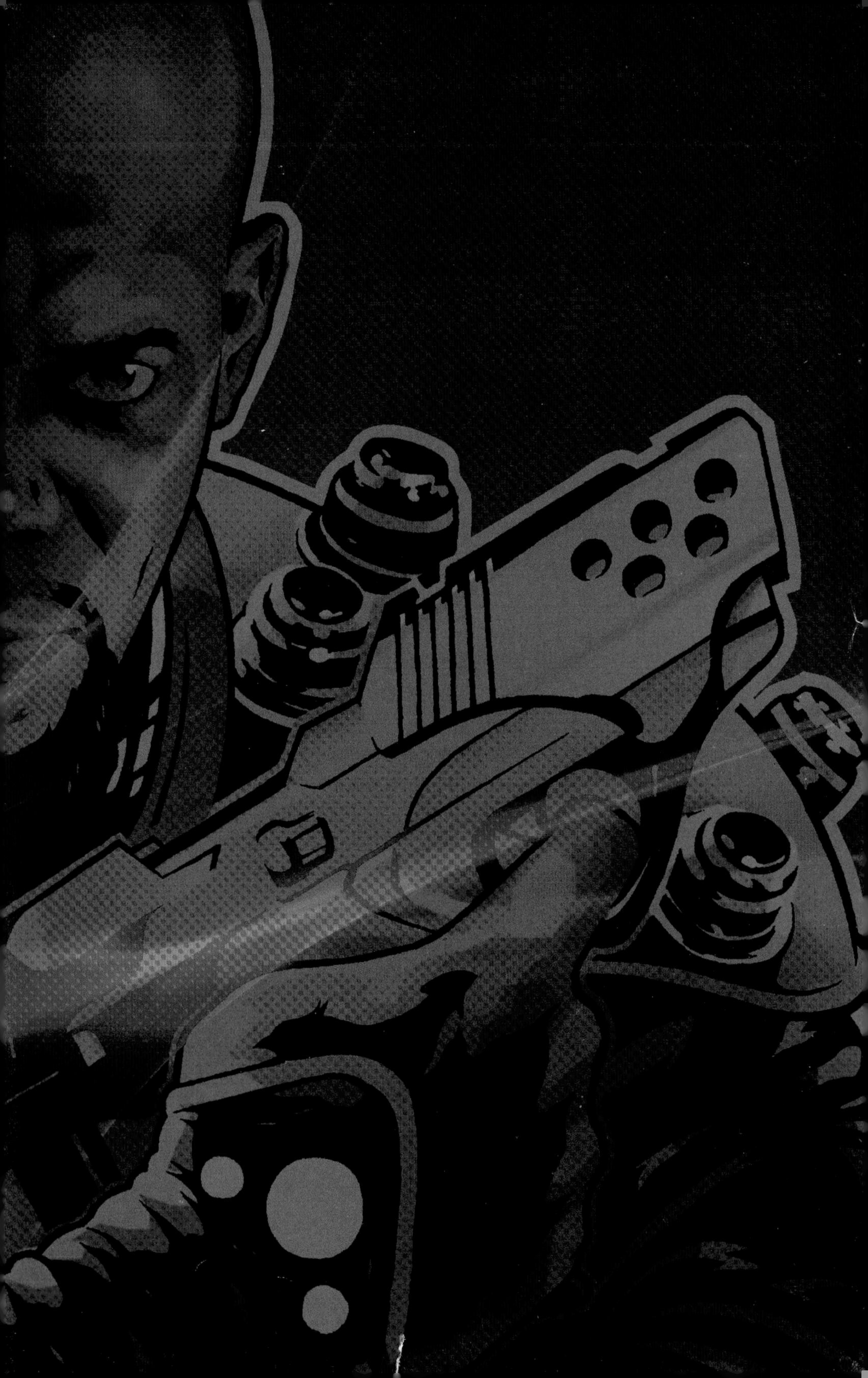

WRITTEN AND CREATED BY
SAMUEL L. JACKSON
ERIC CALDERON

ART
JEREMY ROCK

COLORS
JUAN MANUEL TUMBURÚS

LETTERS
TROY PETERI

COVER
JEFFREY SPOKES

INTRODUCTION
SAMUEL L. JACKSON

EDITOR
BRYCE CARLSON

DESIGNER
BRIAN LATIMER

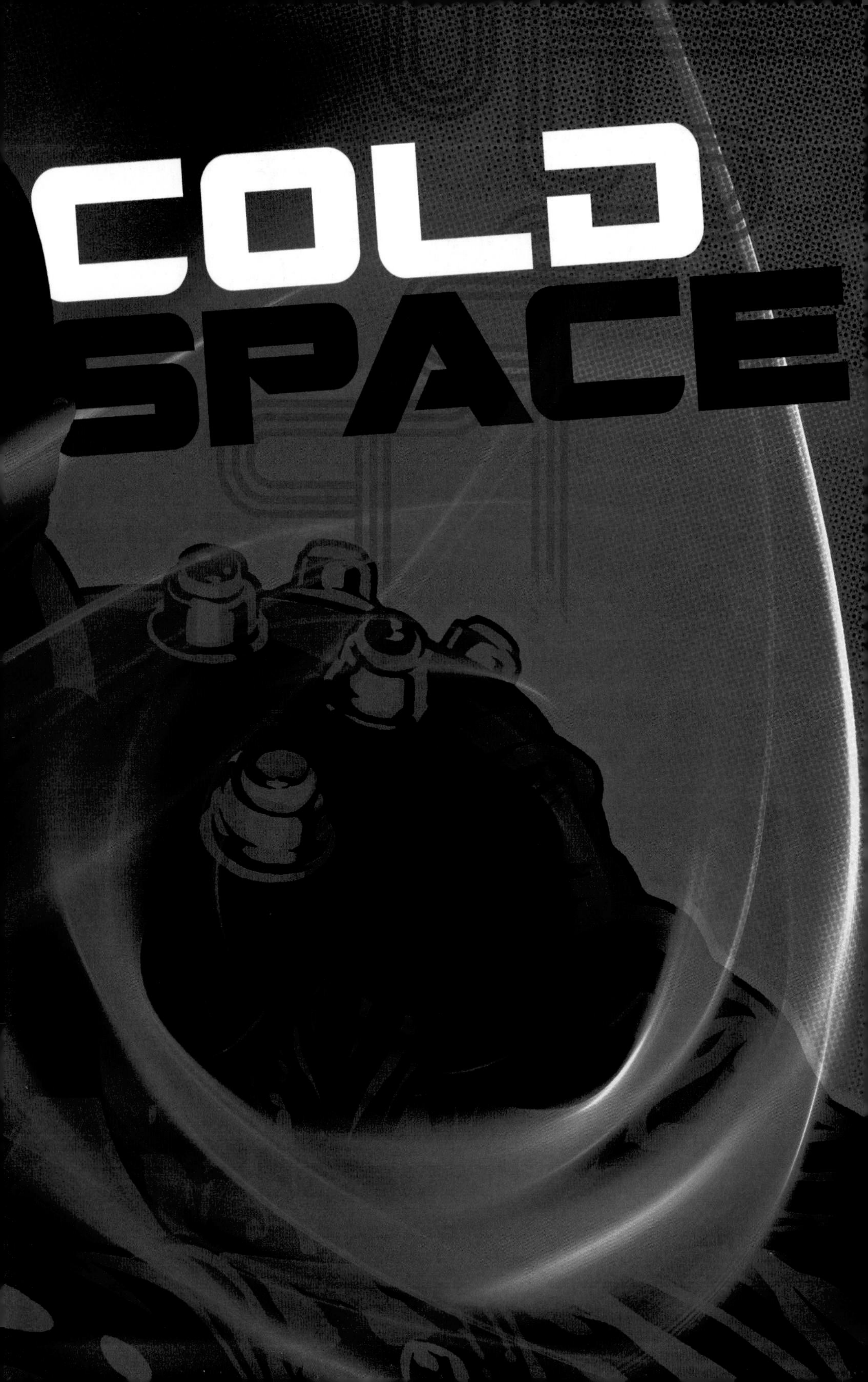
COLD
SPACE

I like comics. Everybody who knows me knows it. You may have heard it before, too. If not—then now you know.

If I'm not working, acting, or playing golf—it's likely I'm reading comics.

Right now, I may be the kind of guy who's always surrounded by people, but growing up as an only child in Chattanooga, Tennessee, escaping into the world of comics was part of how I explored my imagination. My mother used to allow me one comic for every "real" book I got. I read the army stuff, horror, westerns, early Marvel heroes, and whatever I could get.

Now, my taste is pretty broad. I read the superhero stuff. Sure, why not. But I dig pretty deep too. I mostly like cop and crime dramas, thrillers, stuff with a foundation in history, and classic samurai manga. But luckily, because of who I am, I also get lots of stuff sent to me—which I'm usually more than happy to read.

So, maybe now you're asking why a guy like me is suddenly making his own comic. I'll tell you why. Go back to the first sentence. Now read it again. You heard me. Read it again. We clear?

Good. 'Cause now I wanna talk about COLD SPACE.

First of all, I gotta thank Eric, the co-creator on COLD SPACE who really got this whole project started. As one of the producers on AFRO SAMURAI, he and I have been working together since around 2004. We dig lots of the same stuff. We refer movie titles, comics, and anime to each other...Mostly me to him. But sometimes he surprises me with something I haven't heard about. It's all good.

Eric came to me with the idea of making an original comic that just puts together all the things we like—science fiction, cowboy westerns, and lone samurai wanderers. In a way, they're all cut from the same mold.

Oh yeah, there's one other thing we like too: money. Ha. That's not what you think. Of course I got no problem with having and making money. But, what I'm talkin' about is a character who loves money. Cause when it gets down to it, that's what our man Mulberry is really after.

Occasionally, it may look like he's trying to do the right thing, falling for a girl, or gettin' angry enough to kill somebody. But what we thought would be funny, tricky, and even a little villainous is to make a hero who wants the big score more than all that other stuff.

Maybe he's got people after him. Maybe he just wants to be left alone with no worries. But for now, he's not saying. What he is saying is that the deal is what matters most. Think of Han Solo if he had no debt and no Luke Skywalker, or the lead character in Akira Kurosawa's classic film YOJIMBO (whose name is NOT "Yojimbo" by the way) if he had a space pistol. From there, the thing really started writing itself. We just drop our man into any kind of world, and he starts to hustle.

As for the worlds, we had an idea there too. Since I've already been in the Star Wars universe, I wasn't so interested in a character who wandered around perfect white towers and high tech cities. I also didn't want a guy who walked around talkin' to diplomats and senators and worrying about galactic wars. So, I threw to Eric that this should take place in the ghettos—in the places off the beaten path. In that sense, it's just a space western. It's all about a nameless guy wandering into a town and trouble begins…

Now read it 'cause I say So!

Samuel L. Jackson

Samuel L. Jackson

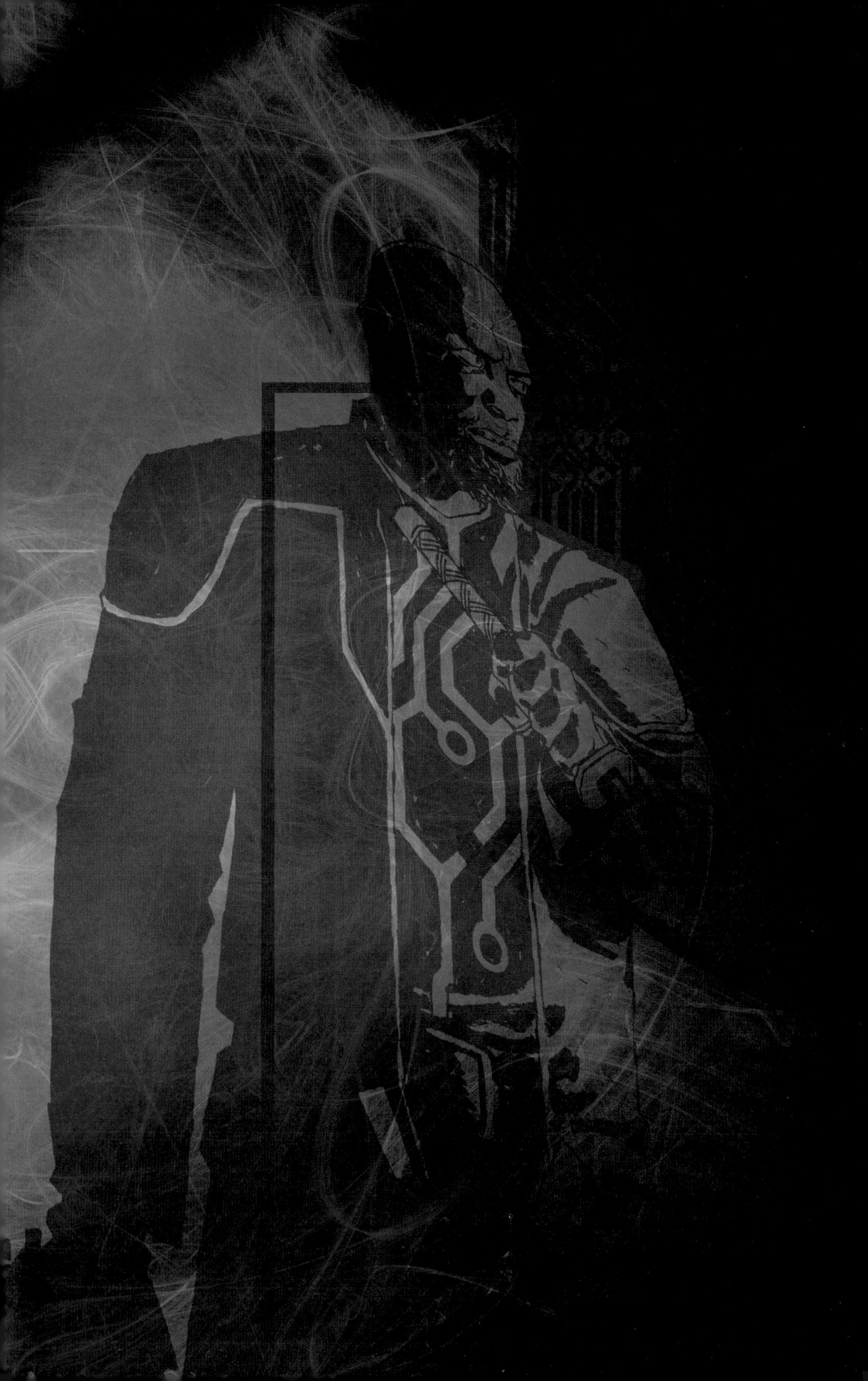

COLD SPACE

CHAPTER 1

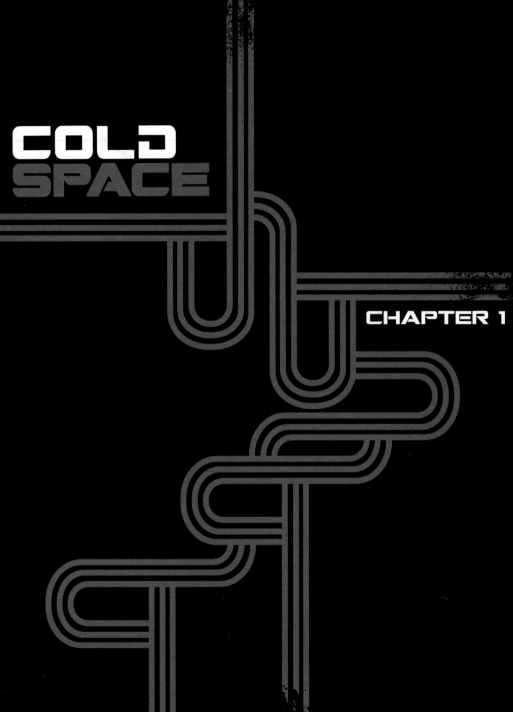

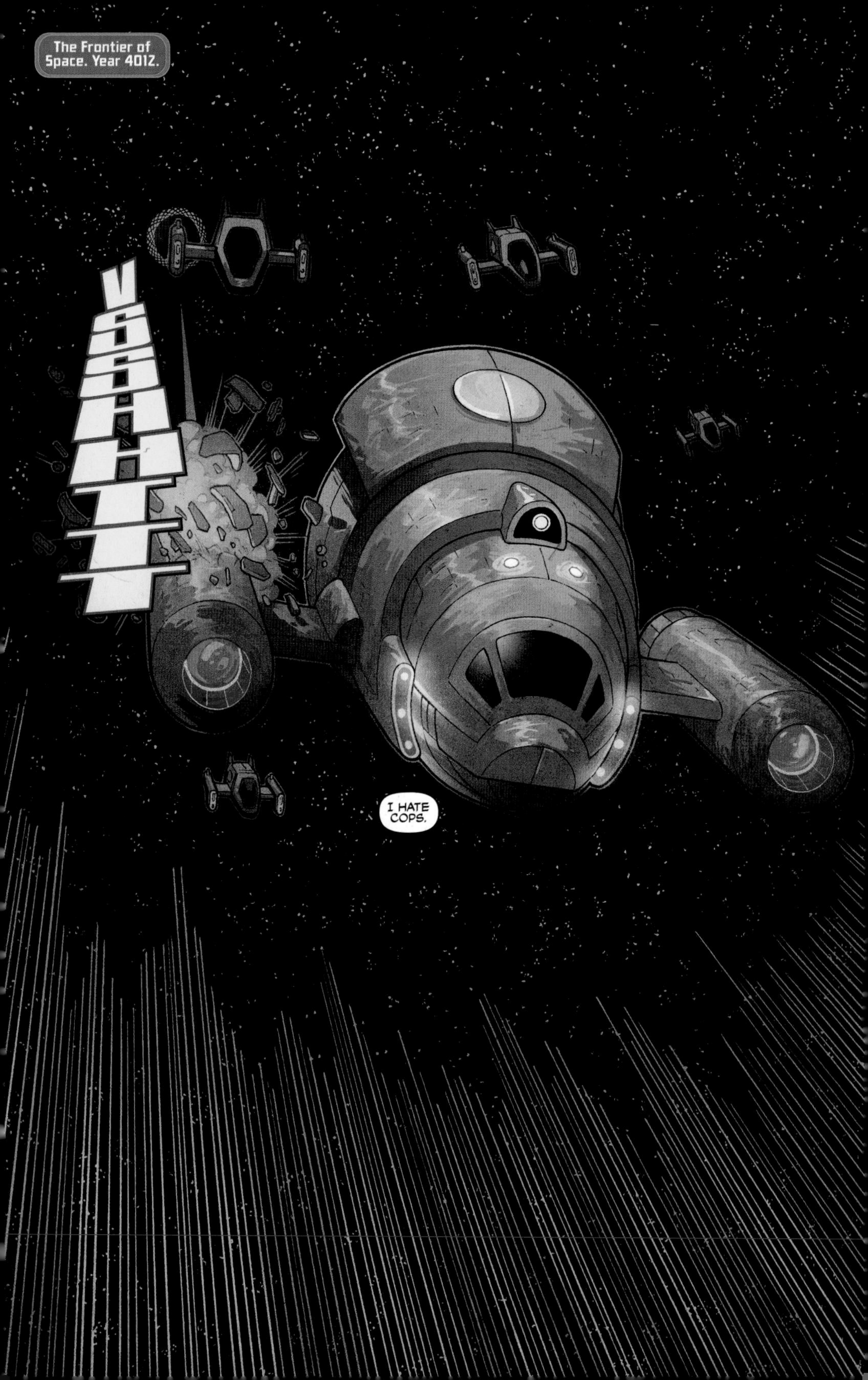
The Frontier of Space. Year 4012.
VSSHHTTT
I HATE COPS.

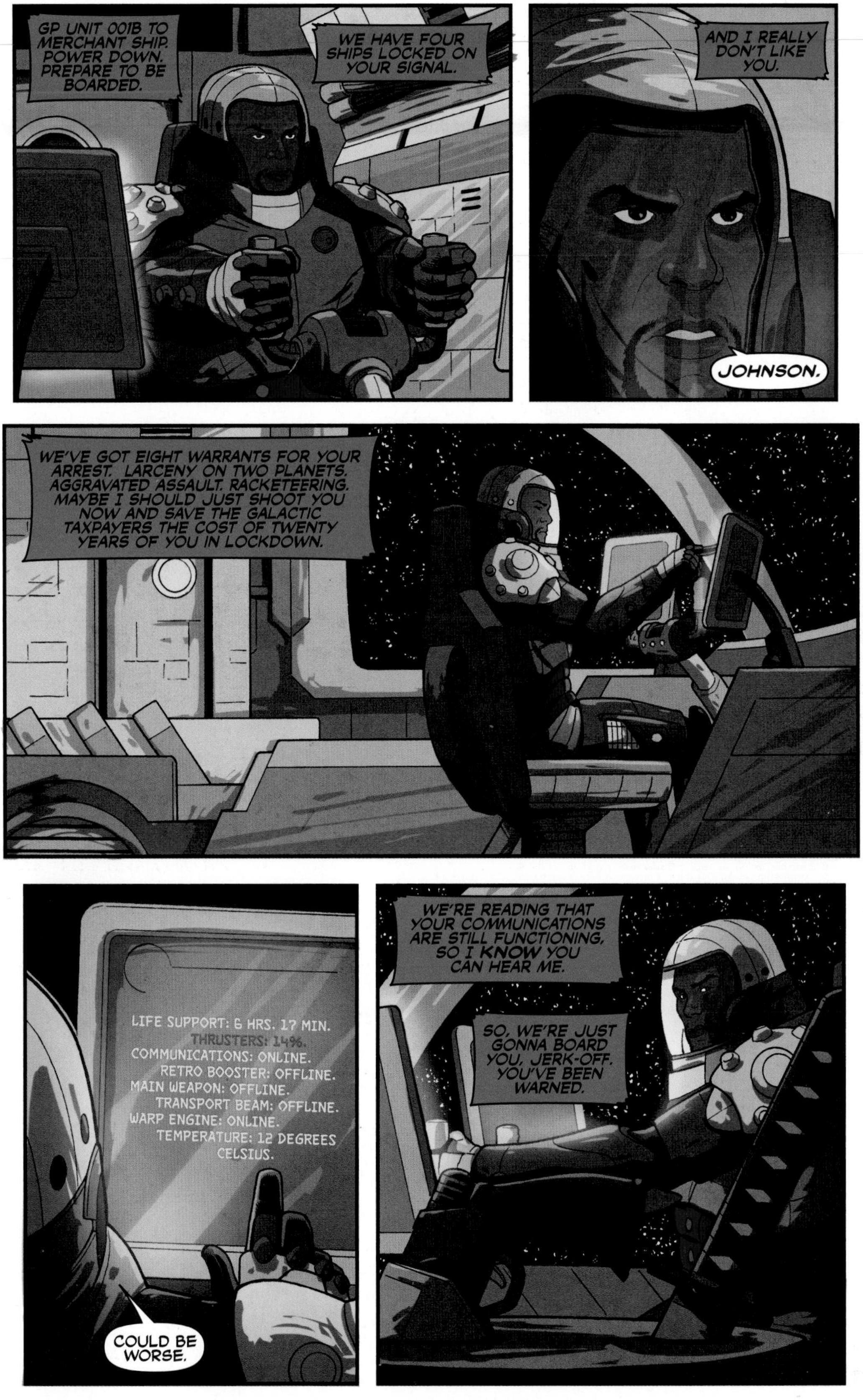
GP UNIT 001B TO MERCHANT SHIP. POWER DOWN. PREPARE TO BE BOARDED.
WE HAVE FOUR SHIPS LOCKED ON YOUR SIGNAL.
AND I REALLY DON'T LIKE YOU.
JOHNSON.
WE'VE GOT EIGHT WARRANTS FOR YOUR ARREST. LARCENY ON TWO PLANETS. AGGRAVATED ASSAULT. RACKETEERING. MAYBE I SHOULD JUST SHOOT YOU NOW AND SAVE THE GALACTIC TAXPAYERS THE COST OF TWENTY YEARS OF YOU IN LOCKDOWN.
LIFE SUPPORT: 6 HRS. 17 MIN.
THRUSTERS: 14%.
COMMUNICATIONS: ONLINE.
RETRO BOOSTER: OFFLINE.
MAIN WEAPON: OFFLINE.
TRANSPORT BEAM: OFFLINE.
WARP ENGINE: ONLINE.
TEMPERATURE: 12 DEGREES CELSIUS.
COULD BE WORSE.
WE'RE READING THAT YOUR COMMUNICATIONS ARE STILL FUNCTIONING, SO I KNOW YOU CAN HEAR ME.
SO, WE'RE JUST GONNA BOARD YOU, JERK-OFF. YOU'VE BEEN WARNED.

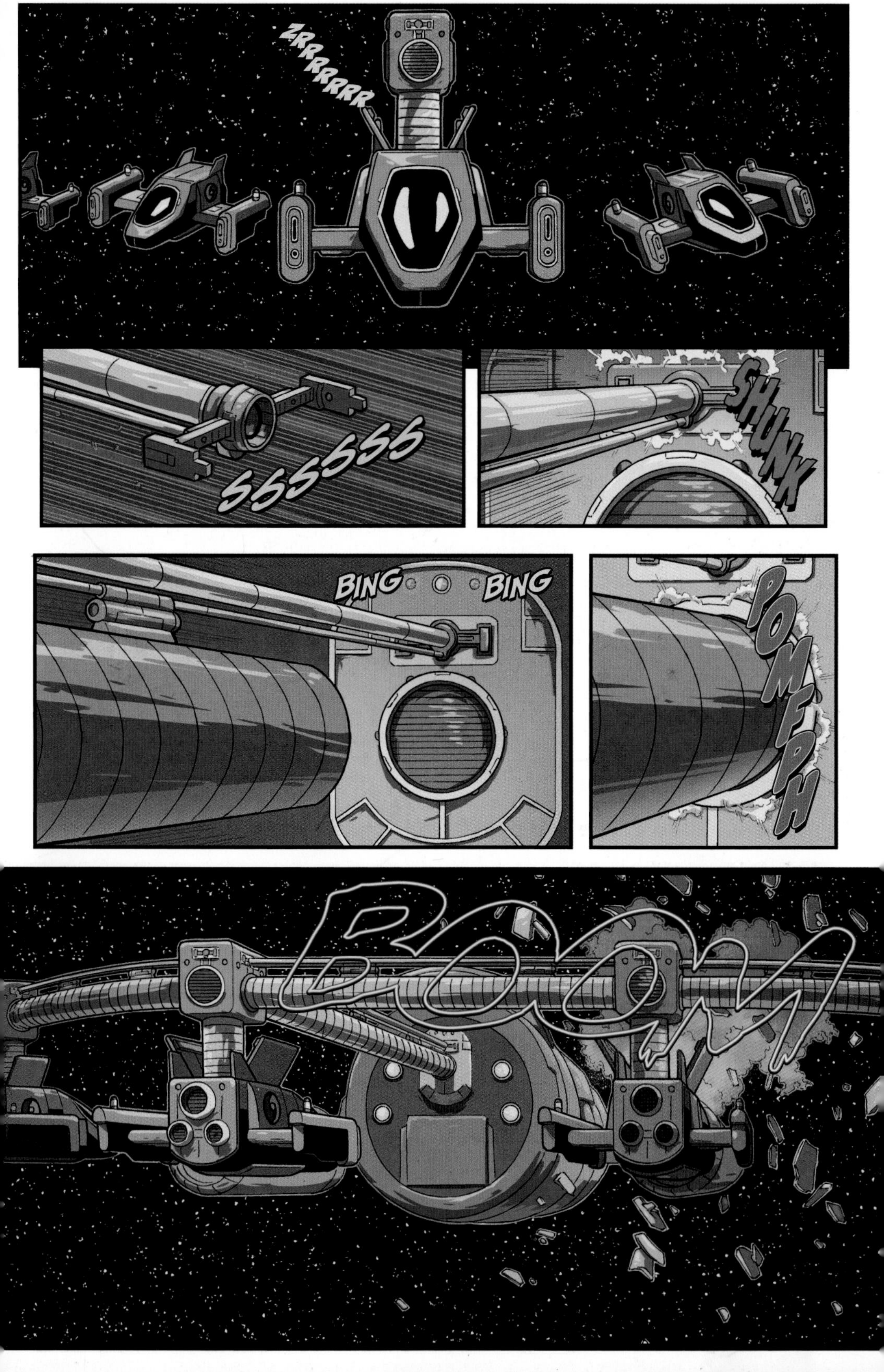
ZRRRRRRR
SSSSSSS
SHUNK
BING
BING
POMFPH
BOOM

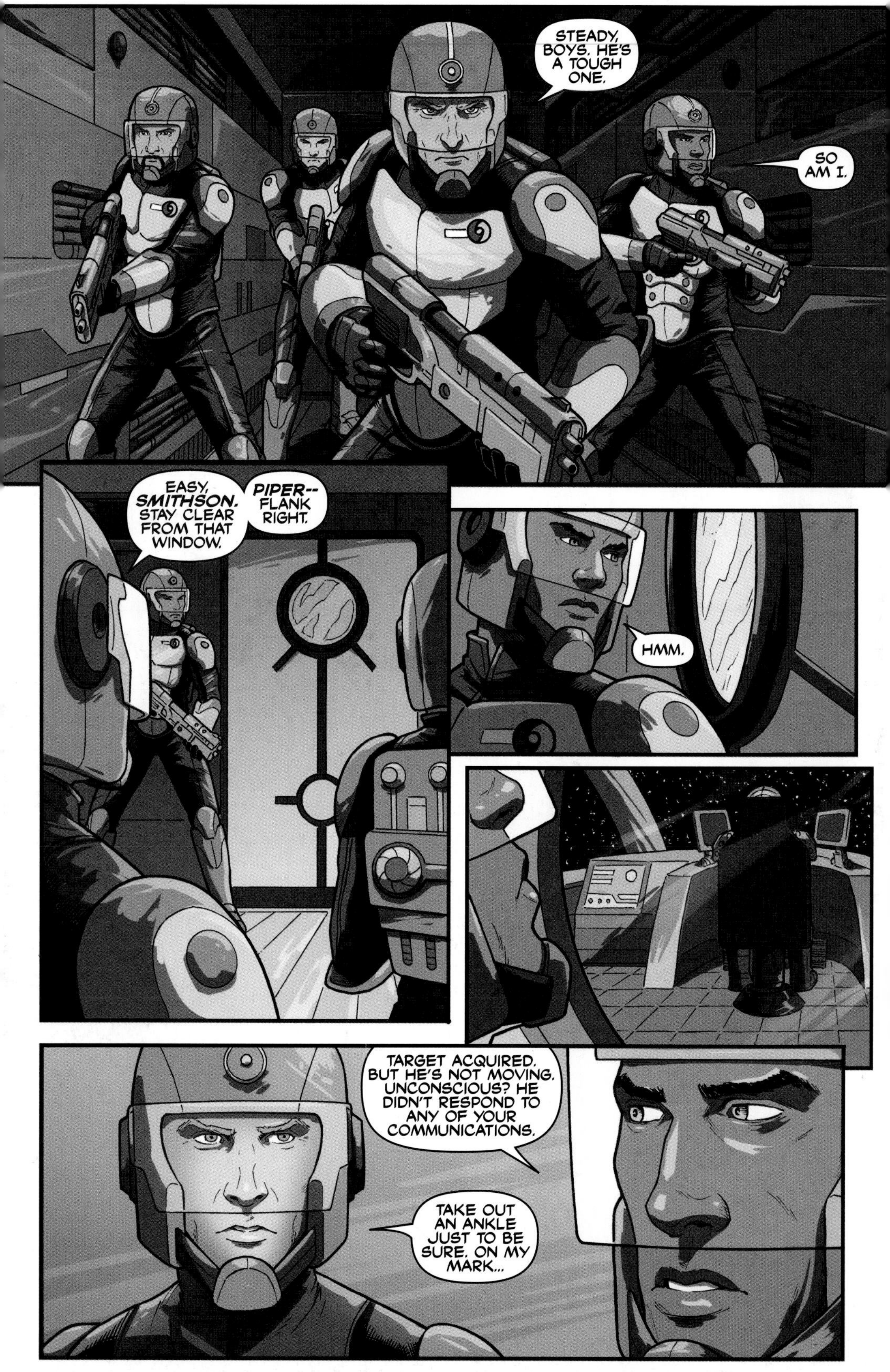

STEADY, BOYS. HE'S A TOUGH ONE.
SO AM I.
EASY, SMITHSON. STAY CLEAR FROM THAT WINDOW.
PIPER-- FLANK RIGHT.
HMM.
TARGET ACQUIRED, BUT HE'S NOT MOVING. UNCONSCIOUS? HE DIDN'T RESPOND TO ANY OF YOUR COMMUNICATIONS.
TAKE OUT AN ANKLE JUST TO BE SURE. ON MY MARK...

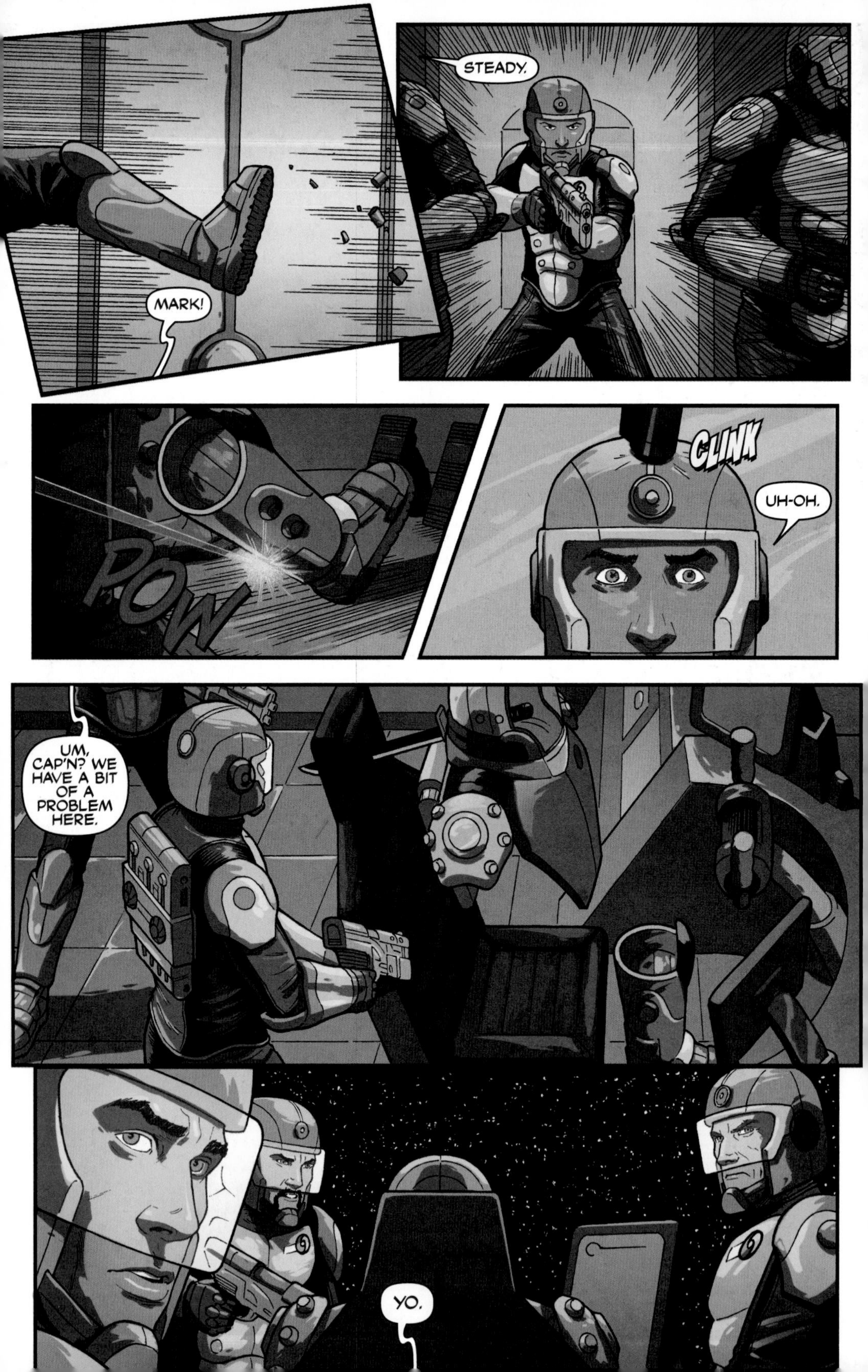
MARK!
STEADY.
POW
CLINK
UH-OH.
UM, CAP'N? WE HAVE A BIT OF A PROBLEM HERE.
YO.

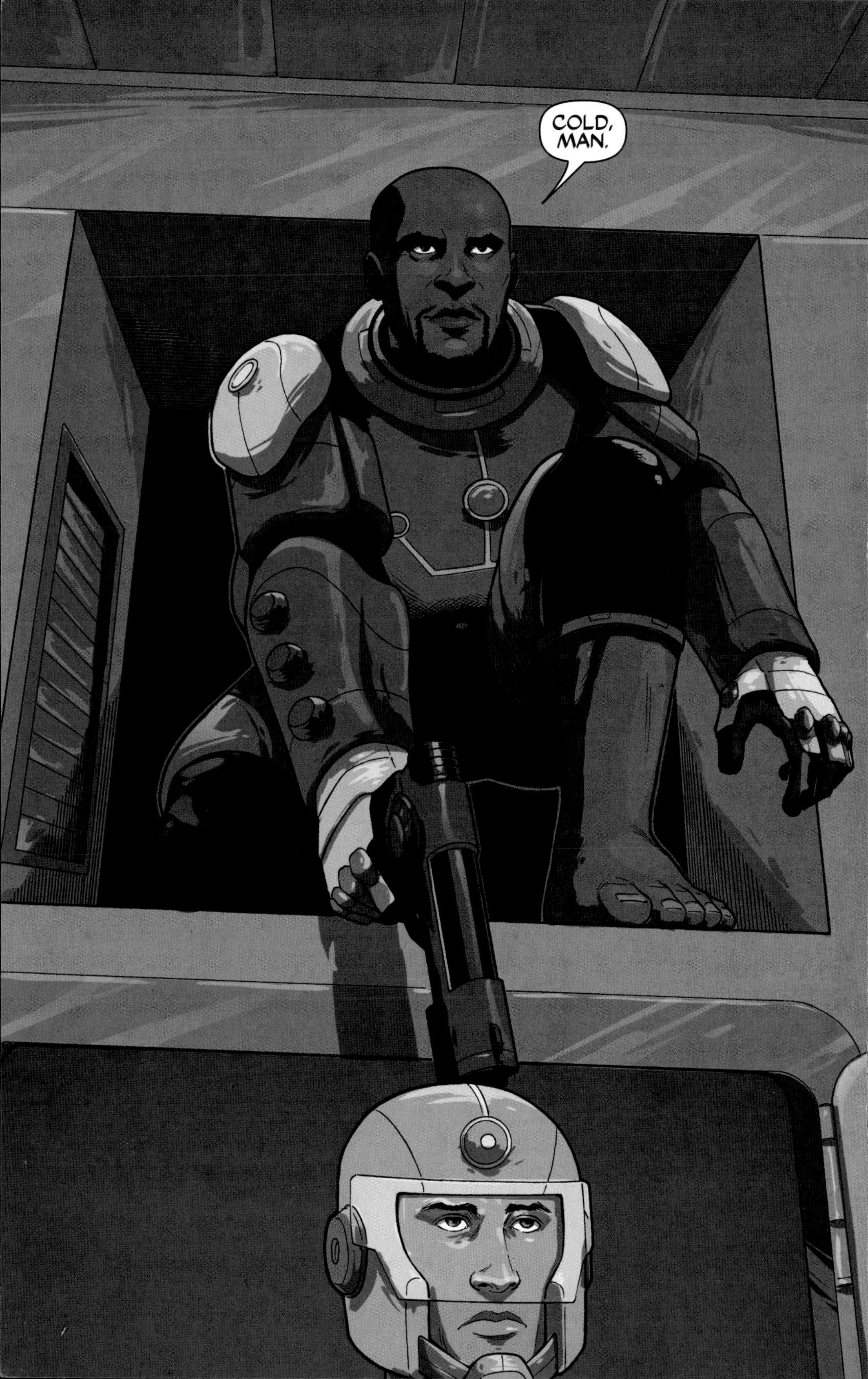
COLD, MAN.

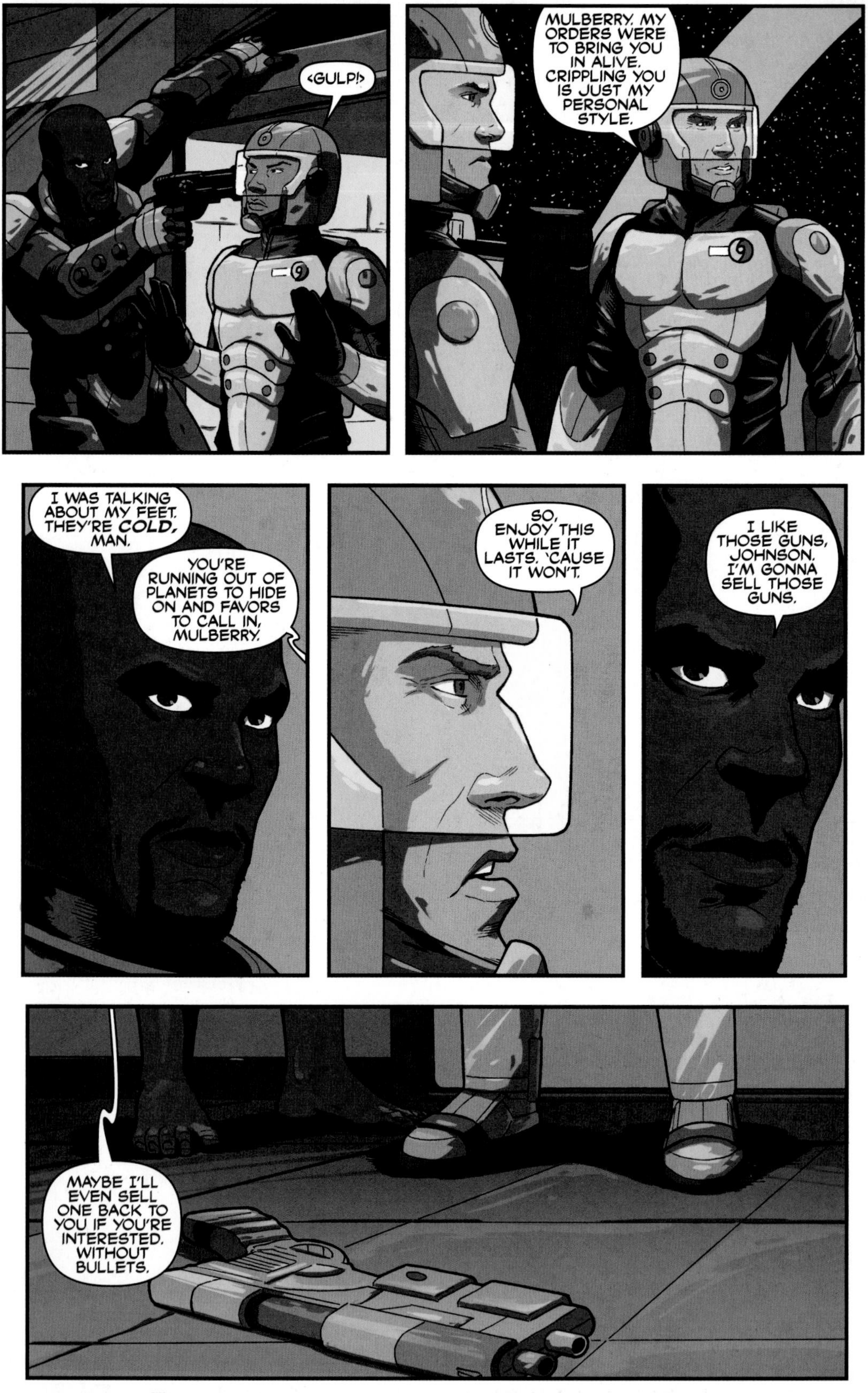
<GULP!>
MULBERRY. MY ORDERS WERE TO BRING YOU IN ALIVE. CRIPPLING YOU IS JUST MY PERSONAL STYLE.
I WAS TALKING ABOUT MY FEET. THEY'RE COLD, MAN.
YOU'RE RUNNING OUT OF PLANETS TO HIDE ON AND FAVORS TO CALL IN, MULBERRY.
SO, ENJOY THIS WHILE IT LASTS. 'CAUSE IT WON'T.
I LIKE THOSE GUNS, JOHNSON. I'M GONNA SELL THOSE GUNS.
MAYBE I'LL EVEN SELL ONE BACK TO YOU IF YOU'RE INTERESTED. WITHOUT BULLETS.

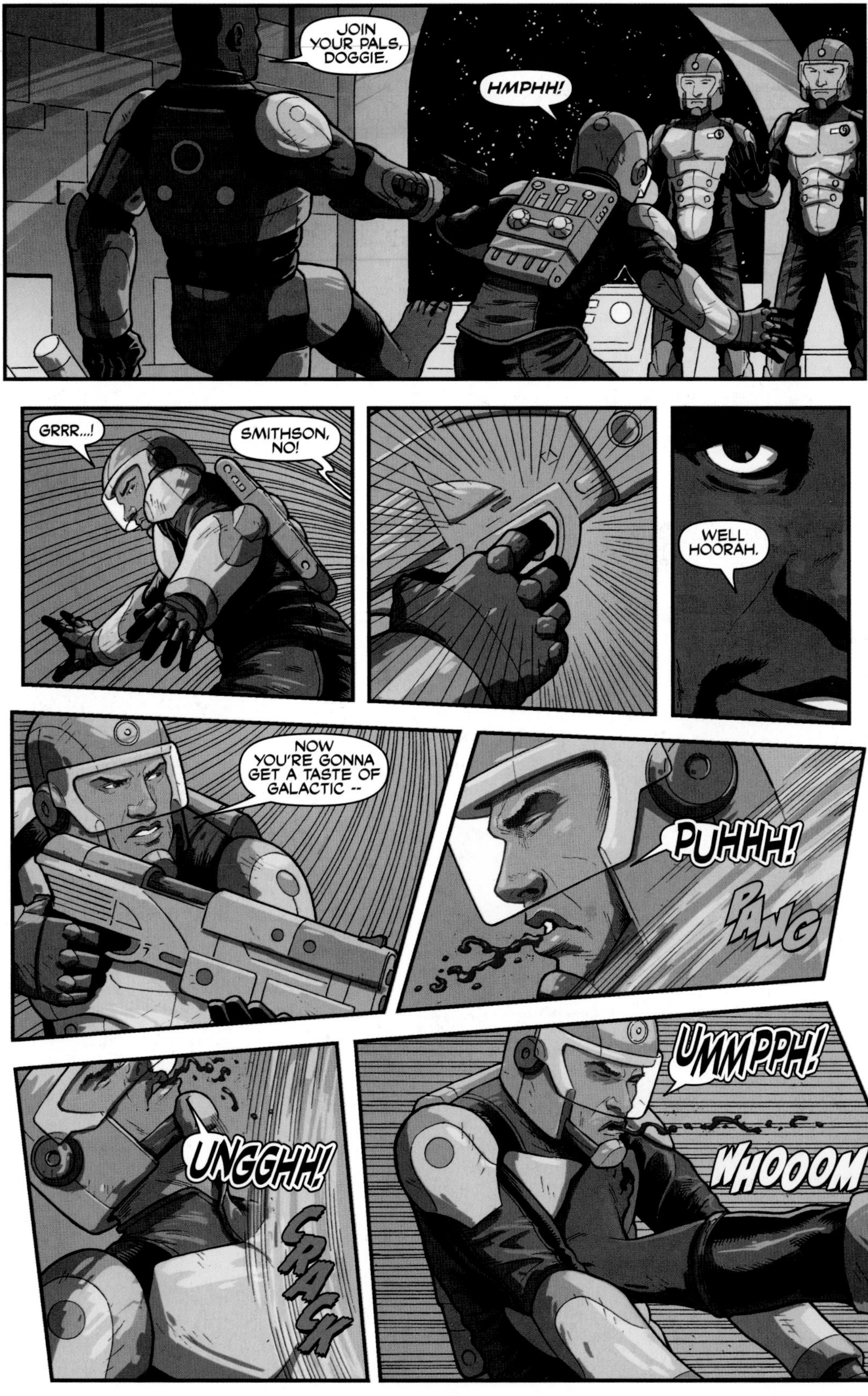

JOIN YOUR PALS, DOGGIE.
HMPHH!
GRRR...!
SMITHSON, NO!
WELL HOORAH.
NOW YOU'RE GONNA GET A TASTE OF GALACTIC --
PUHHH!
PANG
UNGGHH!
CRACK
UMMPPH!
WHOOOM

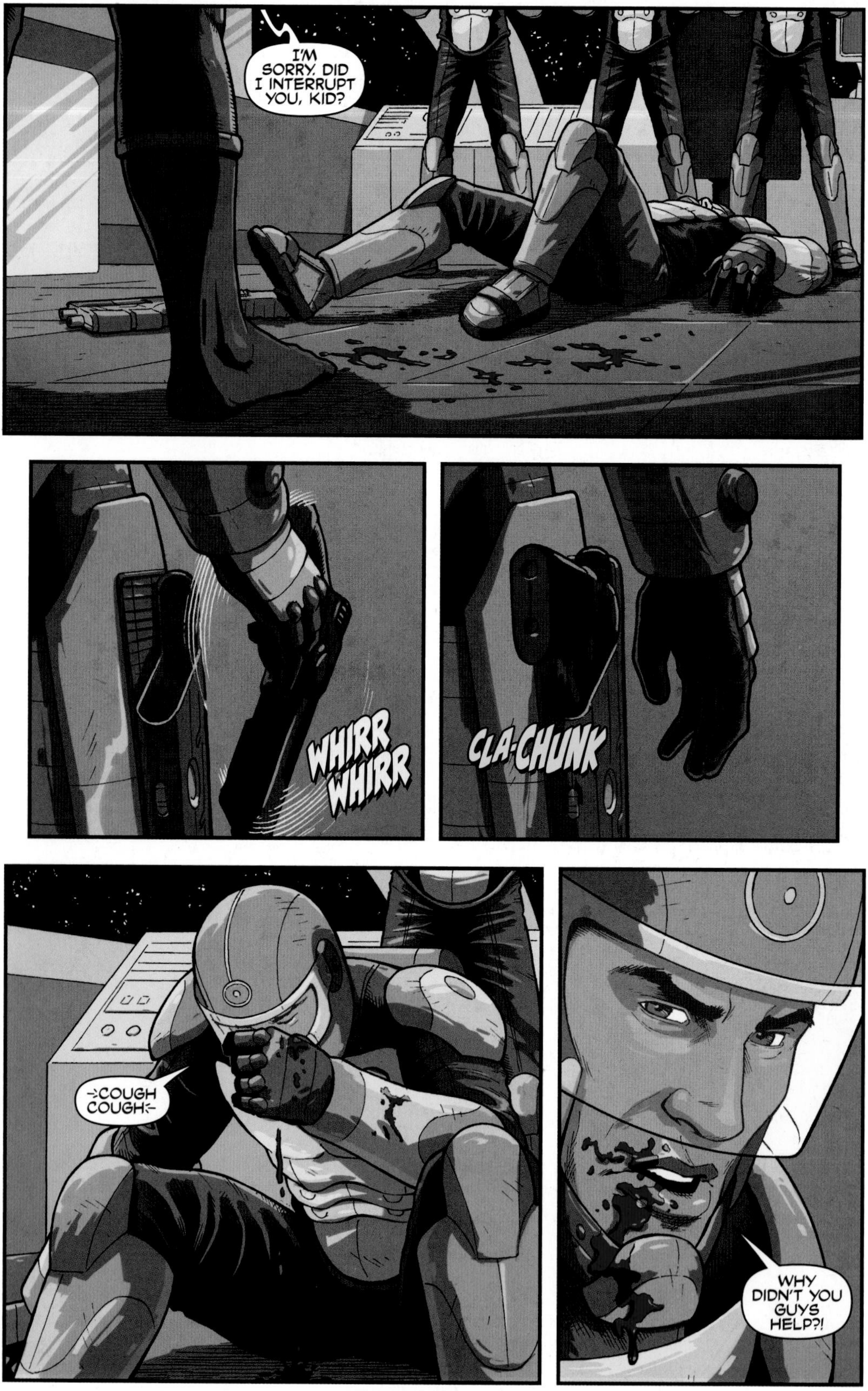
I'M SORRY. DID I INTERRUPT YOU, KID?
WHIRR WHIRR
CLA-CHUNK
COUGH COUGH
WHY DIDN'T YOU GUYS HELP?!

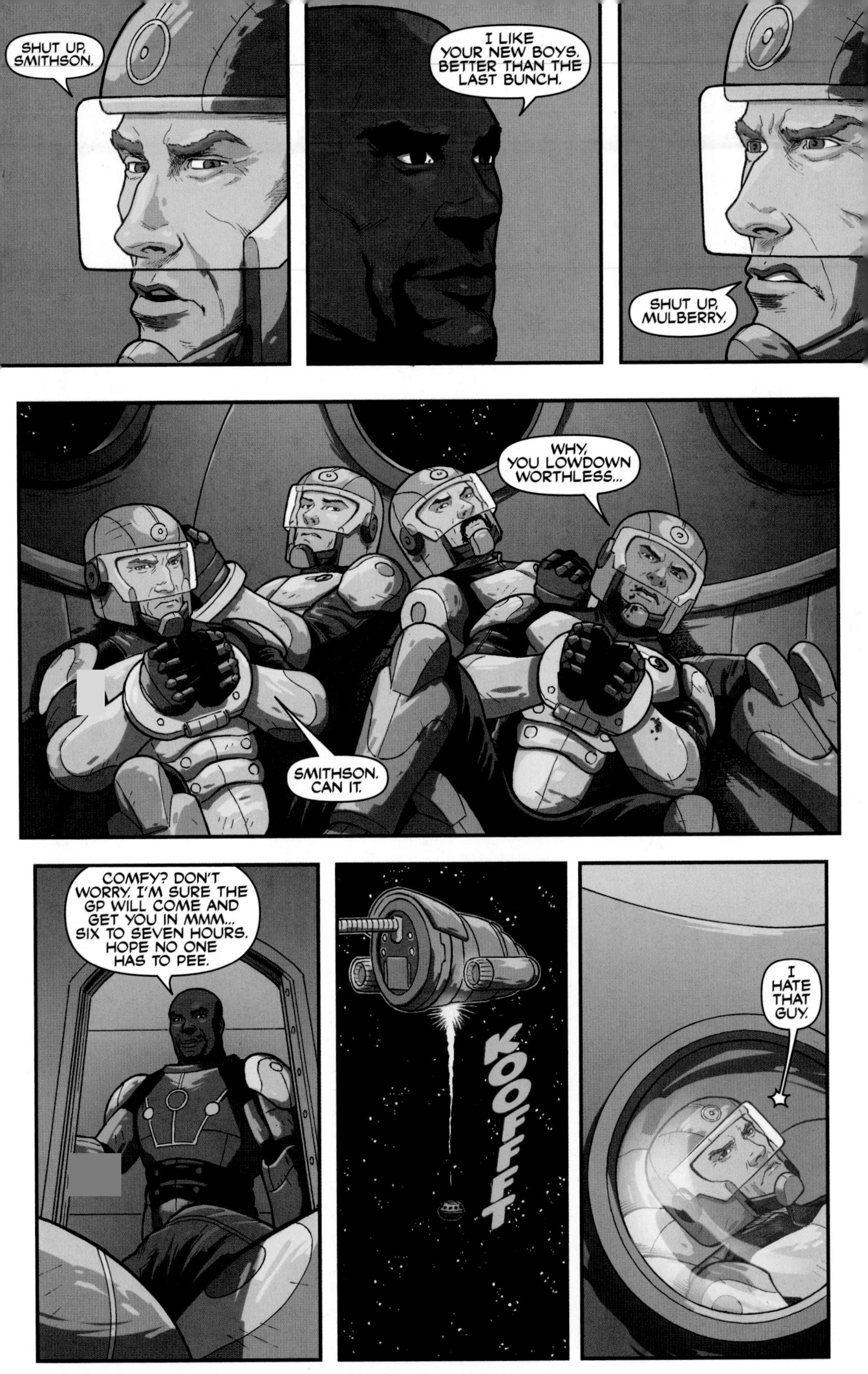

SHUT UP, SMITHSON.
I LIKE YOUR NEW BOYS. BETTER THAN THE LAST BUNCH.
SHUT UP, MULBERRY.
WHY, YOU LOWDOWN WORTHLESS...
SMITHSON. CAN IT.
COMFY? DON'T WORRY. I'M SURE THE GP WILL COME AND GET YOU IN MMM... SIX TO SEVEN HOURS. HOPE NO ONE HAS TO PEE.
KOOFFFT
I HATE THAT GUY.

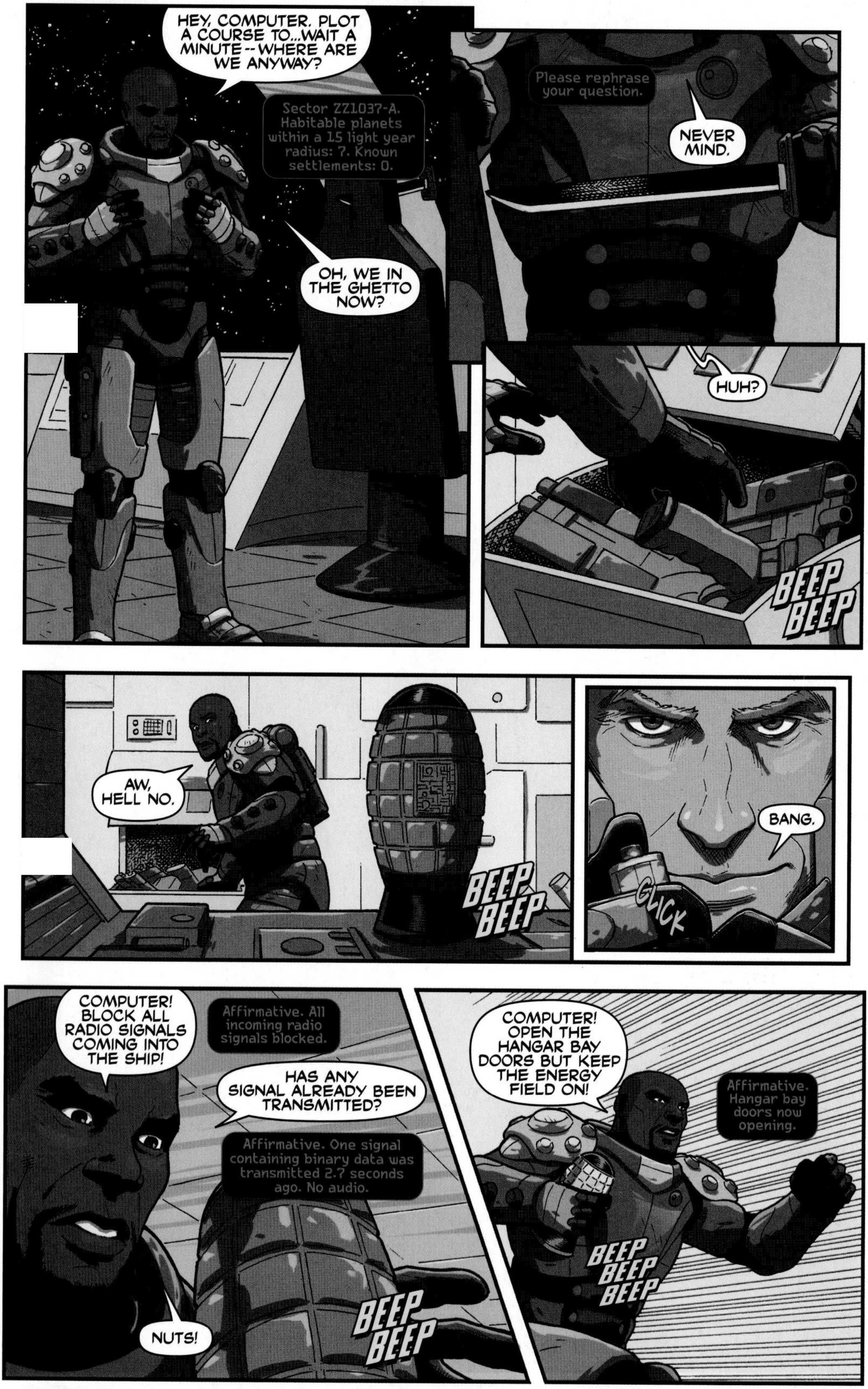

HEY, COMPUTER. PLOT A COURSE TO...WAIT A MINUTE--WHERE ARE WE ANYWAY?
Sector ZZ1037-A. Habitable planets within a 15 light year radius: 7. Known settlements: 0.
OH, WE IN THE GHETTO NOW?
Please rephrase your question.
NEVER MIND.
HUH?
BEEP BEEP
AW, HELL NO.
BEEP BEEP
BANG.
CLICK
COMPUTER! BLOCK ALL RADIO SIGNALS COMING INTO THE SHIP!
Affirmative. All incoming radio signals blocked.
HAS ANY SIGNAL ALREADY BEEN TRANSMITTED?
Affirmative. One signal containing binary data was transmitted 2.7 seconds ago. No audio.
NUTS!
BEEP BEEP
COMPUTER! OPEN THE HANGAR BAY DOORS BUT KEEP THE ENERGY FIELD ON!
Affirmative. Hangar bay doors now opening.
BEEP BEEP BEEP

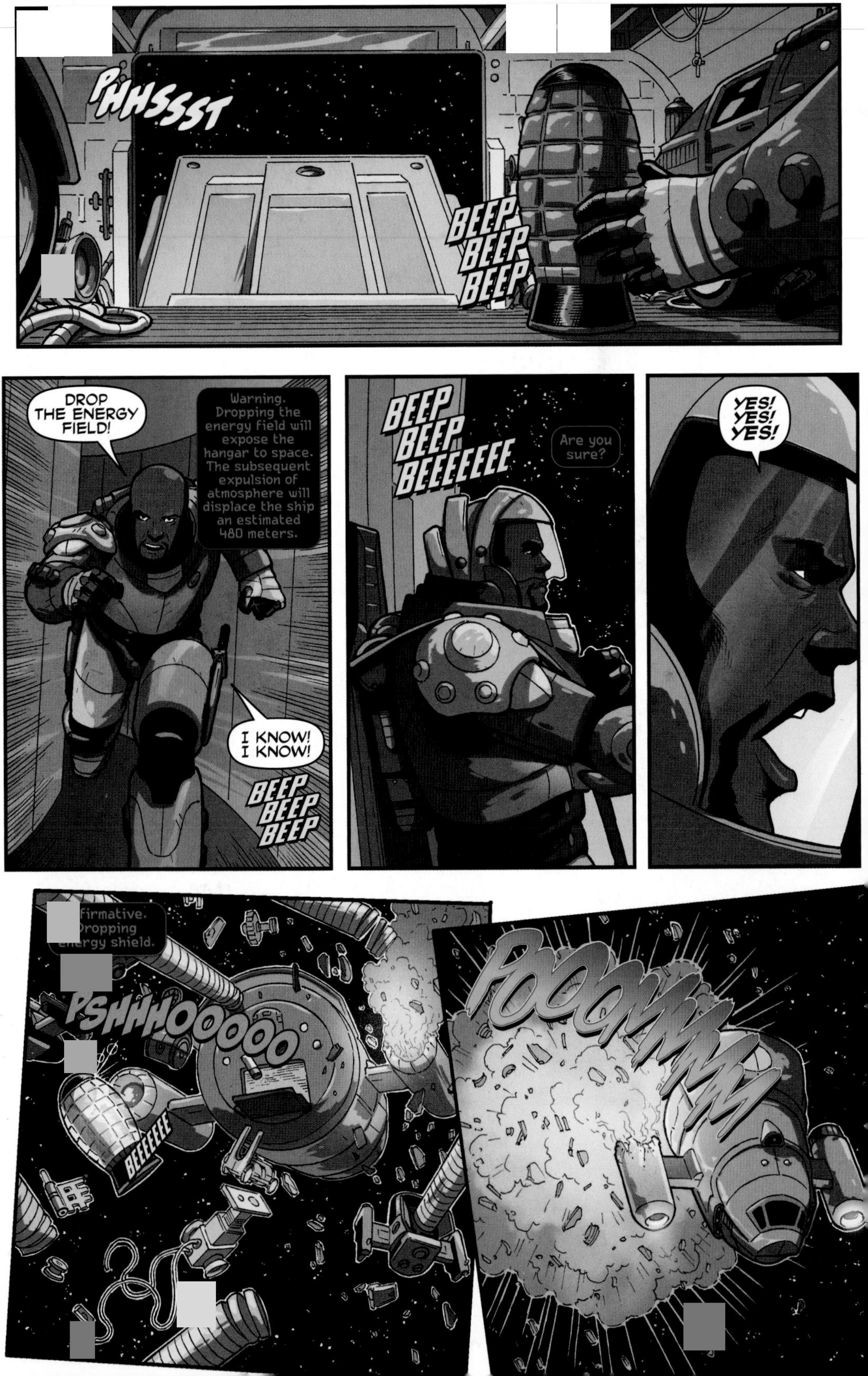
PHHSSST
BEEP BEEP BEEP
DROP THE ENERGY FIELD!
Warning. Dropping the energy field will expose the hangar to space. The subsequent expulsion of atmosphere will displace the ship an estimated 480 meters.
I KNOW! I KNOW!
BEEP BEEP BEEP
BEEP BEEP BEEEEEEE
Are you sure?
YES! YES! YES!
firmative. Dropping energy shield.
PSHHHOOOOOO
BEEEEEEE
POOOMMMM

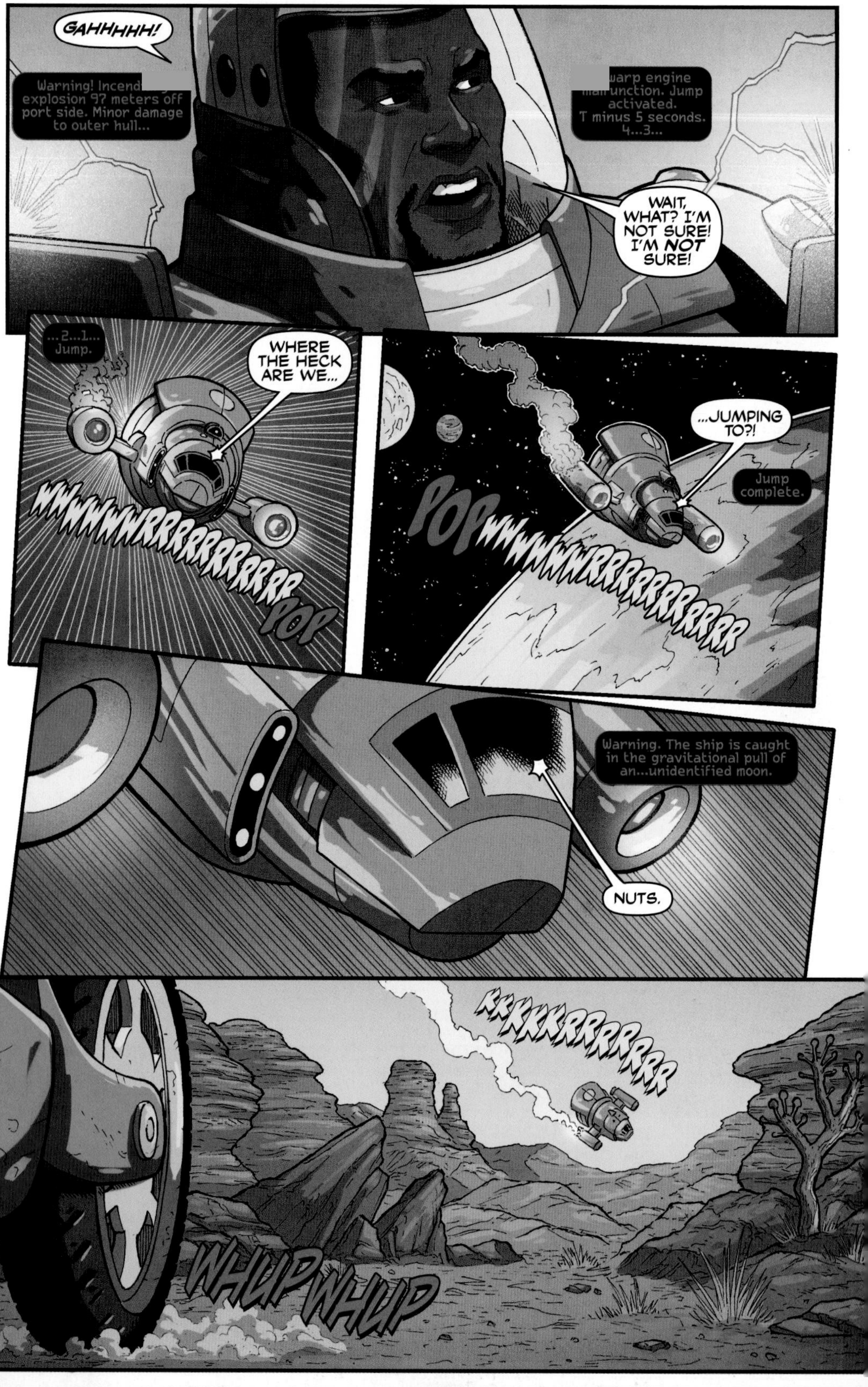
GAHHHHH!
Warning! Incend
explosion 97 meters off port side. Minor damage to outer hull...
warp engine malfunction. Jump activated.
T minus 5 seconds.
4...3...
WAIT, WHAT? I'M NOT SURE! I'M NOT SURE!
...2...1... Jump.
WHERE THE HECK ARE WE...
WWWWWWRRRRRRRRRR
POP
POP
WWWWWWRRRRRRRRRR
...JUMPING TO?!
Jump complete.
Warning. The ship is caught in the gravitational pull of an...unidentified moon.
NUTS.
KKKKKRRRRRRRRR
WHUP WHUP

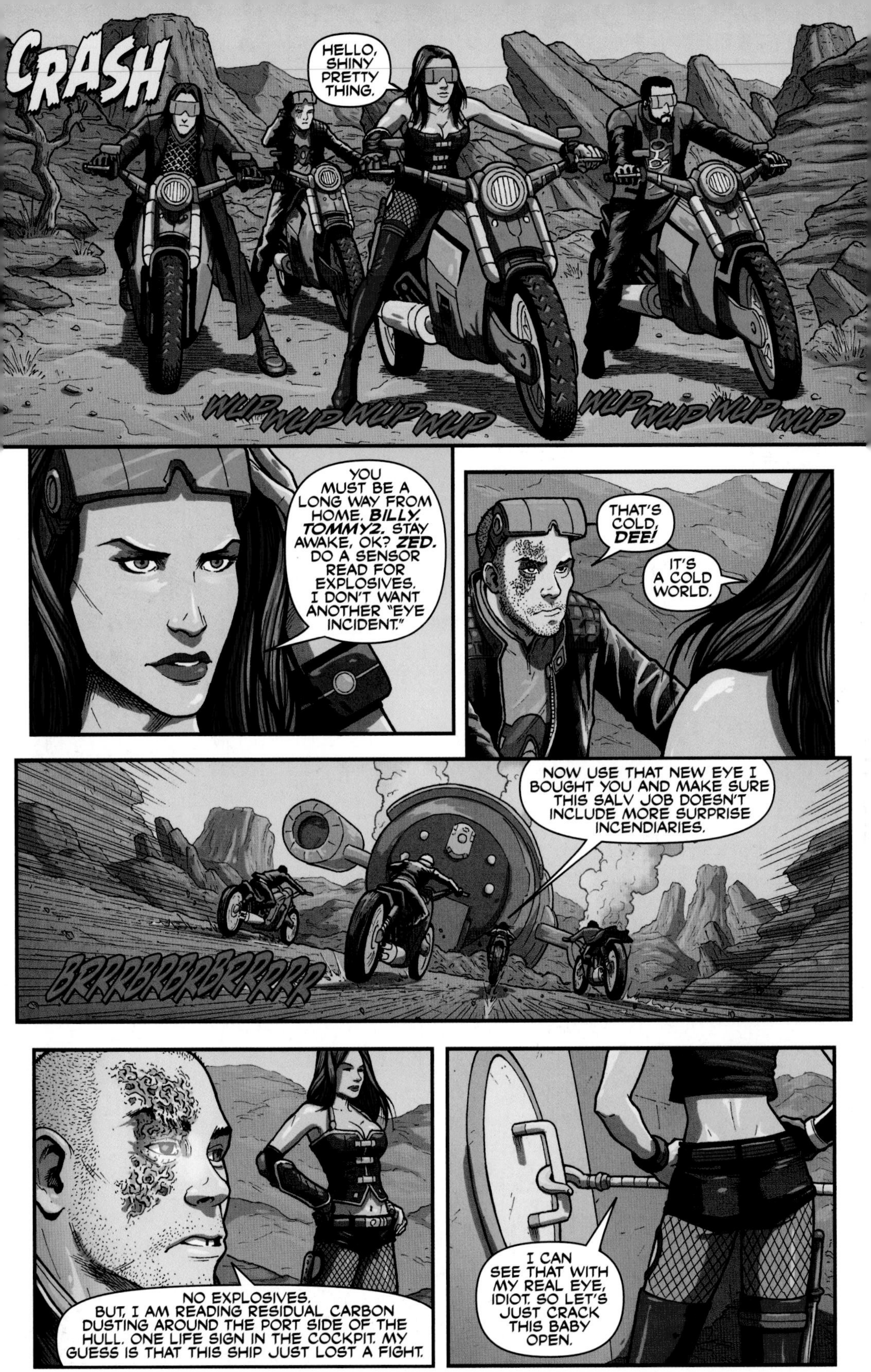
CRASH
HELLO, SHINY PRETTY THING.
WUP WUP WUP WUP
WUP WUP WUP WUP
YOU MUST BE A LONG WAY FROM HOME. BILLY. TOMMY2. STAY AWAKE, OK? ZED. DO A SENSOR READ FOR EXPLOSIVES. I DON'T WANT ANOTHER "EYE INCIDENT."
THAT'S COLD, DEE!
IT'S A COLD WORLD.
NOW USE THAT NEW EYE I BOUGHT YOU AND MAKE SURE THIS SALV JOB DOESN'T INCLUDE MORE SURPRISE INCENDIARIES.
BRRRBRBRBRBRRRRRR
NO EXPLOSIVES. BUT, I AM READING RESIDUAL CARBON DUSTING AROUND THE PORT SIDE OF THE HULL. ONE LIFE SIGN IN THE COCKPIT. MY GUESS IS THAT THIS SHIP JUST LOST A FIGHT.
I CAN SEE THAT WITH MY REAL EYE, IDIOT. SO LET'S JUST CRACK THIS BABY OPEN.

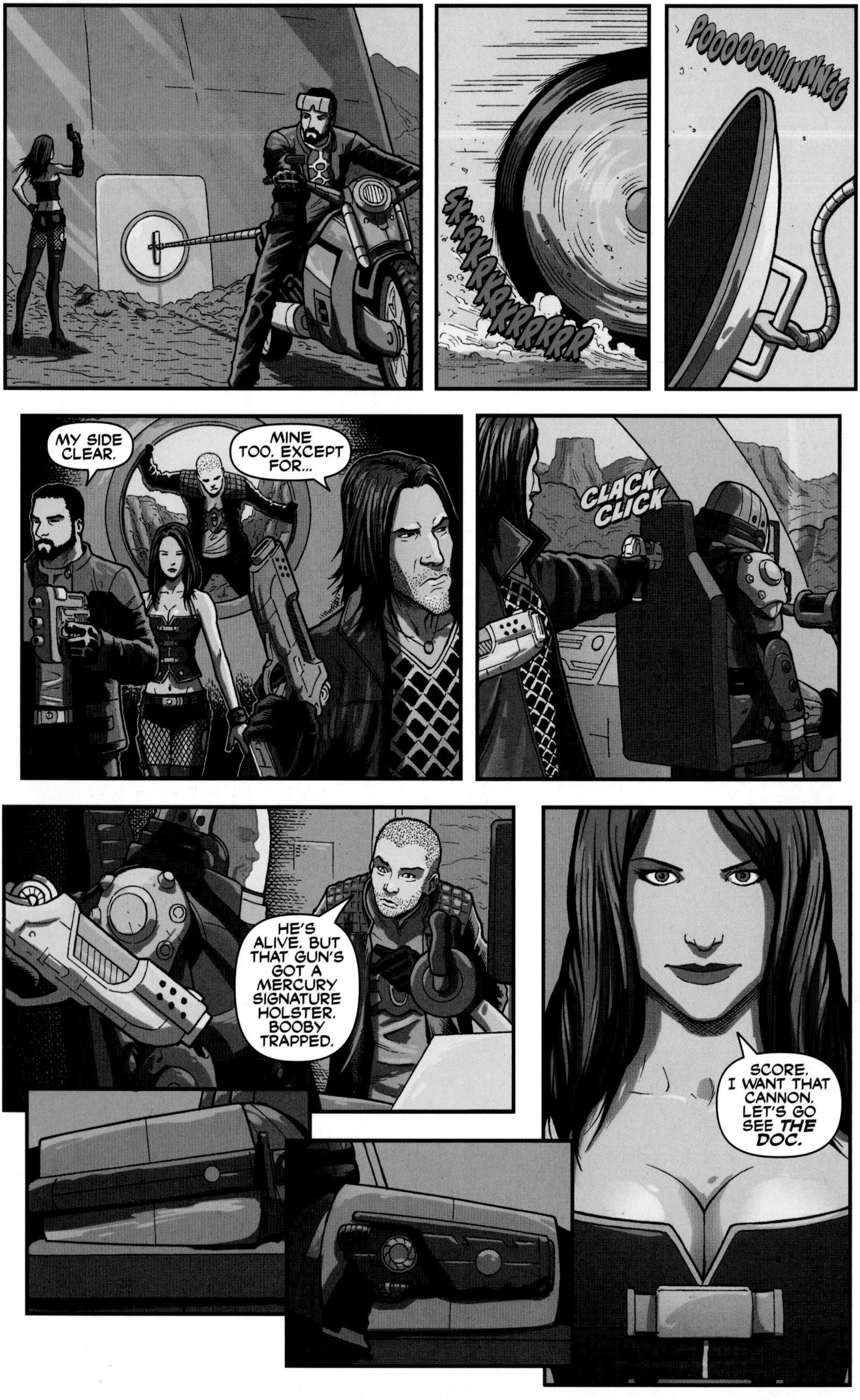
SKRKRKRKRKRKRRRR
POOOOOOIIINNNGG
MY SIDE CLEAR.
MINE TOO. EXCEPT FOR...
CLACK CLICK
HE'S ALIVE. BUT THAT GUN'S GOT A MERCURY SIGNATURE HOLSTER. BOOBY TRAPPED.
SCORE. I WANT THAT CANNON. LET'S GO SEE *THE DOC.*

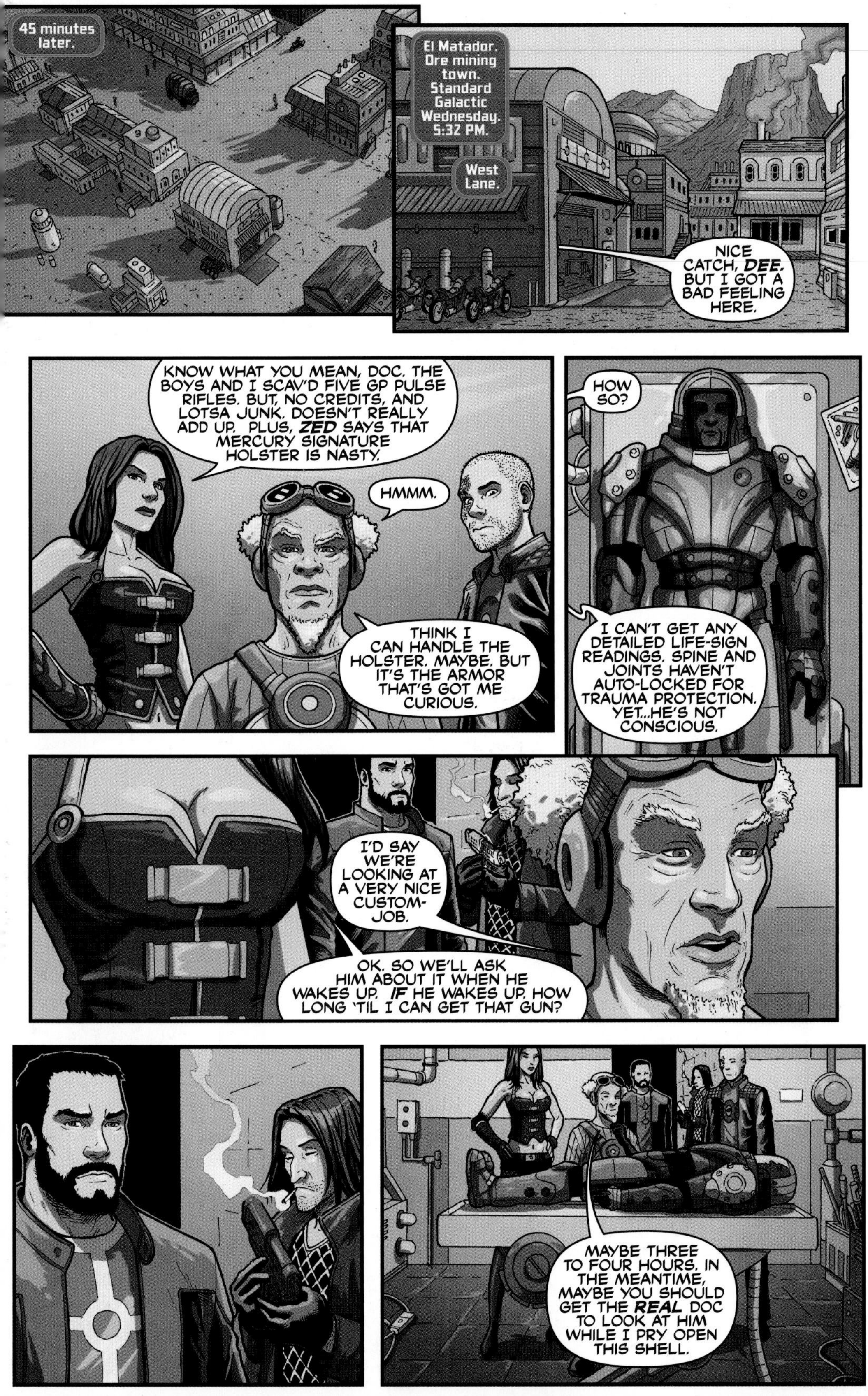
45 minutes later.
El Matador. Ore mining town. Standard Galactic Wednesday. 5:32 PM.
West Lane.
NICE CATCH, DEE. BUT I GOT A BAD FEELING HERE.
KNOW WHAT YOU MEAN, DOC. THE BOYS AND I SCAV'D FIVE GP PULSE RIFLES. BUT, NO CREDITS, AND LOTSA JUNK. DOESN'T REALLY ADD UP. PLUS, ZED SAYS THAT MERCURY SIGNATURE HOLSTER IS NASTY.
HMMM.
THINK I CAN HANDLE THE HOLSTER. MAYBE. BUT IT'S THE ARMOR THAT'S GOT ME CURIOUS.
HOW SO?
I CAN'T GET ANY DETAILED LIFE-SIGN READINGS. SPINE AND JOINTS HAVEN'T AUTO-LOCKED FOR TRAUMA PROTECTION. YET...HE'S NOT CONSCIOUS.
I'D SAY WE'RE LOOKING AT A VERY NICE CUSTOM-JOB.
OK. SO WE'LL ASK HIM ABOUT IT WHEN HE WAKES UP. IF HE WAKES UP. HOW LONG 'TIL I CAN GET THAT GUN?
MAYBE THREE TO FOUR HOURS. IN THE MEANTIME, MAYBE YOU SHOULD GET THE REAL DOC TO LOOK AT HIM WHILE I PRY OPEN THIS SHELL.

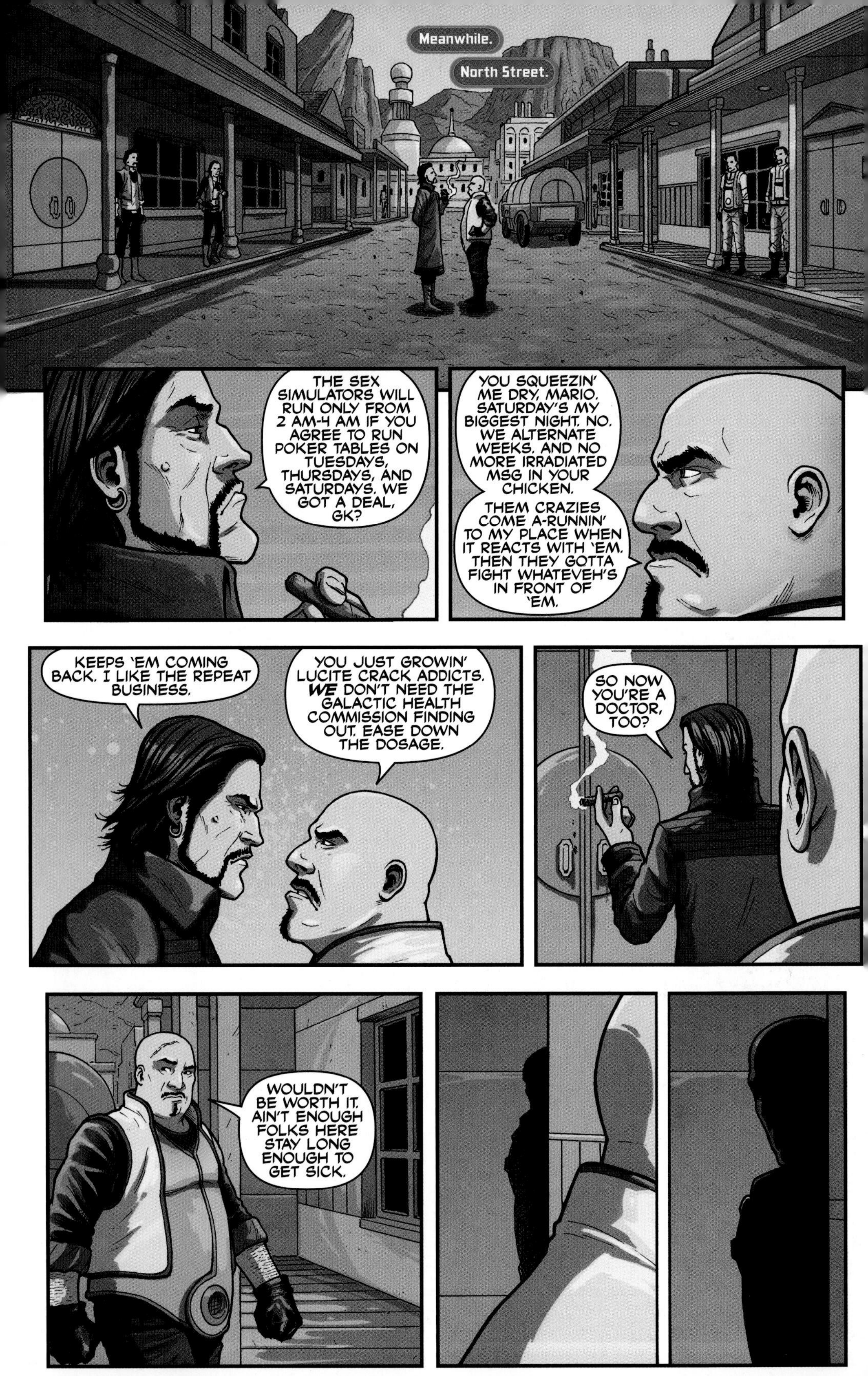
Meanwhile.
North Street.
THE SEX SIMULATORS WILL RUN ONLY FROM 2 AM-4 AM IF YOU AGREE TO RUN POKER TABLES ON TUESDAYS, THURSDAYS, AND SATURDAYS. WE GOT A DEAL, GK?
YOU SQUEEZIN' ME DRY, MARIO. SATURDAY'S MY BIGGEST NIGHT. NO. WE ALTERNATE WEEKS. AND NO MORE IRRADIATED MSG IN YOUR CHICKEN.
THEM CRAZIES COME A-RUNNIN' TO MY PLACE WHEN IT REACTS WITH 'EM. THEN THEY GOTTA FIGHT WHATEVEH'S IN FRONT OF 'EM.
KEEPS 'EM COMING BACK. I LIKE THE REPEAT BUSINESS.
YOU JUST GROWIN' LUCITE CRACK ADDICTS. WE DON'T NEED THE GALACTIC HEALTH COMMISSION FINDING OUT. EASE DOWN THE DOSAGE.
SO NOW YOU'RE A DOCTOR, TOO?
WOULDN'T BE WORTH IT. AIN'T ENOUGH FOLKS HERE STAY LONG ENOUGH TO GET SICK.

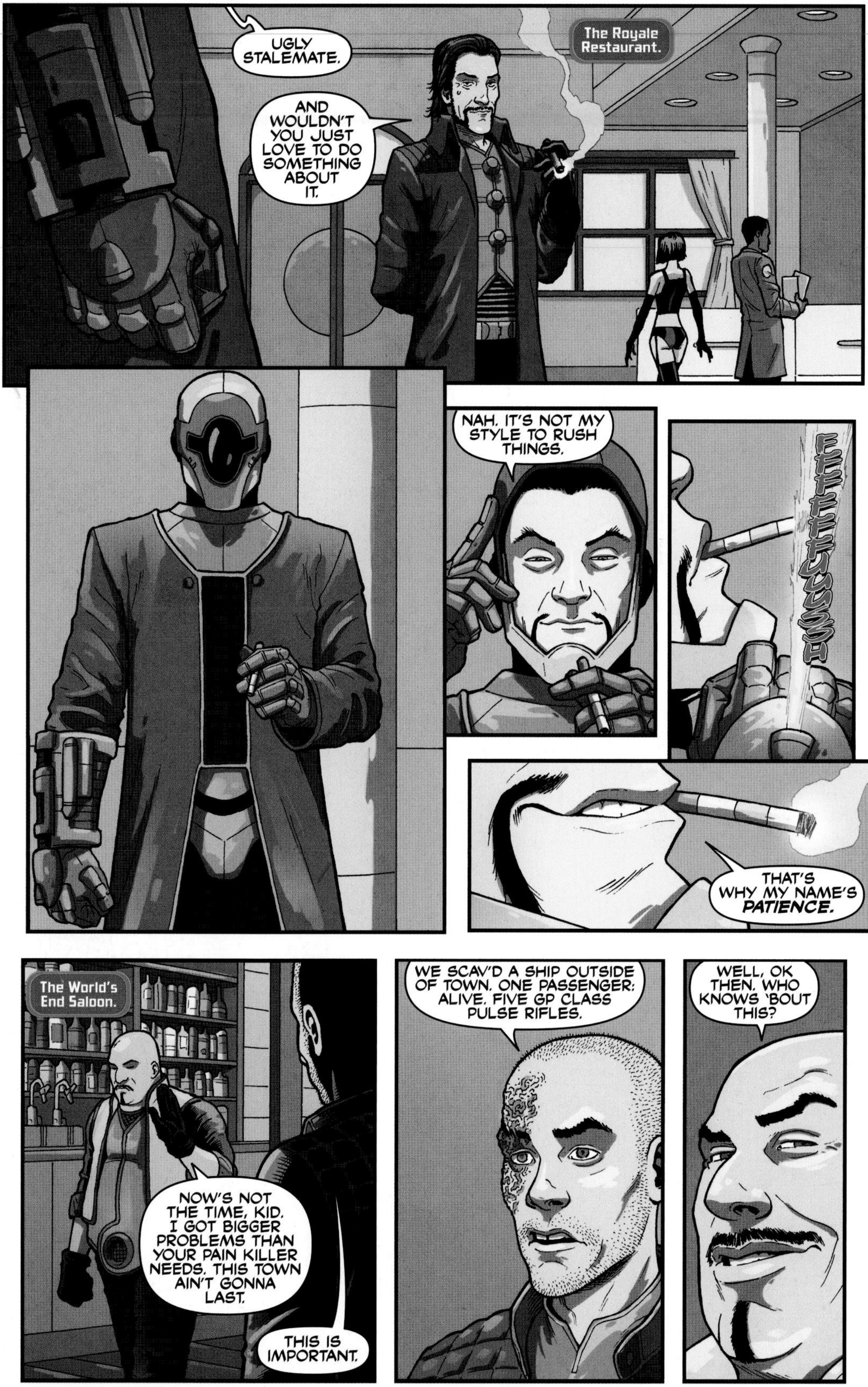

The Royale Restaurant.
UGLY STALEMATE.
AND WOULDN'T YOU JUST LOVE TO DO SOMETHING ABOUT IT.
NAH, IT'S NOT MY STYLE TO RUSH THINGS.
FFFFFFUUUSSH
THAT'S WHY MY NAME'S PATIENCE.
The World's End Saloon.
NOW'S NOT THE TIME, KID. I GOT BIGGER PROBLEMS THAN YOUR PAIN KILLER NEEDS. THIS TOWN AIN'T GONNA LAST.
THIS IS IMPORTANT.
WE SCAV'D A SHIP OUTSIDE OF TOWN. ONE PASSENGER: ALIVE. FIVE GP CLASS PULSE RIFLES.
WELL, OK THEN. WHO KNOWS 'BOUT THIS?

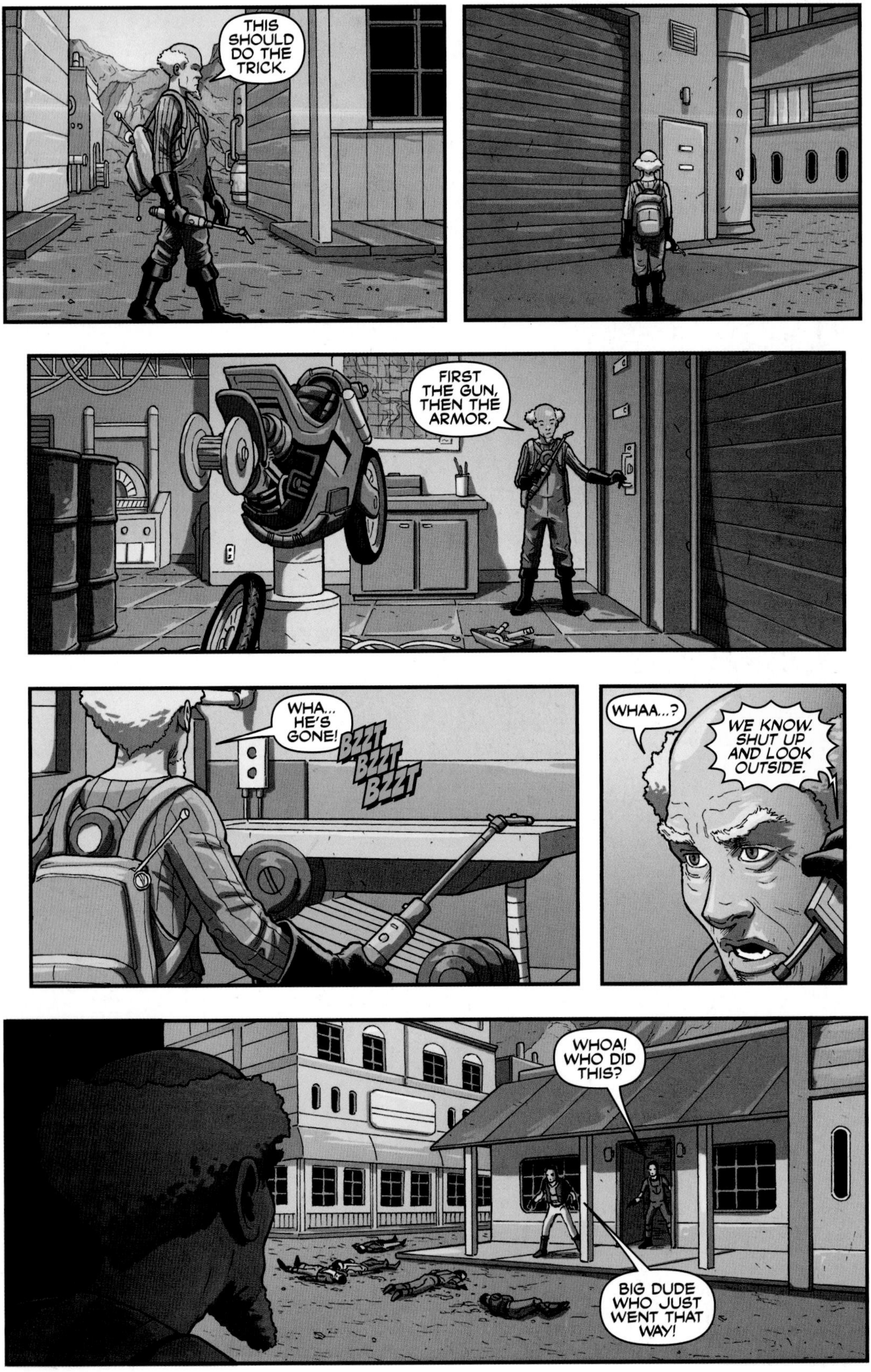
THIS SHOULD DO THE TRICK.
FIRST THE GUN, THEN THE ARMOR.
WHA... HE'S GONE!
BZZT BZZT BZZT
WHAA...?
WE KNOW. SHUT UP AND LOOK OUTSIDE.
WHOA! WHO DID THIS?
BIG DUDE WHO JUST WENT THAT WAY!

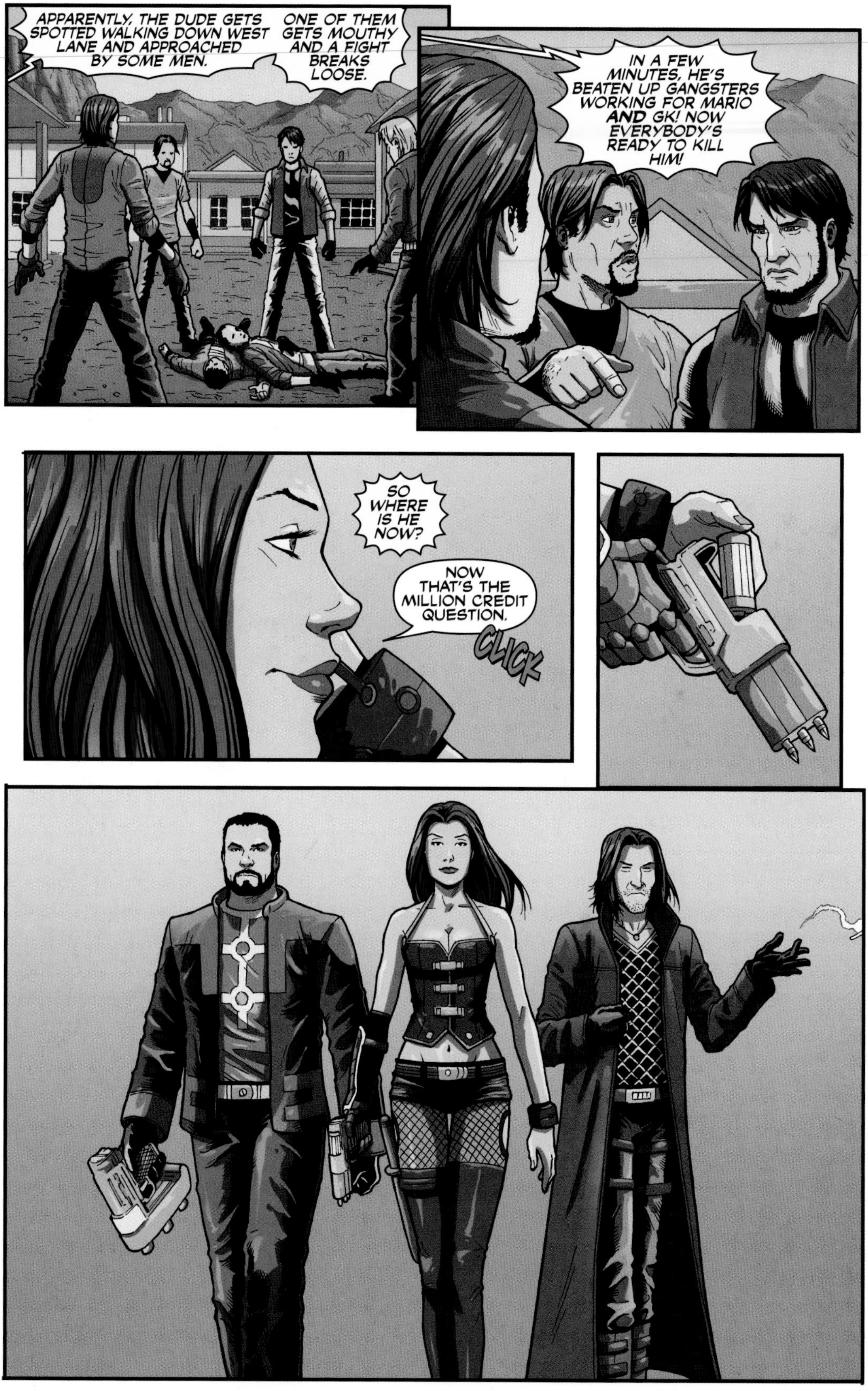
APPARENTLY, THE DUDE GETS SPOTTED WALKING DOWN WEST LANE AND APPROACHED BY SOME MEN.
ONE OF THEM GETS MOUTHY AND A FIGHT BREAKS LOOSE.
IN A FEW MINUTES, HE'S BEATEN UP GANGSTERS WORKING FOR MARIO **AND** GK! NOW EVERYBODY'S READY TO KILL HIM!
SO WHERE IS HE NOW?
NOW THAT'S THE MILLION CREDIT QUESTION.
CLICK

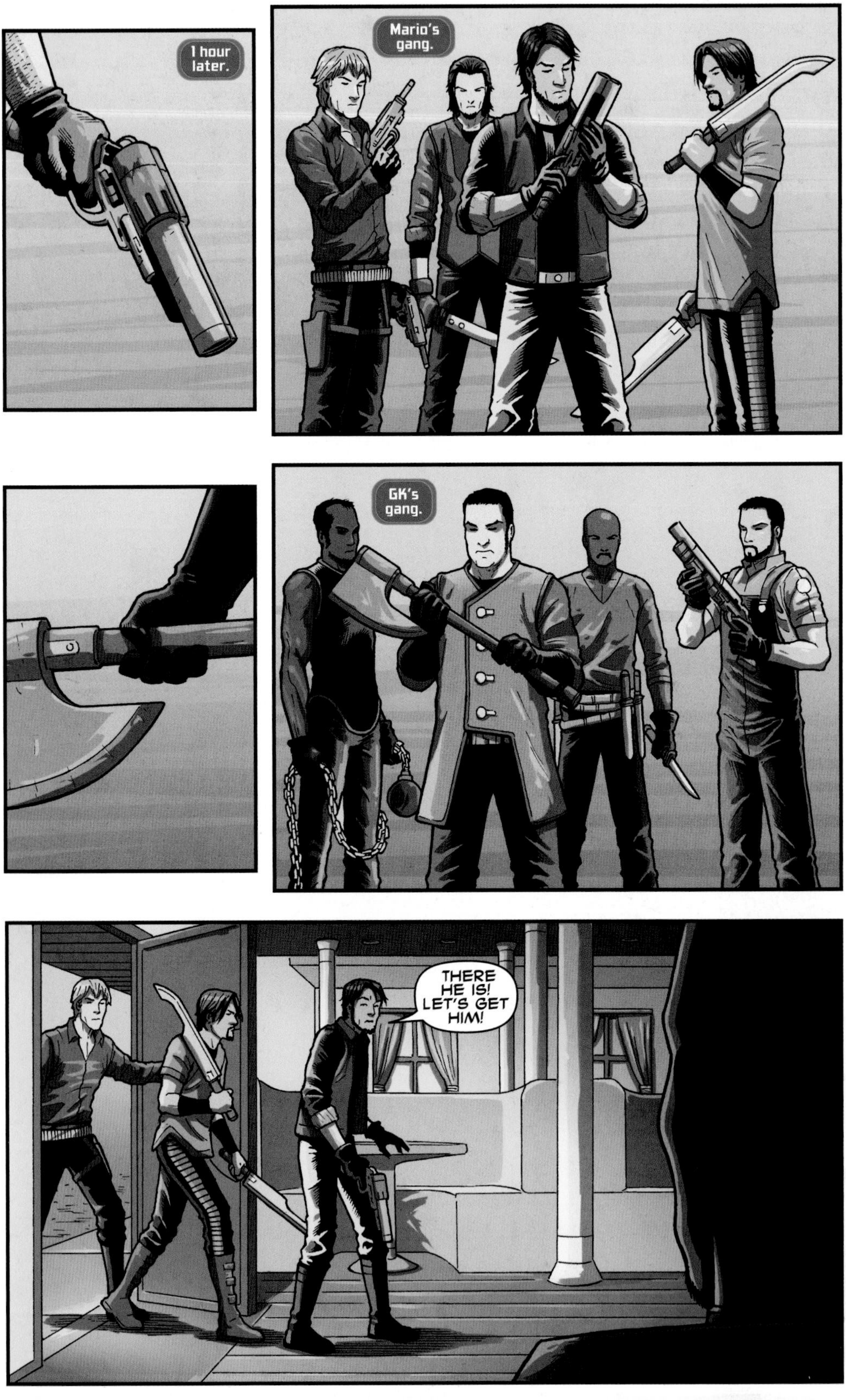
1 hour later.
Mario's gang.
GK's gang.
THERE HE IS! LET'S GET HIM!

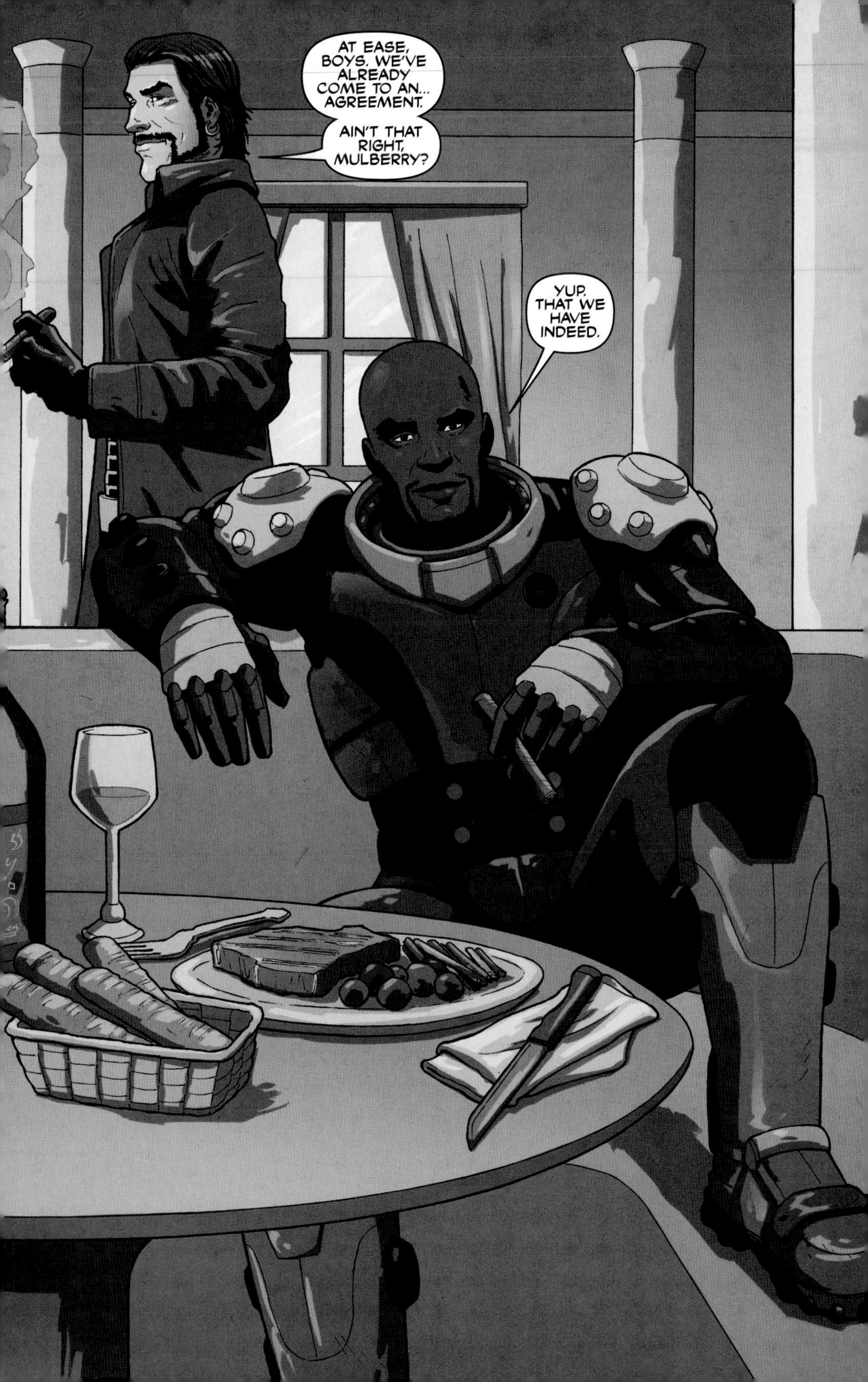
AT EASE, BOYS. WE'VE ALREADY COME TO AN... AGREEMENT.
AIN'T THAT RIGHT, MULBERRY?
YUP, THAT WE HAVE INDEED.

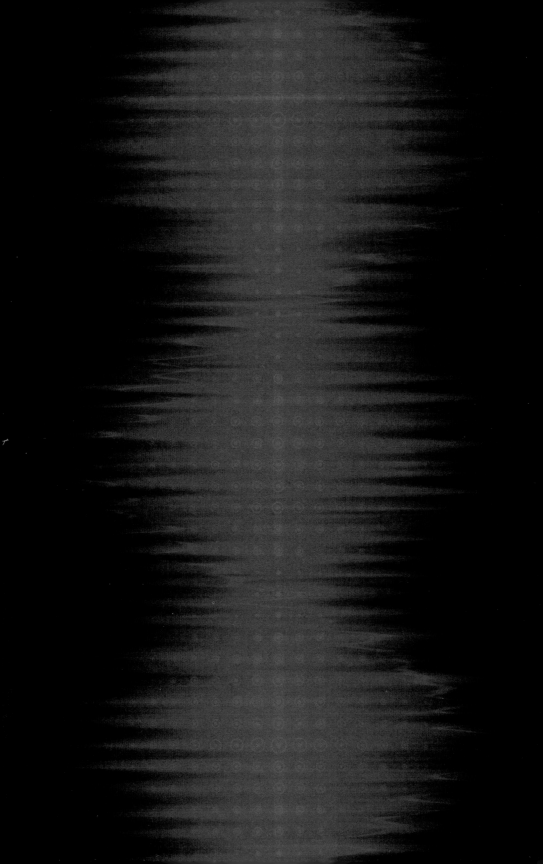

COLD SPACE

CHAPTER 2

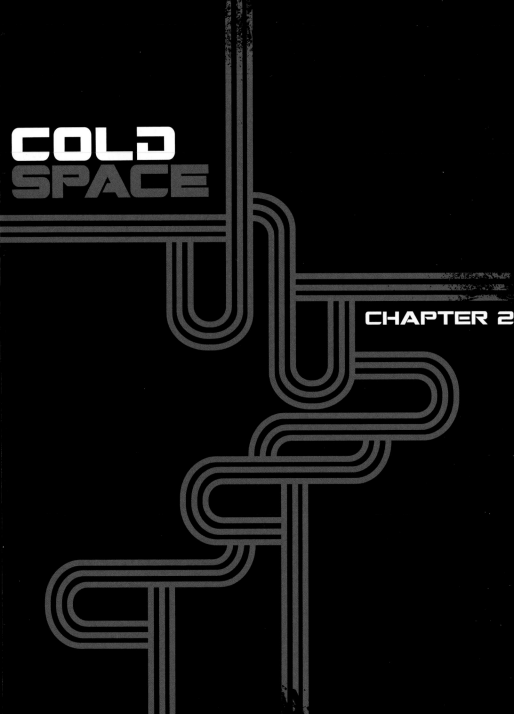

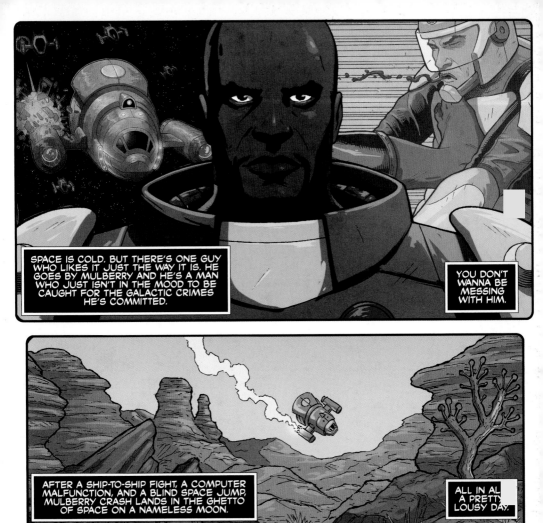

SPACE IS COLD. BUT THERE'S ONE GUY WHO LIKES IT JUST THE WAY IT IS. HE GOES BY MULBERRY AND HE'S A MAN WHO JUST ISN'T IN THE MOOD TO BE CAUGHT FOR THE GALACTIC CRIMES HE'S COMMITTED.

YOU DON'T WANNA BE MESSING WITH HIM.

AFTER A SHIP-TO-SHIP FIGHT, A COMPUTER MALFUNCTION, AND A BLIND SPACE JUMP, MULBERRY CRASH LANDS IN THE GHETTO OF SPACE ON A NAMELESS MOON.

ALL IN ALL A PRETTY LOUSY DAY.

BUT WITH DRAMA COMES OPPORTUNITY AND MULBERRY QUICKLY FINDS A GANG LEADER WITH A FULL WALLET JUST ITCHING TO HIRE THE NEW GUN IN TOWN. THINGS ARE ABOUT TO GET COMPLICATED...

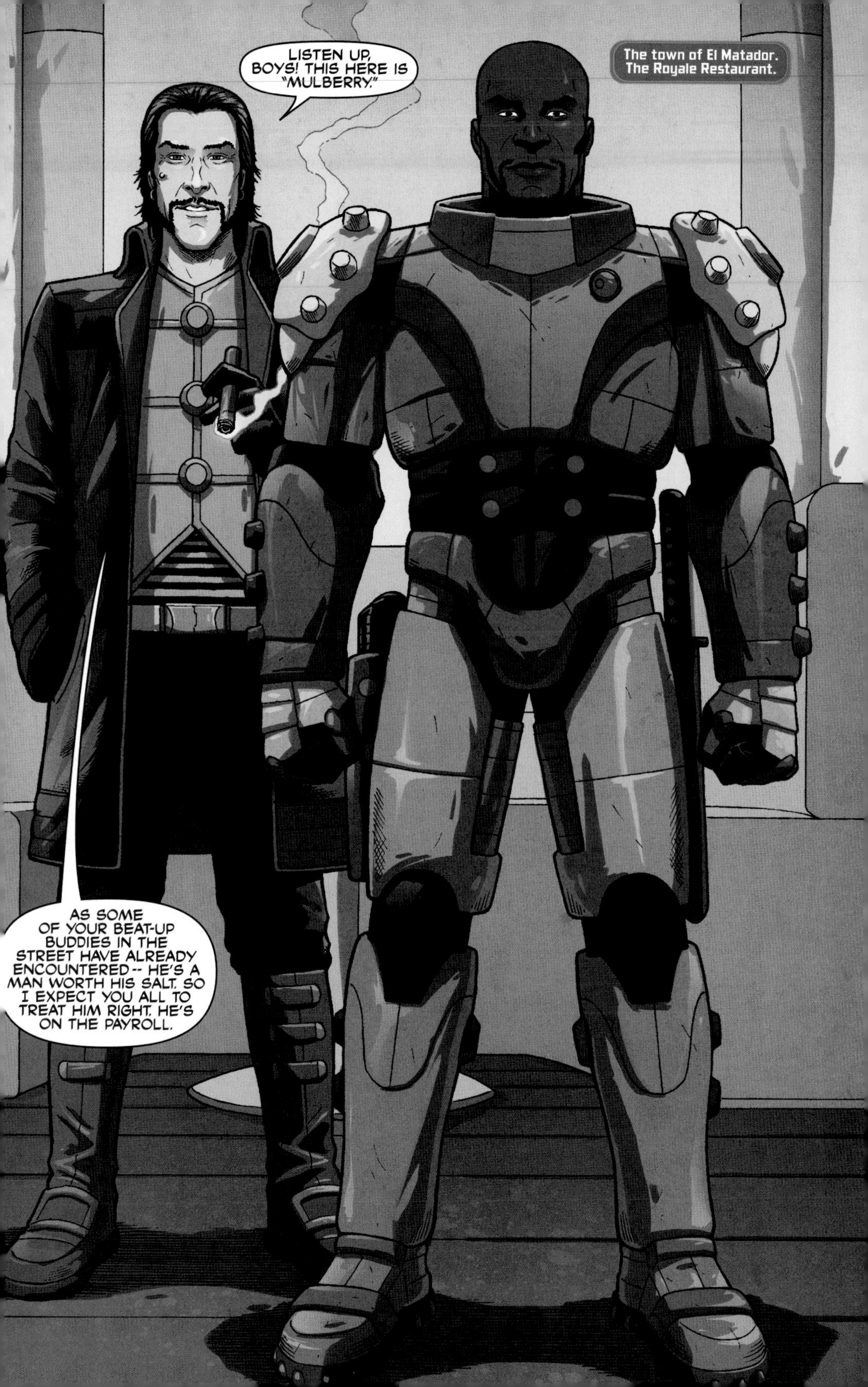
The town of El Matador.
The Royale Restaurant.
LISTEN UP, BOYS! THIS HERE IS "MULBERRY."
AS SOME OF YOUR BEAT-UP BUDDIES IN THE STREET HAVE ALREADY ENCOUNTERED-- HE'S A MAN WORTH HIS SALT. SO I EXPECT YOU ALL TO TREAT HIM RIGHT. HE'S ON THE PAYROLL.

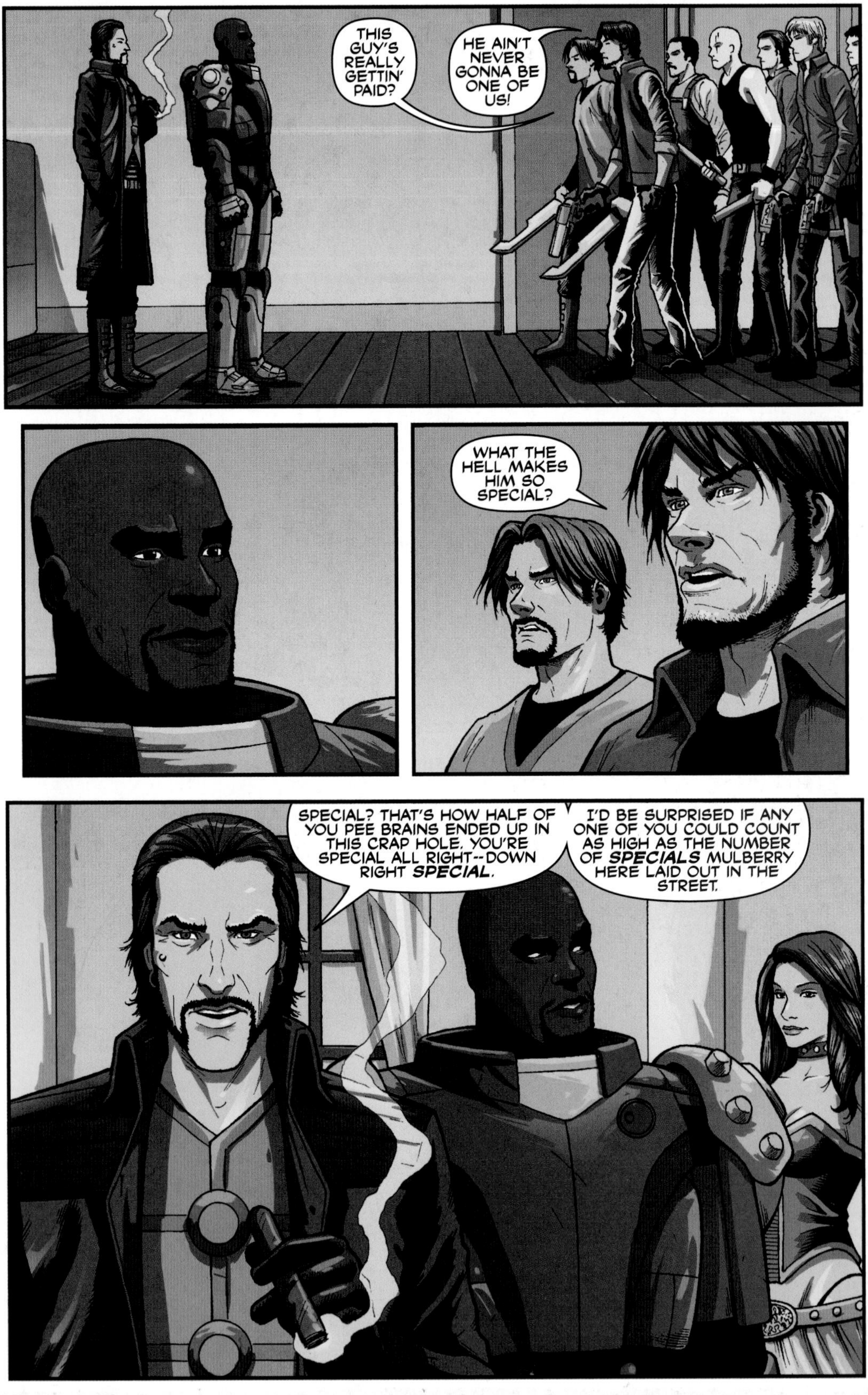

THIS GUY'S REALLY GETTIN' PAID?
HE AIN'T NEVER GONNA BE ONE OF US!
WHAT THE HELL MAKES HIM SO SPECIAL?
SPECIAL? THAT'S HOW HALF OF YOU PEE BRAINS ENDED UP IN THIS CRAP HOLE. YOU'RE SPECIAL ALL RIGHT--DOWN RIGHT SPECIAL.
I'D BE SURPRISED IF ANY ONE OF YOU COULD COUNT AS HIGH AS THE NUMBER OF SPECIALS MULBERRY HERE LAID OUT IN THE STREET.

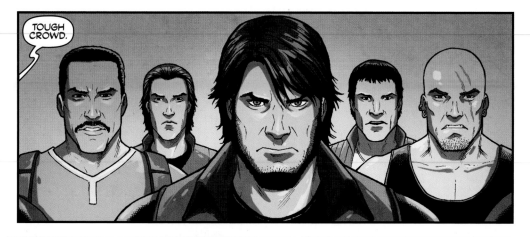

TOUGH CROWD.

HEY, BABY. WHAT DO THEY CALL YOU?

CANDY. I DON'T DO FAVORS.

THAT'S ORIGINAL. WELL THEN, I'M PAYING FOR A QUICK TRICK.

MMMM? YOU DON'T SEEM LIKE THE QUICK TRICK TYPE.

JUST PICK UP THE CARDS.

WE GONNA PLAY THIS IN FRONT OF ALL THE BOYS? 'CAUSE THAT'LL COST YOU EXTRA.

JUST TOSS 'EM IN THE AIR. THE CARDS, THAT IS.

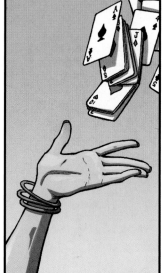

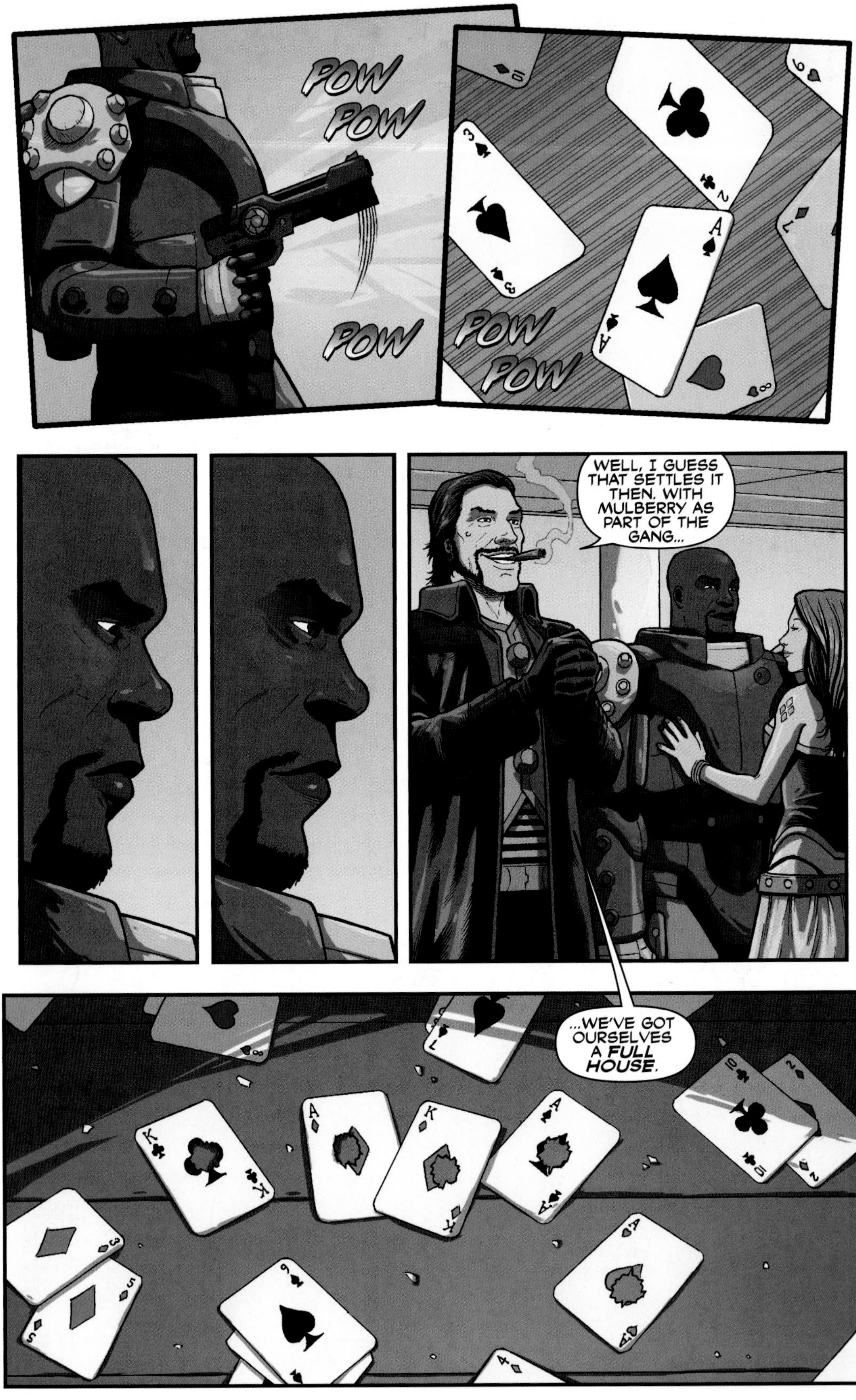
POW
POW
POW
POW
POW
WELL, I GUESS THAT SETTLES IT THEN. WITH MULBERRY AS PART OF THE GANG...
...WE'VE GOT OURSELVES A FULL HOUSE.

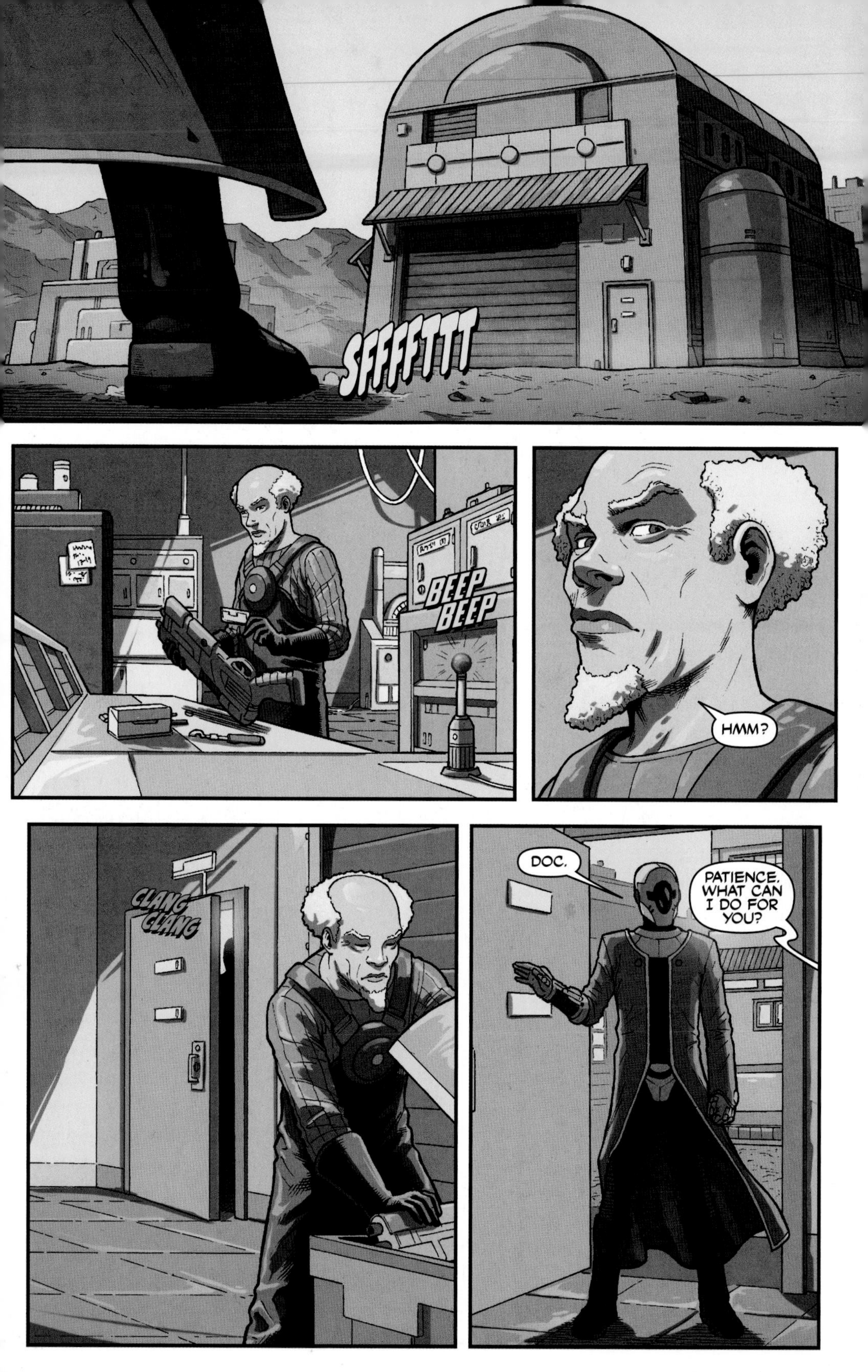
SFFFFTTT
BEEP BEEP
HMM?
CLANG CLANG
DOC.
PATIENCE. WHAT CAN I DO FOR YOU?

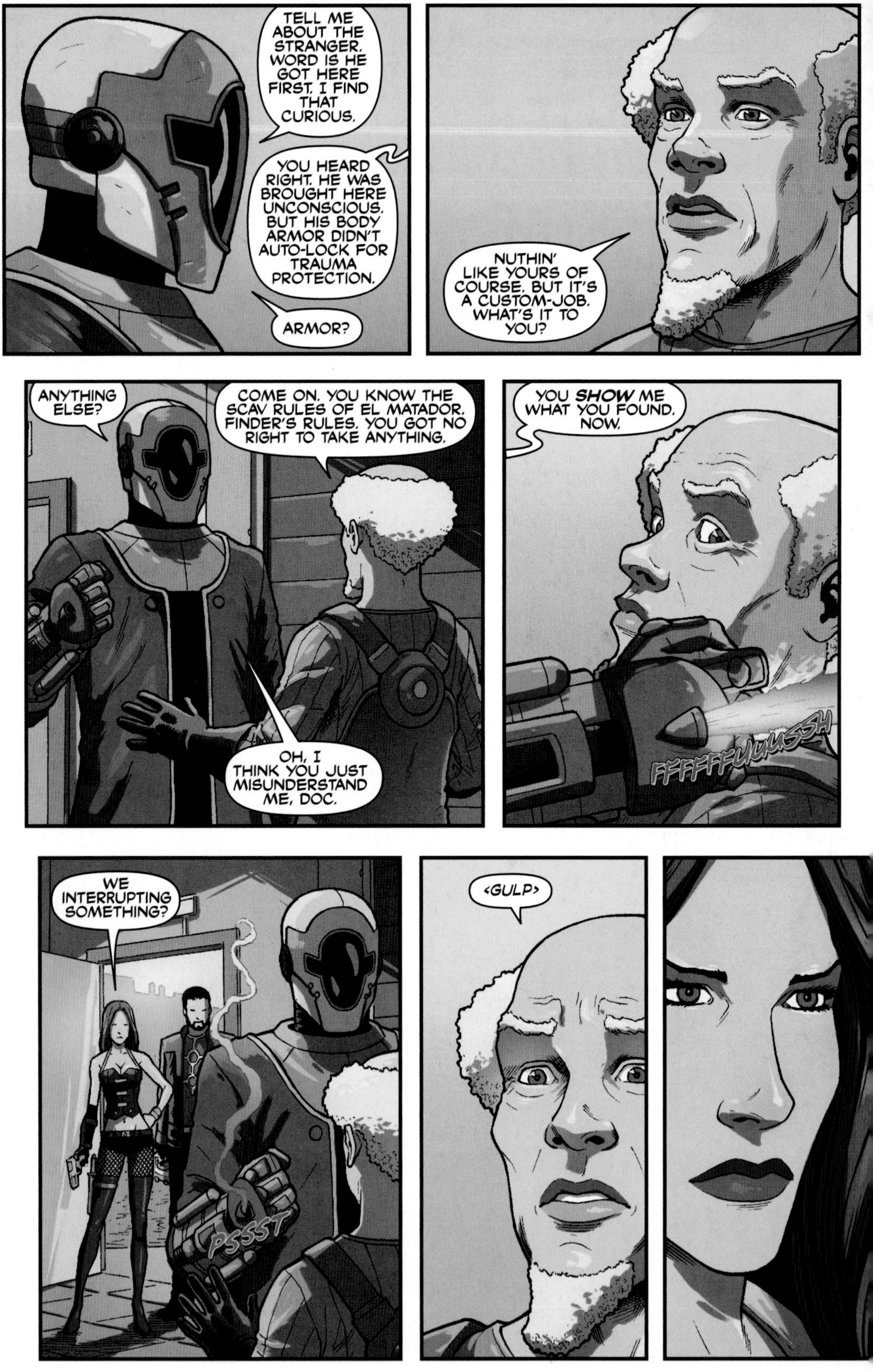

TELL ME ABOUT THE STRANGER. WORD IS HE GOT HERE FIRST. I FIND THAT CURIOUS.
YOU HEARD RIGHT. HE WAS BROUGHT HERE UNCONSCIOUS. BUT HIS BODY ARMOR DIDN'T AUTO-LOCK FOR TRAUMA PROTECTION.
ARMOR?
NUTHIN' LIKE YOURS OF COURSE. BUT IT'S A CUSTOM-JOB. WHAT'S IT TO YOU?
ANYTHING ELSE?
COME ON. YOU KNOW THE SCAV RULES OF EL MATADOR. FINDER'S RULES. YOU GOT NO RIGHT TO TAKE ANYTHING.
OH, I THINK YOU JUST MISUNDERSTAND ME, DOC.
YOU ***SHOW*** ME WHAT YOU FOUND. NOW.
FFFFFFUUUSSH
WE INTERRUPTING SOMETHING?
PSSST
<GULP>

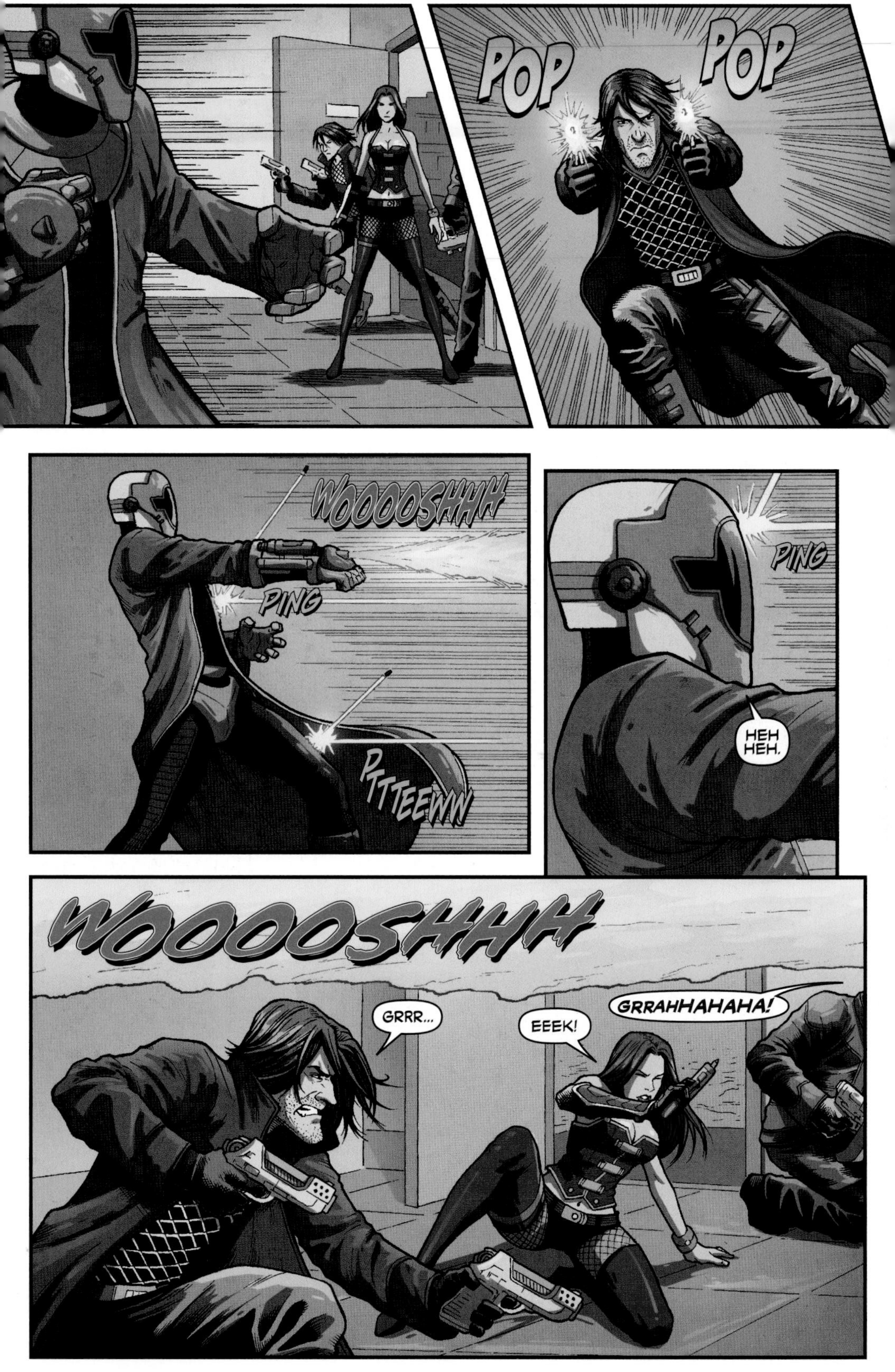
POP
POP
WOOOOSHHH
PING
PTTTEEWN
PING
HEH HEH.
WOOOOSHHH
GRRR...
EEEK!
GRRAHHAHAHA!

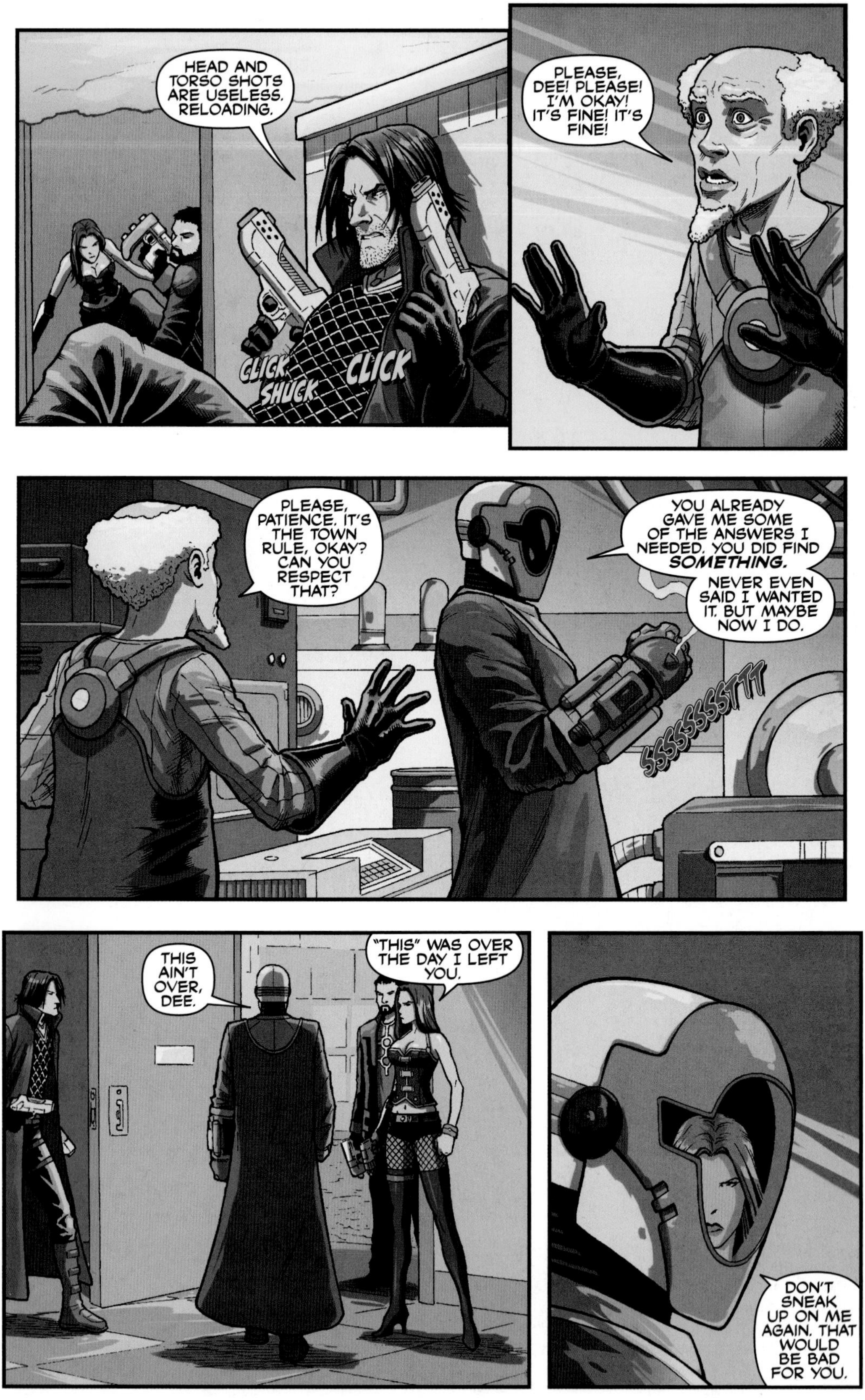
HEAD AND TORSO SHOTS ARE USELESS. RELOADING.
CLICK
SHUCK
CLICK
PLEASE, DEE! PLEASE! I'M OKAY! IT'S FINE! IT'S FINE!
PLEASE, PATIENCE. IT'S THE TOWN RULE, OKAY? CAN YOU RESPECT THAT?
YOU ALREADY GAVE ME SOME OF THE ANSWERS I NEEDED. YOU DID FIND *SOMETHING.*
NEVER EVEN SAID I WANTED IT. BUT MAYBE NOW I DO.
SSSSSSSSSTTT
THIS AIN'T OVER, DEE.
"THIS" WAS OVER THE DAY I LEFT YOU.
DON'T SNEAK UP ON ME AGAIN. THAT WOULD BE BAD FOR YOU.

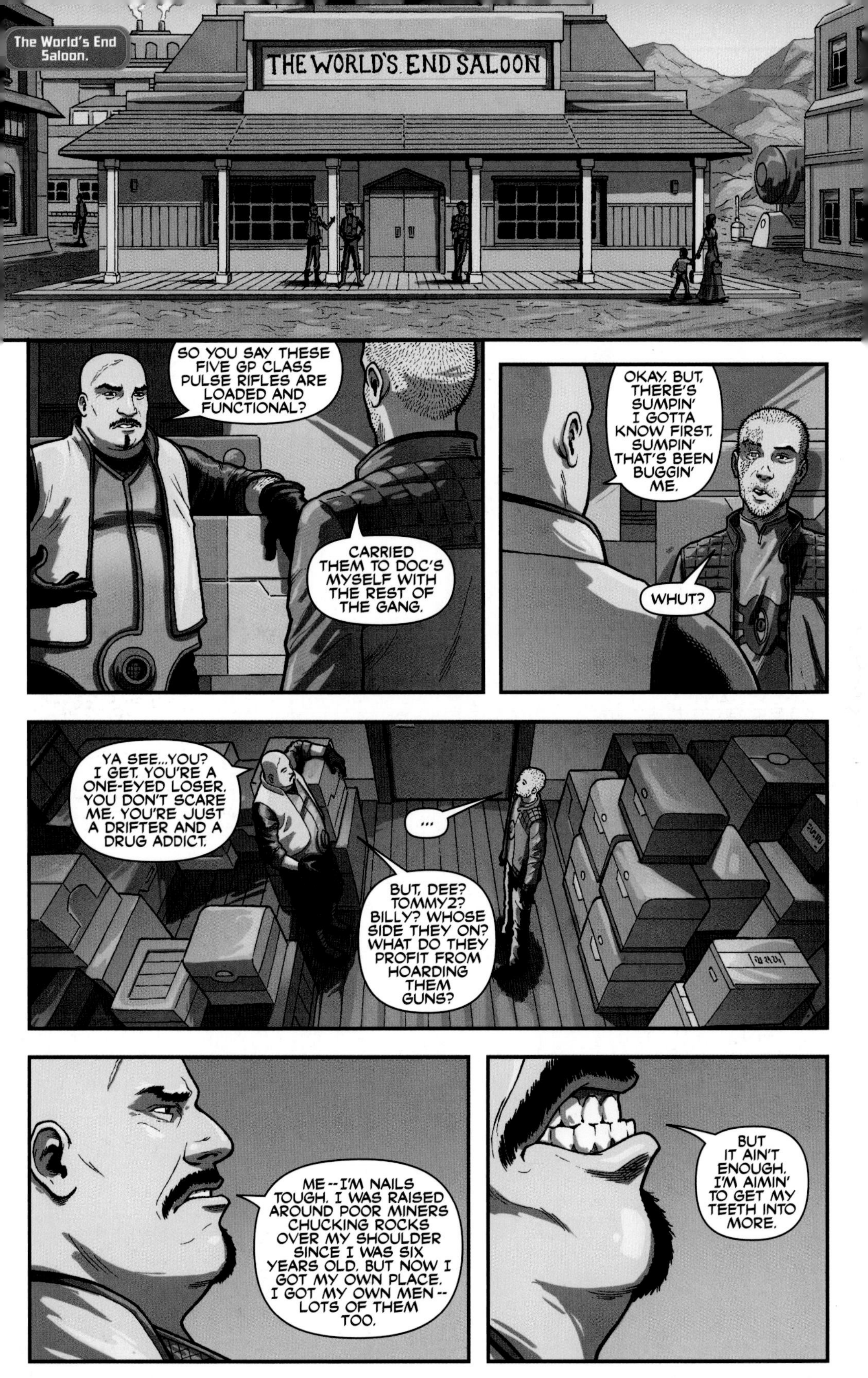
The World's End Saloon.
THE WORLD'S END SALOON
SO YOU SAY THESE FIVE GP CLASS PULSE RIFLES ARE LOADED AND FUNCTIONAL?
CARRIED THEM TO DOC'S MYSELF WITH THE REST OF THE GANG.
OKAY. BUT, THERE'S SUMPIN' I GOTTA KNOW FIRST. SUMPIN' THAT'S BEEN BUGGIN' ME.
WHUT?
YA SEE...YOU? I GET. YOU'RE A ONE-EYED LOSER. YOU DON'T SCARE ME. YOU'RE JUST A DRIFTER AND A DRUG ADDICT.
...
BUT, DEE? TOMMY2? BILLY? WHOSE SIDE THEY ON? WHAT DO THEY PROFIT FROM HOARDING THEM GUNS?
ME -- I'M NAILS TOUGH. I WAS RAISED AROUND POOR MINERS CHUCKING ROCKS OVER MY SHOULDER SINCE I WAS SIX YEARS OLD. BUT NOW I GOT MY OWN PLACE. I GOT MY OWN MEN -- LOTS OF THEM TOO.
BUT IT AIN'T ENOUGH. I'M AIMIN' TO GET MY TEETH INTO MORE.

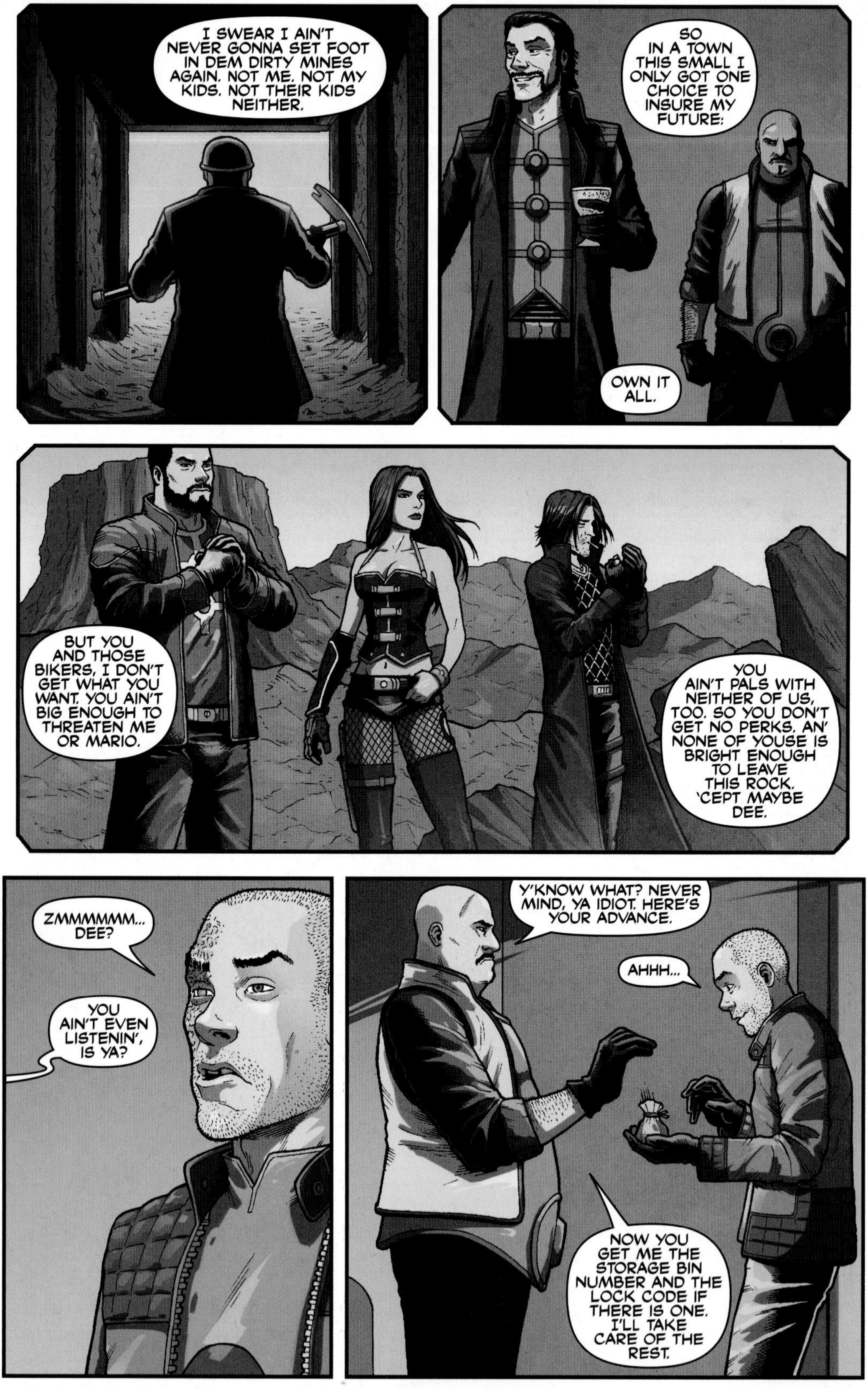
I SWEAR I AIN'T NEVER GONNA SET FOOT IN DEM DIRTY MINES AGAIN. NOT ME. NOT MY KIDS. NOT THEIR KIDS NEITHER.
SO IN A TOWN THIS SMALL I ONLY GOT ONE CHOICE TO INSURE MY FUTURE:
OWN IT ALL.
BUT YOU AND THOSE BIKERS, I DON'T GET WHAT YOU WANT. YOU AIN'T BIG ENOUGH TO THREATEN ME OR MARIO.
YOU AIN'T PALS WITH NEITHER OF US, TOO. SO YOU DON'T GET NO PERKS. AN' NONE OF YOUSE IS BRIGHT ENOUGH TO LEAVE THIS ROCK. 'CEPT MAYBE DEE.
ZMMMMMM... DEE?
YOU AIN'T EVEN LISTENIN', IS YA?
Y'KNOW WHAT? NEVER MIND, YA IDIOT. HERE'S YOUR ADVANCE.
AHHH...
NOW YOU GET ME THE STORAGE BIN NUMBER AND THE LOCK CODE IF THERE IS ONE. I'LL TAKE CARE OF THE REST.

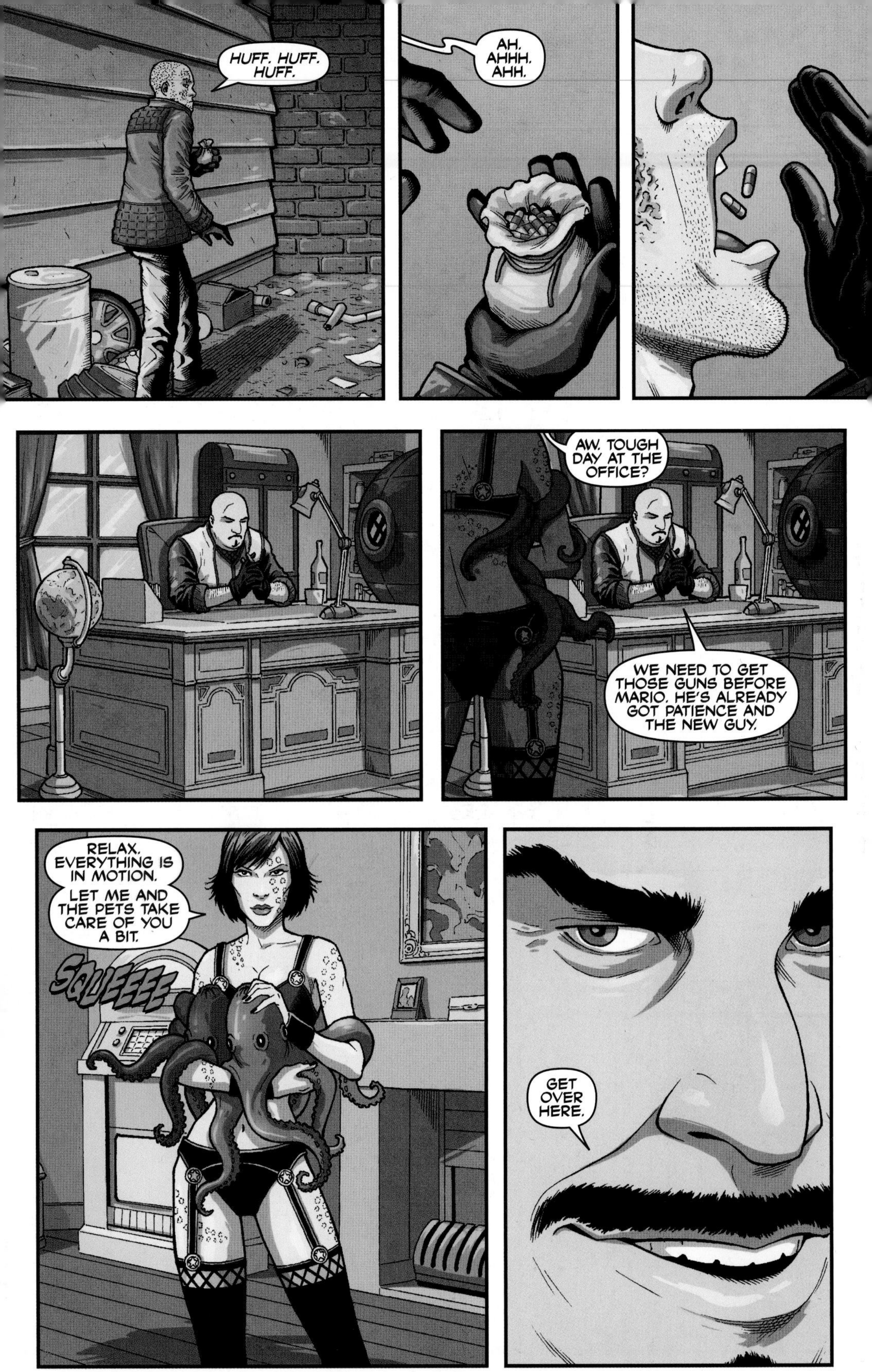
HUFF. HUFF. HUFF.
AH. AHHH. AHH.
AW. TOUGH DAY AT THE OFFICE?
WE NEED TO GET THOSE GUNS BEFORE MARIO. HE'S ALREADY GOT PATIENCE AND THE NEW GUY.
RELAX. EVERYTHING IS IN MOTION.
LET ME AND THE PETS TAKE CARE OF YOU A BIT.
SQUEEEE
GET OVER HERE.

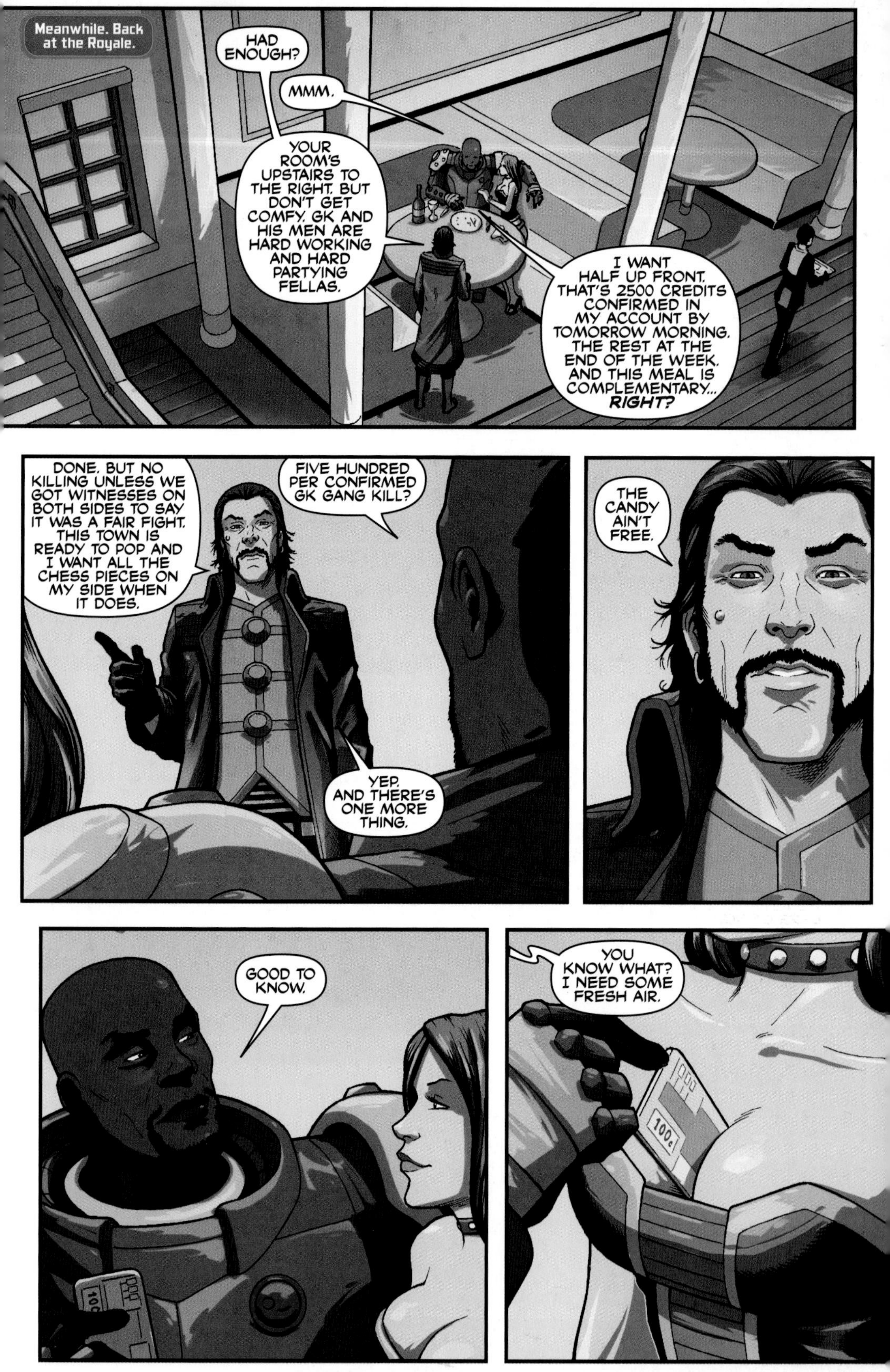
Meanwhile. Back at the Royale.
HAD ENOUGH?
MMM.
YOUR ROOM'S UPSTAIRS TO THE RIGHT. BUT DON'T GET COMFY. GK AND HIS MEN ARE HARD WORKING AND HARD PARTYING FELLAS.
I WANT HALF UP FRONT. THAT'S 2500 CREDITS CONFIRMED IN MY ACCOUNT BY TOMORROW MORNING. THE REST AT THE END OF THE WEEK. AND THIS MEAL IS COMPLEMENTARY... RIGHT?
FIVE HUNDRED PER CONFIRMED GK GANG KILL?
DONE. BUT NO KILLING UNLESS WE GOT WITNESSES ON BOTH SIDES TO SAY IT WAS A FAIR FIGHT. THIS TOWN IS READY TO POP AND I WANT ALL THE CHESS PIECES ON MY SIDE WHEN IT DOES.
YEP. AND THERE'S ONE MORE THING.
THE CANDY AIN'T FREE.
GOOD TO KNOW.
YOU KNOW WHAT? I NEED SOME FRESH AIR.
100¢

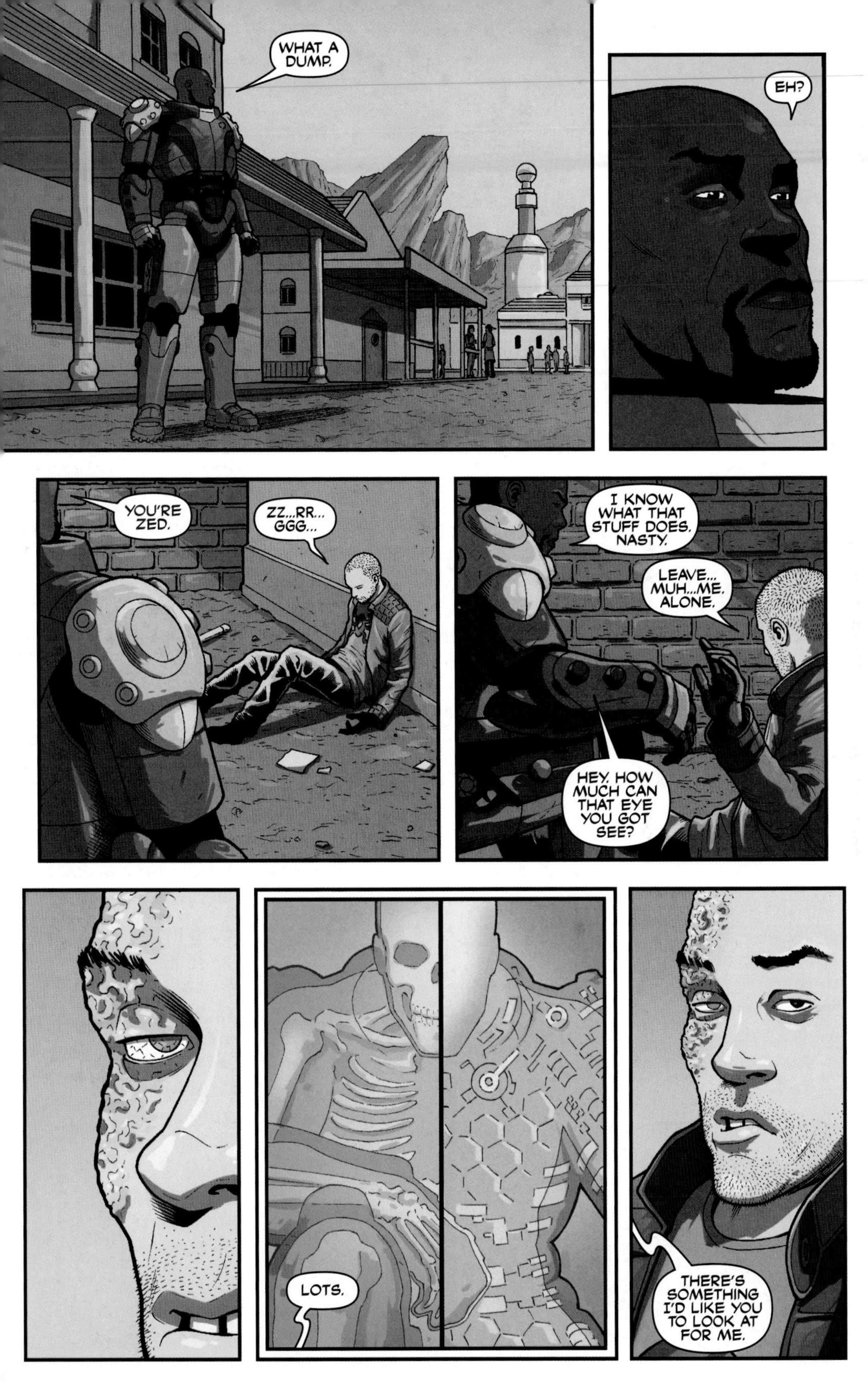
WHAT A DUMP.
EH?
YOU'RE ZED.
ZZ...RR... GGG...
I KNOW WHAT THAT STUFF DOES. NASTY.
LEAVE... MUH...ME. ALONE.
HEY. HOW MUCH CAN THAT EYE YOU GOT SEE?
LOTS.
THERE'S SOMETHING I'D LIKE YOU TO LOOK AT FOR ME.

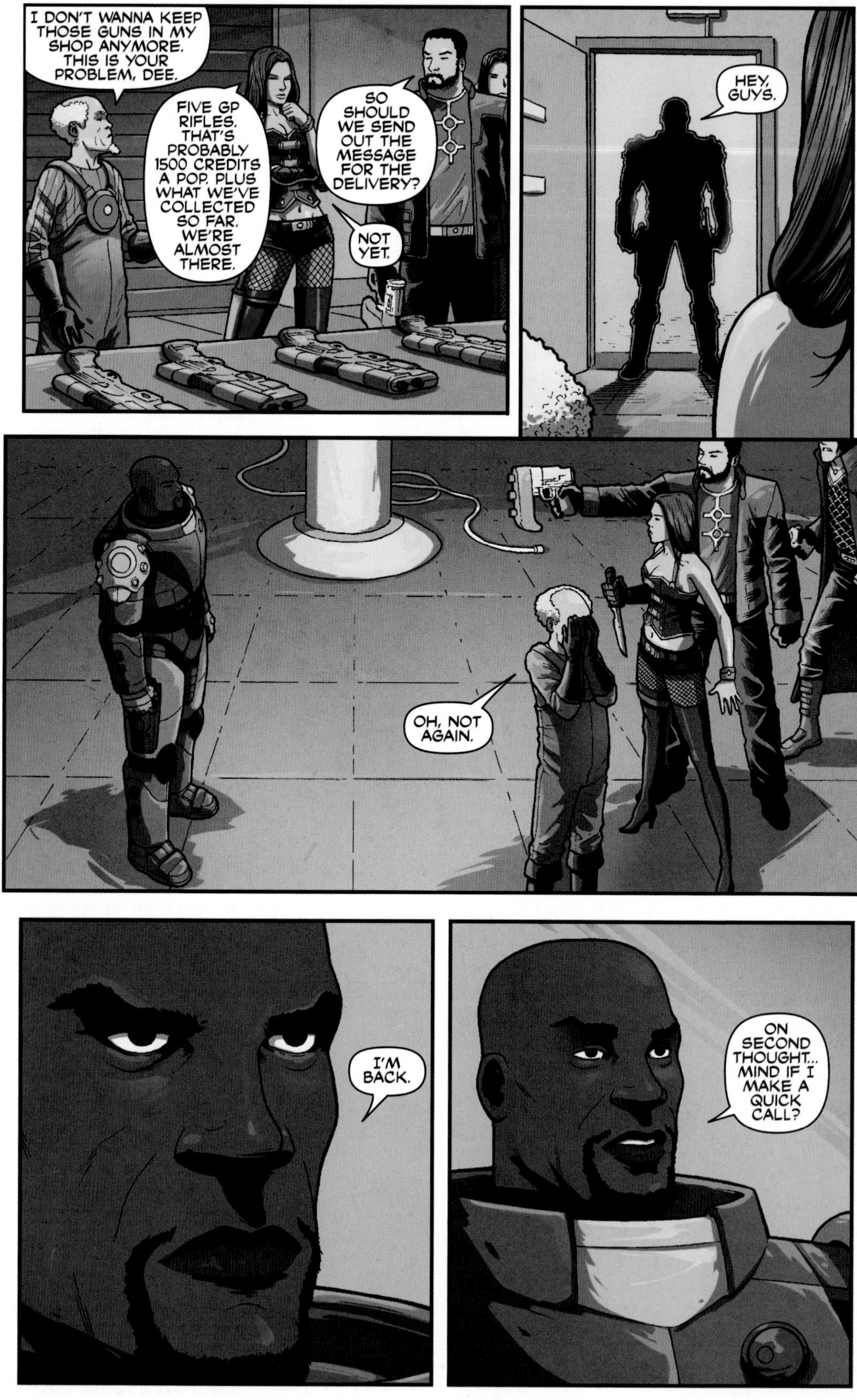

I DON'T WANNA KEEP THOSE GUNS IN MY SHOP ANYMORE. THIS IS YOUR PROBLEM, DEE.
FIVE GP RIFLES. THAT'S PROBABLY 1500 CREDITS A POP. PLUS WHAT WE'VE COLLECTED SO FAR. WE'RE ALMOST THERE.
SO SHOULD WE SEND OUT THE MESSAGE FOR THE DELIVERY?
NOT YET.
HEY, GUYS.
OH, NOT AGAIN.
I'M BACK.
ON SECOND THOUGHT... MIND IF I MAKE A QUICK CALL?

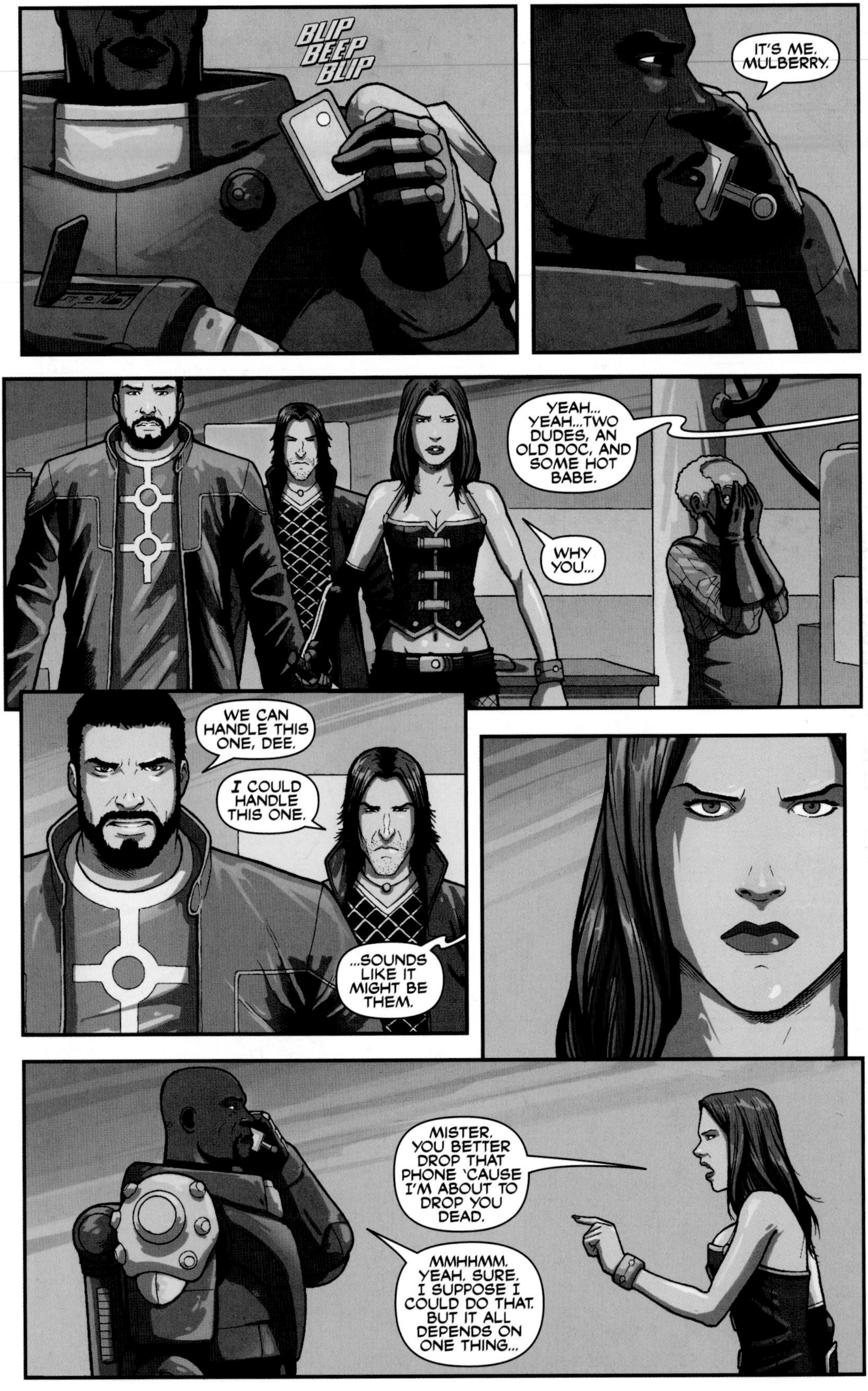
BLIP BEEP BLIP
IT'S ME. MULBERRY.
YEAH... YEAH...TWO DUDES, AN OLD DOC, AND SOME HOT BABE.
WHY YOU...
WE CAN HANDLE THIS ONE, DEE.
I COULD HANDLE THIS ONE.
...SOUNDS LIKE IT MIGHT BE THEM.
MISTER. YOU BETTER DROP THAT PHONE 'CAUSE I'M ABOUT TO DROP YOU DEAD.
MMHHMM. YEAH. SURE. I SUPPOSE I COULD DO THAT. BUT IT ALL DEPENDS ON ONE THING...

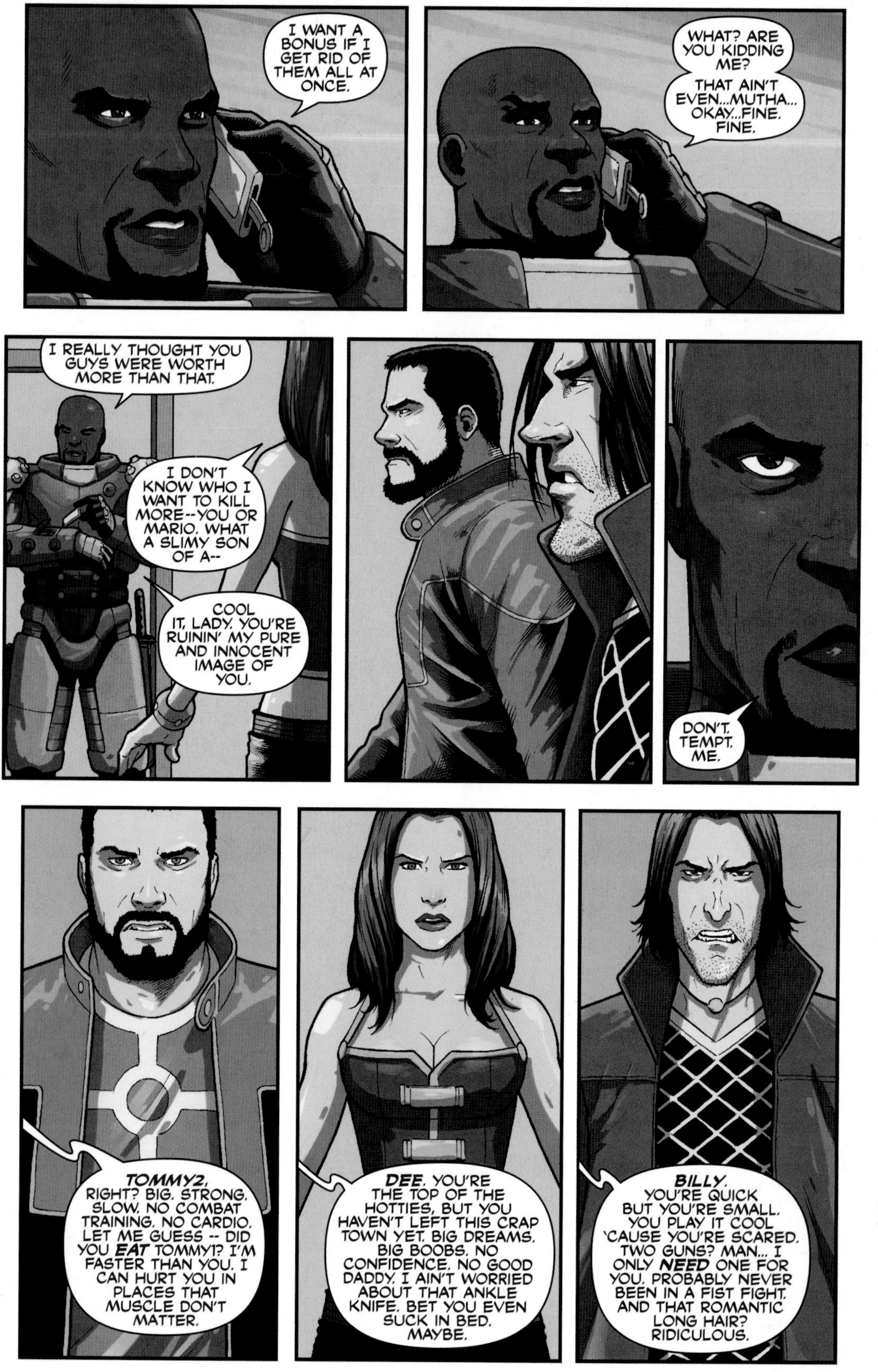

I WANT A BONUS IF I GET RID OF THEM ALL AT ONCE.
WHAT? ARE YOU KIDDING ME?
THAT AIN'T EVEN...MUTHA... OKAY...FINE. FINE.
I REALLY THOUGHT YOU GUYS WERE WORTH MORE THAN THAT.
I DON'T KNOW WHO I WANT TO KILL MORE--YOU OR MARIO. WHAT A SLIMY SON OF A--
COOL IT, LADY. YOU'RE RUININ' MY PURE AND INNOCENT IMAGE OF YOU.
DON'T. TEMPT. ME.
TOMMY2, RIGHT? BIG. STRONG. SLOW. NO COMBAT TRAINING. NO CARDIO. LET ME GUESS -- DID YOU EAT TOMMY1? I'M FASTER THAN YOU. I CAN HURT YOU IN PLACES THAT MUSCLE DON'T MATTER.
DEE. YOU'RE THE TOP OF THE HOTTIES, BUT YOU HAVEN'T LEFT THIS CRAP TOWN YET. BIG DREAMS. BIG BOOBS. NO CONFIDENCE. NO GOOD DADDY. I AIN'T WORRIED ABOUT THAT ANKLE KNIFE. BET YOU EVEN SUCK IN BED. MAYBE.
BILLY. YOU'RE QUICK BUT YOU'RE SMALL. YOU PLAY IT COOL 'CAUSE YOU'RE SCARED. TWO GUNS? MAN... I ONLY NEED ONE FOR YOU. PROBABLY NEVER BEEN IN A FIST FIGHT. AND THAT ROMANTIC LONG HAIR? RIDICULOUS.

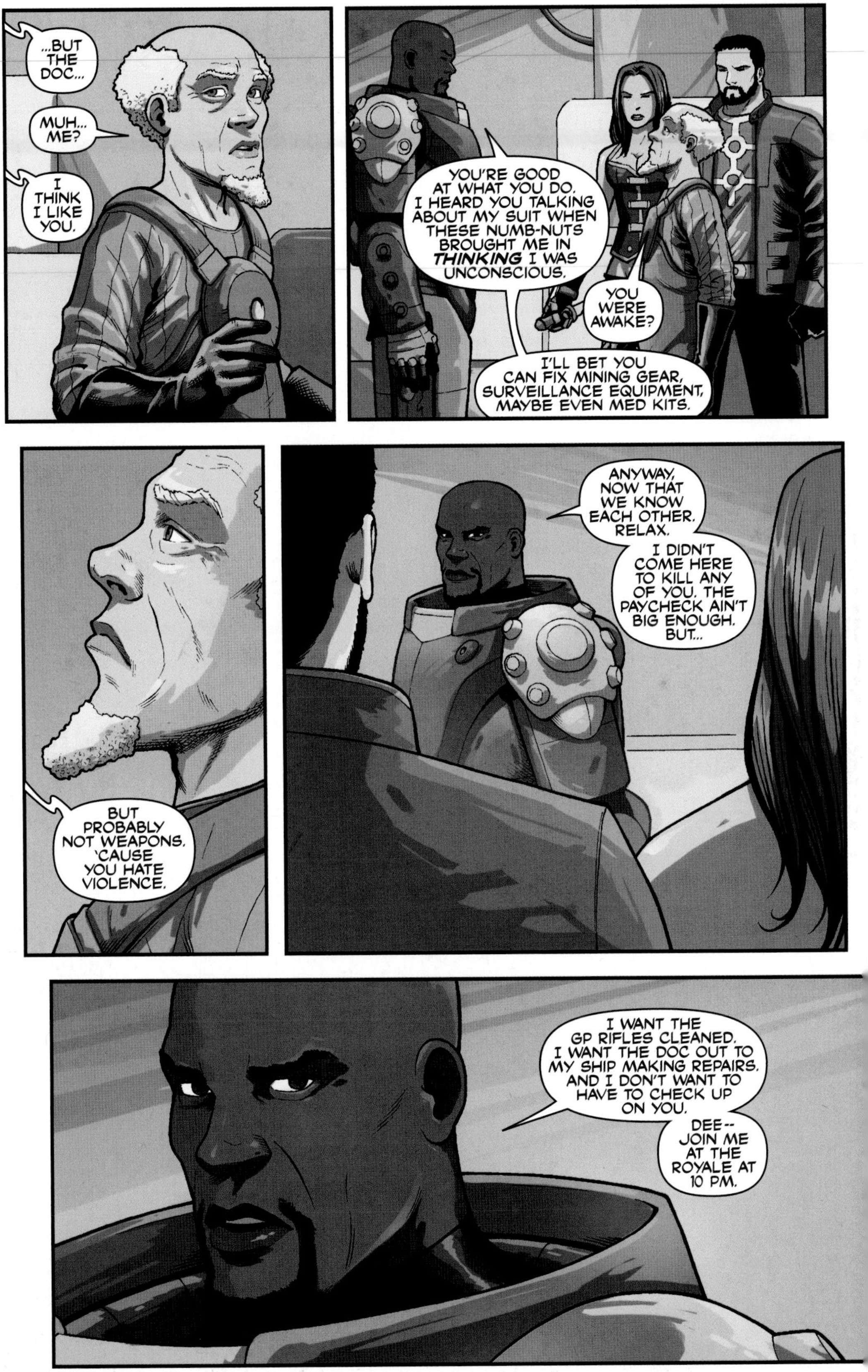
...BUT THE DOC...
MUH... ME?
I THINK I LIKE YOU.
YOU'RE GOOD AT WHAT YOU DO. I HEARD YOU TALKING ABOUT MY SUIT WHEN THESE NUMB-NUTS BROUGHT ME IN *THINKING* I WAS UNCONSCIOUS.
YOU WERE AWAKE?
I'LL BET YOU CAN FIX MINING GEAR, SURVEILLANCE EQUIPMENT, MAYBE EVEN MED KITS.
BUT PROBABLY NOT WEAPONS. 'CAUSE YOU HATE VIOLENCE.
ANYWAY, NOW THAT WE KNOW EACH OTHER, RELAX.
I DIDN'T COME HERE TO KILL ANY OF YOU. THE PAYCHECK AIN'T BIG ENOUGH. BUT...
I WANT THE GP RIFLES CLEANED. I WANT THE DOC OUT TO MY SHIP MAKING REPAIRS. AND I DON'T WANT TO HAVE TO CHECK UP ON YOU.
DEE-- JOIN ME AT THE ROYALE AT 10 PM.

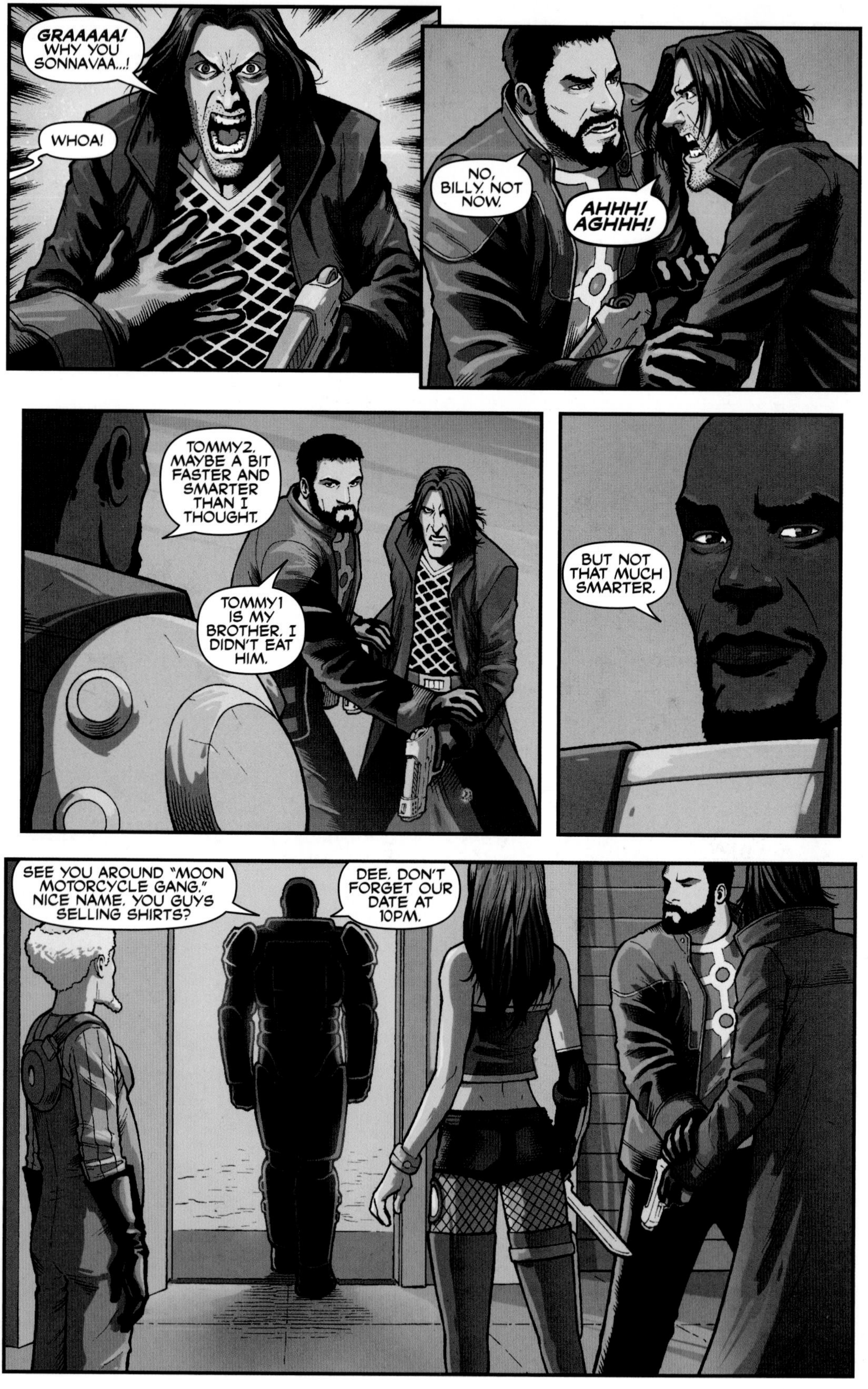
GRAAAAA! WHY YOU SONNAVAA...!
WHOA!
NO, BILLY. NOT NOW.
AHHH! AGHHH!
TOMMY2. MAYBE A BIT FASTER AND SMARTER THAN I THOUGHT.
TOMMY1 IS MY BROTHER. I DIDN'T EAT HIM.
BUT NOT THAT MUCH SMARTER.
SEE YOU AROUND "MOON MOTORCYCLE GANG." NICE NAME. YOU GUYS SELLING SHIRTS?
DEE. DON'T FORGET OUR DATE AT 10PM.

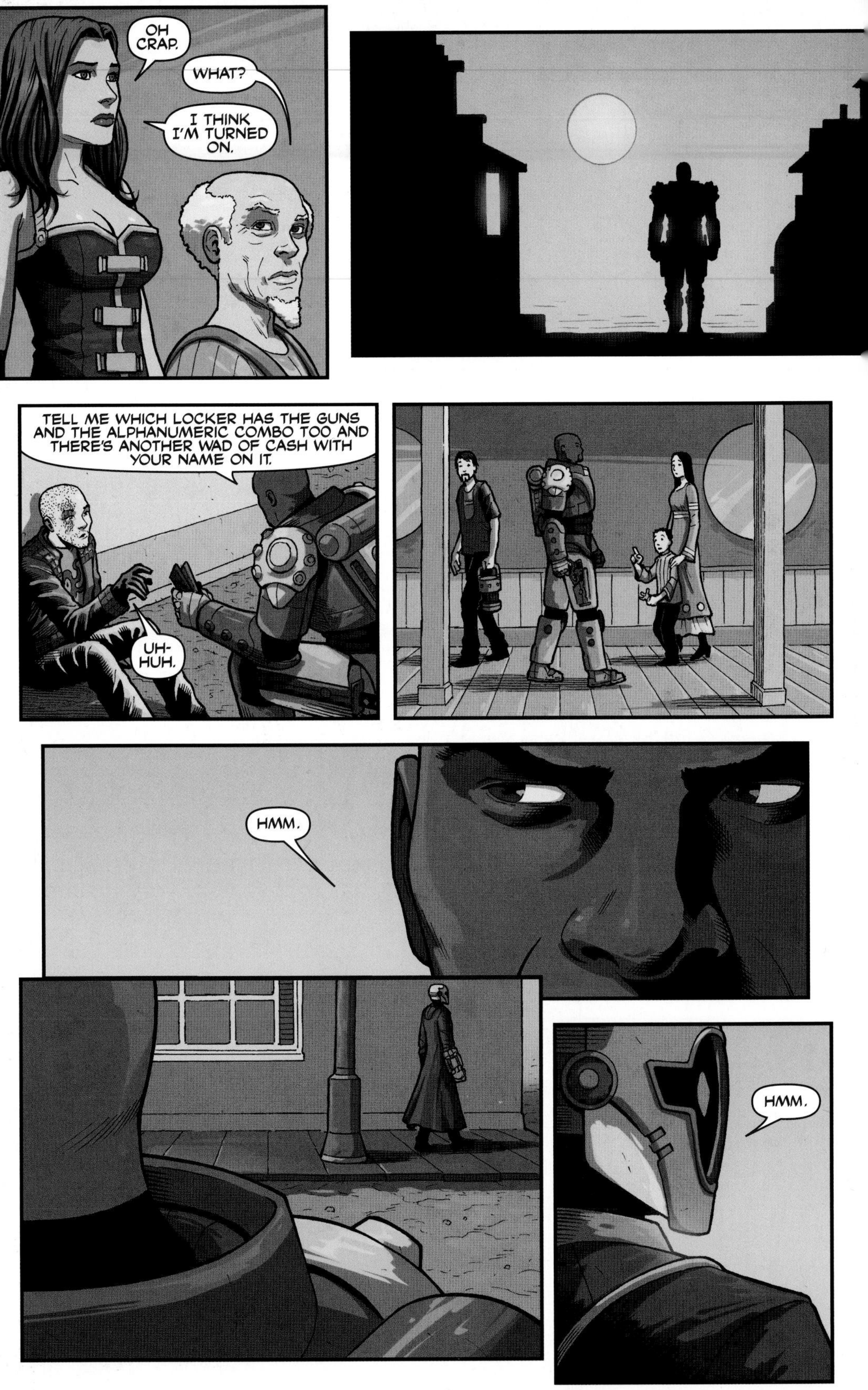
OH CRAP.
WHAT?
I THINK I'M TURNED ON.
TELL ME WHICH LOCKER HAS THE GUNS AND THE ALPHANUMERIC COMBO TOO AND THERE'S ANOTHER WAD OF CASH WITH YOUR NAME ON IT.
UH-HUH.
HMM.
HMM.

CLICK CLACK

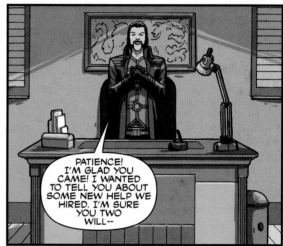

PATIENCE! I'M GLAD YOU CAME! I WANTED TO TELL YOU ABOUT SOME NEW HELP WE HIRED. I'M SURE YOU TWO WILL--

WOOOOSSSHHH

AGH! AHHHH! AHHHHHHHH!

"-- GET ALONG NICELY?" YEAH. SURE WE WILL.

LSSSSTTT

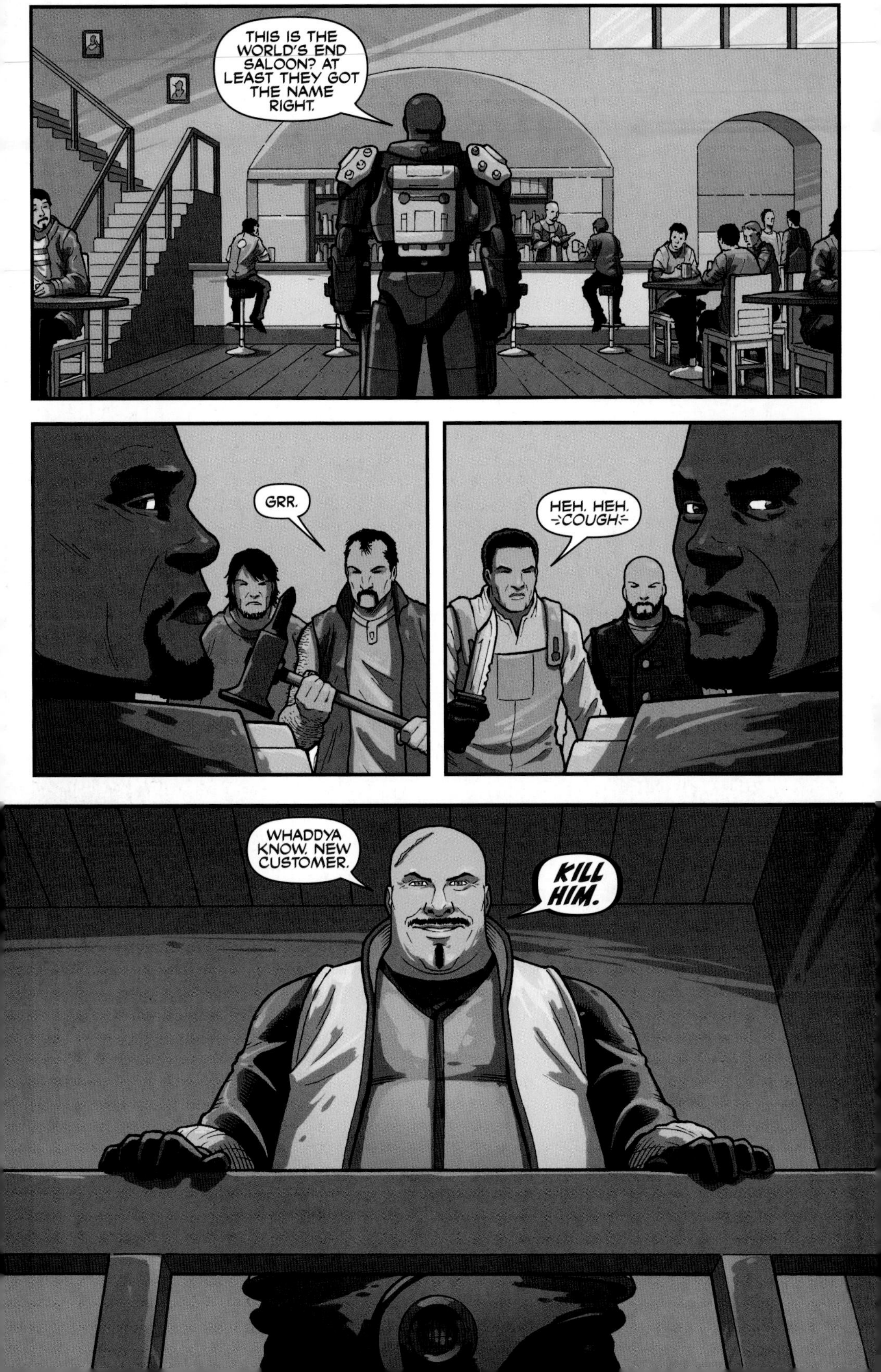
THIS IS THE WORLD'S END SALOON? AT LEAST THEY GOT THE NAME RIGHT.
GRR.
HEH. HEH. COUGH
WHADDYA KNOW. NEW CUSTOMER.
KILL HIM.

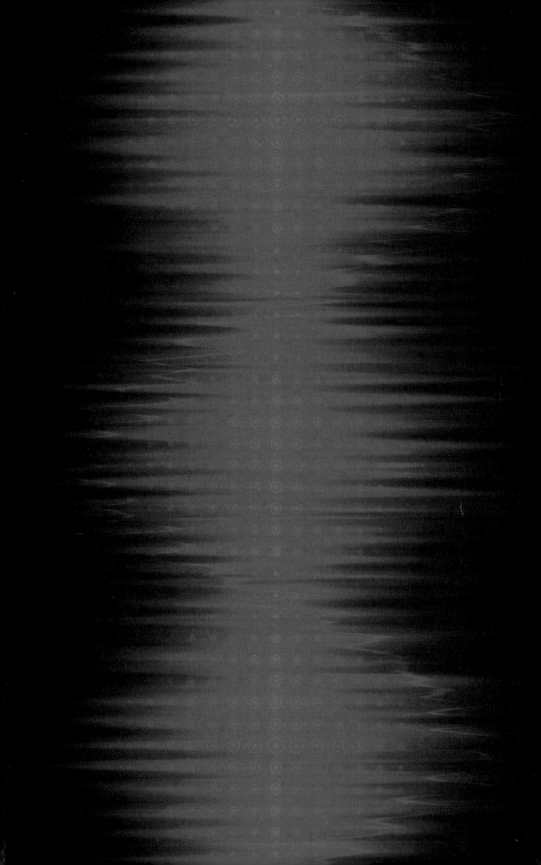

COLD SPACE

CHAPTER 3

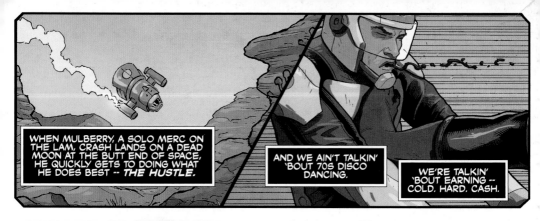

WHEN MULBERRY, A SOLO MERC ON THE LAM, CRASH LANDS ON A DEAD MOON AT THE BUTT END OF SPACE, HE QUICKLY GETS TO DOING WHAT HE DOES BEST -- *THE HUSTLE.*

AND WE AIN'T TALKIN' 'BOUT 70S DISCO DANCING.

WE'RE TALKIN' 'BOUT EARNING -- COLD. HARD. CASH.

BUT FRIENDS AND FOES QUICKLY APPEAR AND OLD MULBERRY FINDS HIMSELF IN THE MIDDLE OF SOMETHING THAT MIGHT TAKE MORE THAN THE QUICK DRAW OF HIS SIDE ARM.

DEE AND THE MOON MOTORCYCLE GANG: A HOT REDHEAD AND HER FREELANCE SCAVENGER PACK -- A TOUGH BUNCH.

MARIO WAID: THE OWNER OF THE ROYALE RESTAURANT AND POWERFUL GANG LEADER. MURDERED MOMENTS AGO.

GK: FORMER MOON MINER, OWNER OF THE WORLD'S END SALOON AND GANG LEADER. MARIO'S ONLY RIVAL. THE PLANET'S HEIR APPARENT.

PATIENCE: A MYSTERY MERC WITH A THING FOR FIRE. WORKED FOR MARIO. THAT IS, UNTIL HE KILLED HIM. EX-BOYFRIEND OF DEE.

DOC: AN OLD FELLOW WHO FIXES STUFF AND IS SCARED OF MOST EVERYTHING ELSE.

THAT'S A LOT OF FOLKS TO NAVIGATE. LUCKY FOR MULBERRY, SHOOTIN' IS HIS SECOND BEST SKILL...

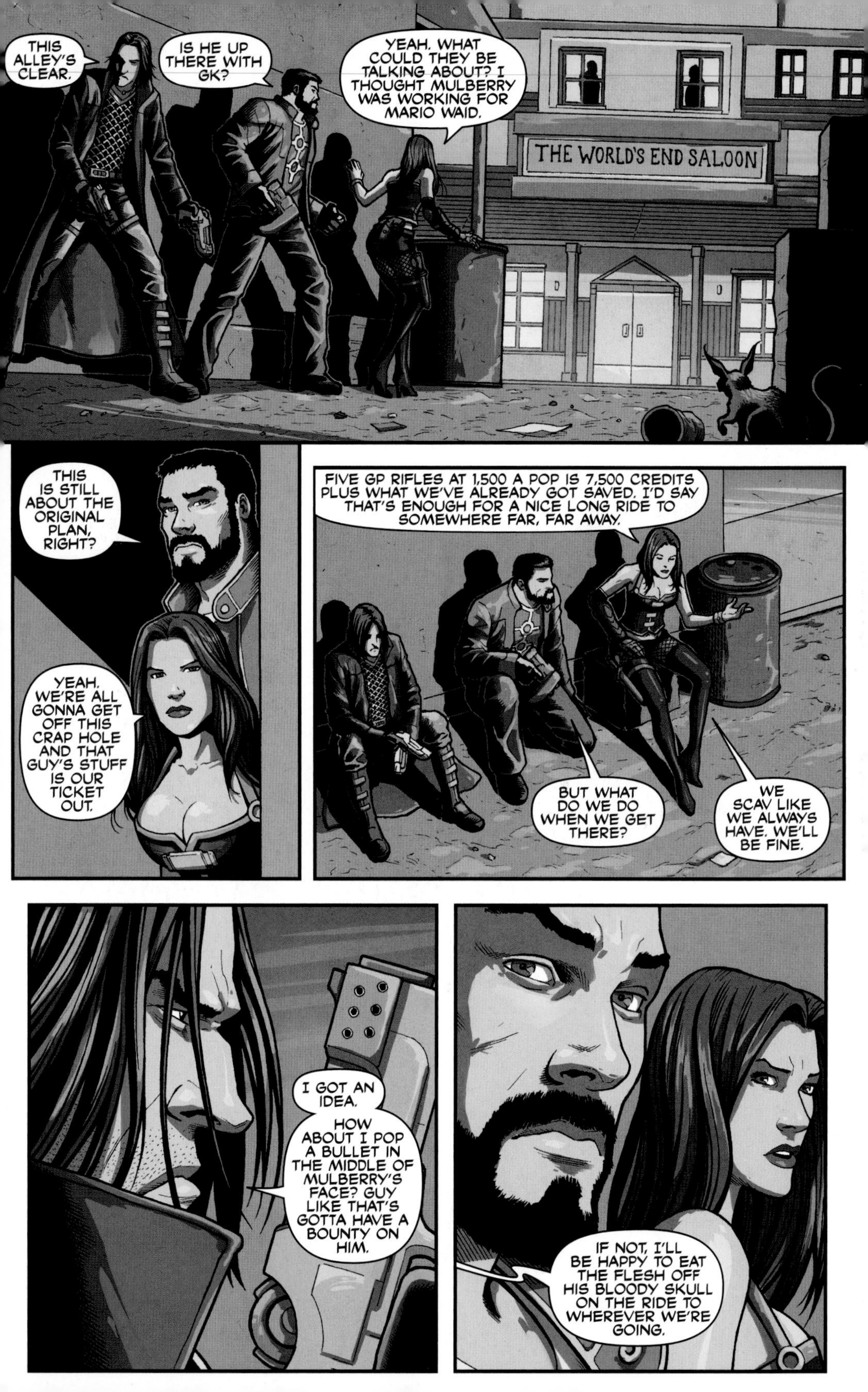

THIS ALLEY'S CLEAR.
IS HE UP THERE WITH GK?
YEAH. WHAT COULD THEY BE TALKING ABOUT? I THOUGHT MULBERRY WAS WORKING FOR MARIO WAID.
THE WORLD'S END SALOON
THIS IS STILL ABOUT THE ORIGINAL PLAN, RIGHT?
YEAH. WE'RE ALL GONNA GET OFF THIS CRAP HOLE AND THAT GUY'S STUFF IS OUR TICKET OUT.
FIVE GP RIFLES AT 1,500 A POP IS 7,500 CREDITS PLUS WHAT WE'VE ALREADY GOT SAVED. I'D SAY THAT'S ENOUGH FOR A NICE LONG RIDE TO SOMEWHERE FAR, FAR AWAY.
BUT WHAT DO WE DO WHEN WE GET THERE?
WE SCAV LIKE WE ALWAYS HAVE. WE'LL BE FINE.
I GOT AN IDEA.
HOW ABOUT I POP A BULLET IN THE MIDDLE OF MULBERRY'S FACE? GUY LIKE THAT'S GOTTA HAVE A BOUNTY ON HIM.
IF NOT, I'LL BE HAPPY TO EAT THE FLESH OFF HIS BLOODY SKULL ON THE RIDE TO WHEREVER WE'RE GOING.

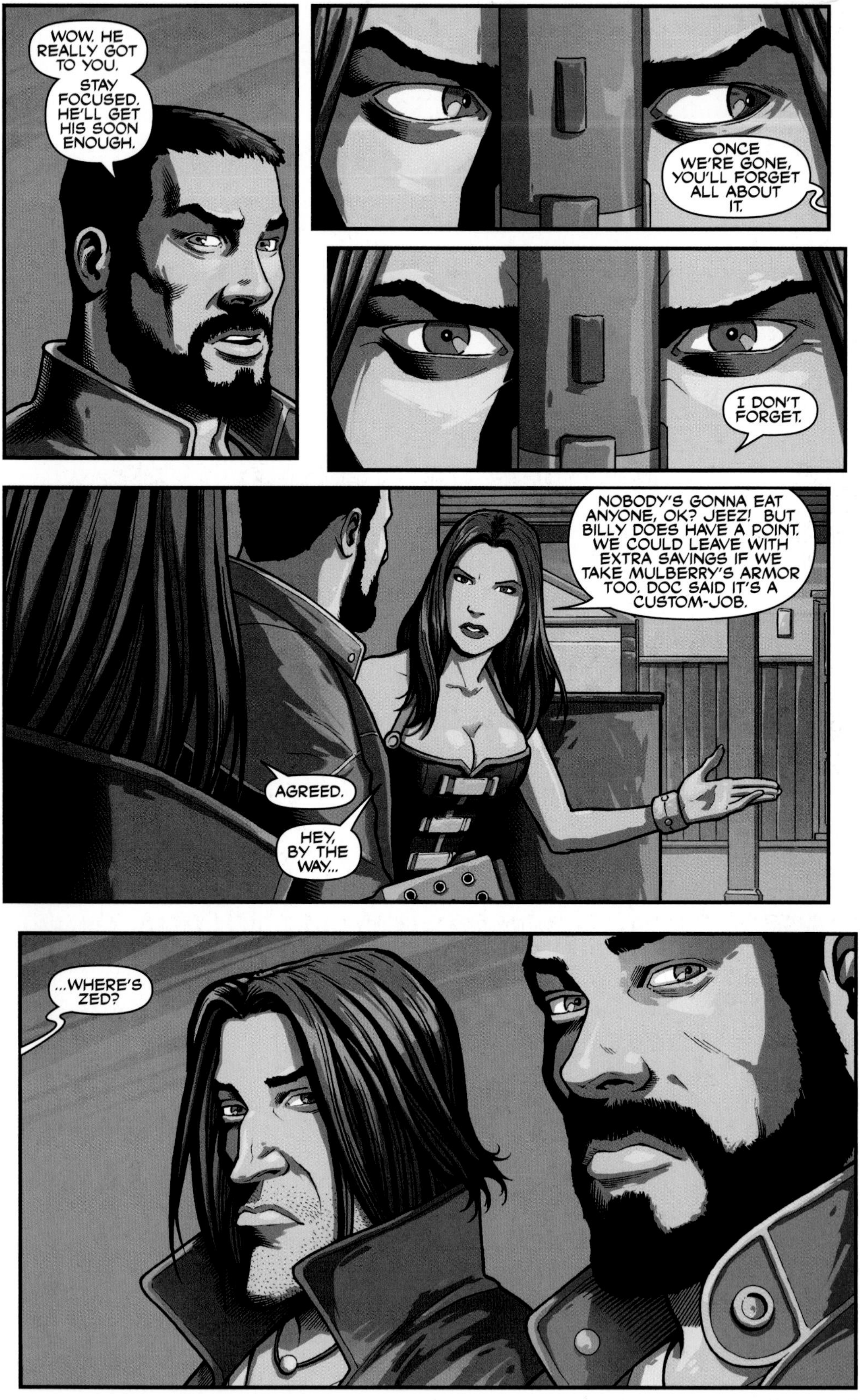
WOW. HE REALLY GOT TO YOU.
STAY FOCUSED. HE'LL GET HIS SOON ENOUGH.
ONCE WE'RE GONE, YOU'LL FORGET ALL ABOUT IT.
I DON'T FORGET.
NOBODY'S GONNA EAT ANYONE, OK? JEEZ! BUT BILLY DOES HAVE A POINT. WE COULD LEAVE WITH EXTRA SAVINGS IF WE TAKE MULBERRY'S ARMOR TOO. DOC SAID IT'S A CUSTOM-JOB.
AGREED.
HEY, BY THE WAY...
...WHERE'S ZED?

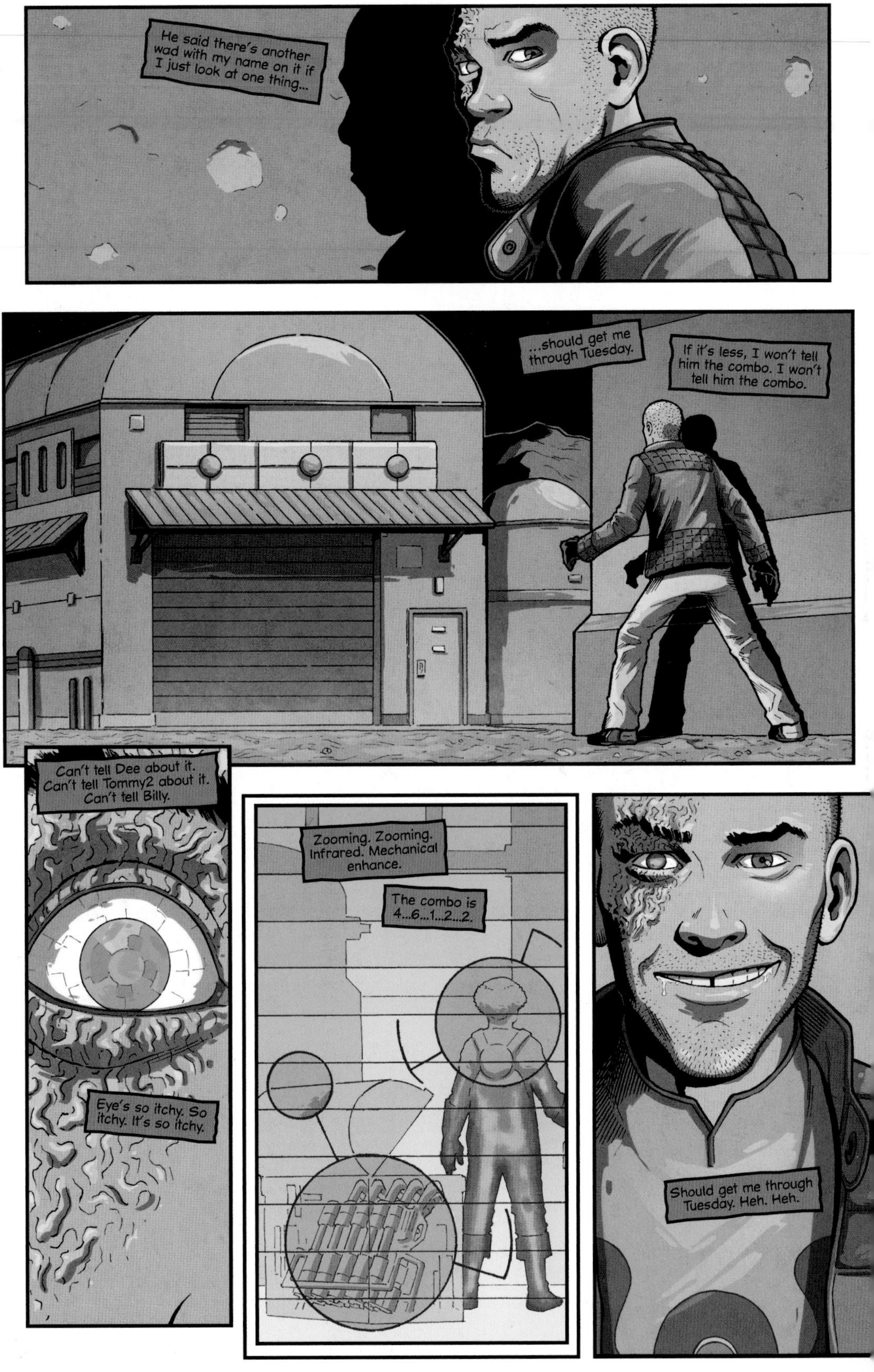
He said there's another wad with my name on it if I just look at one thing...
...should get me through Tuesday.
If it's less, I won't tell him the combo. I won't tell him the combo.
Can't tell Dee about it. Can't tell Tommy2 about it. Can't tell Billy.
Eye's so itchy. So itchy. It's so itchy.
Zooming. Zooming. Infrared. Mechanical enhance.
The combo is 4...6...1...2...2.
Should get me through Tuesday. Heh. Heh.

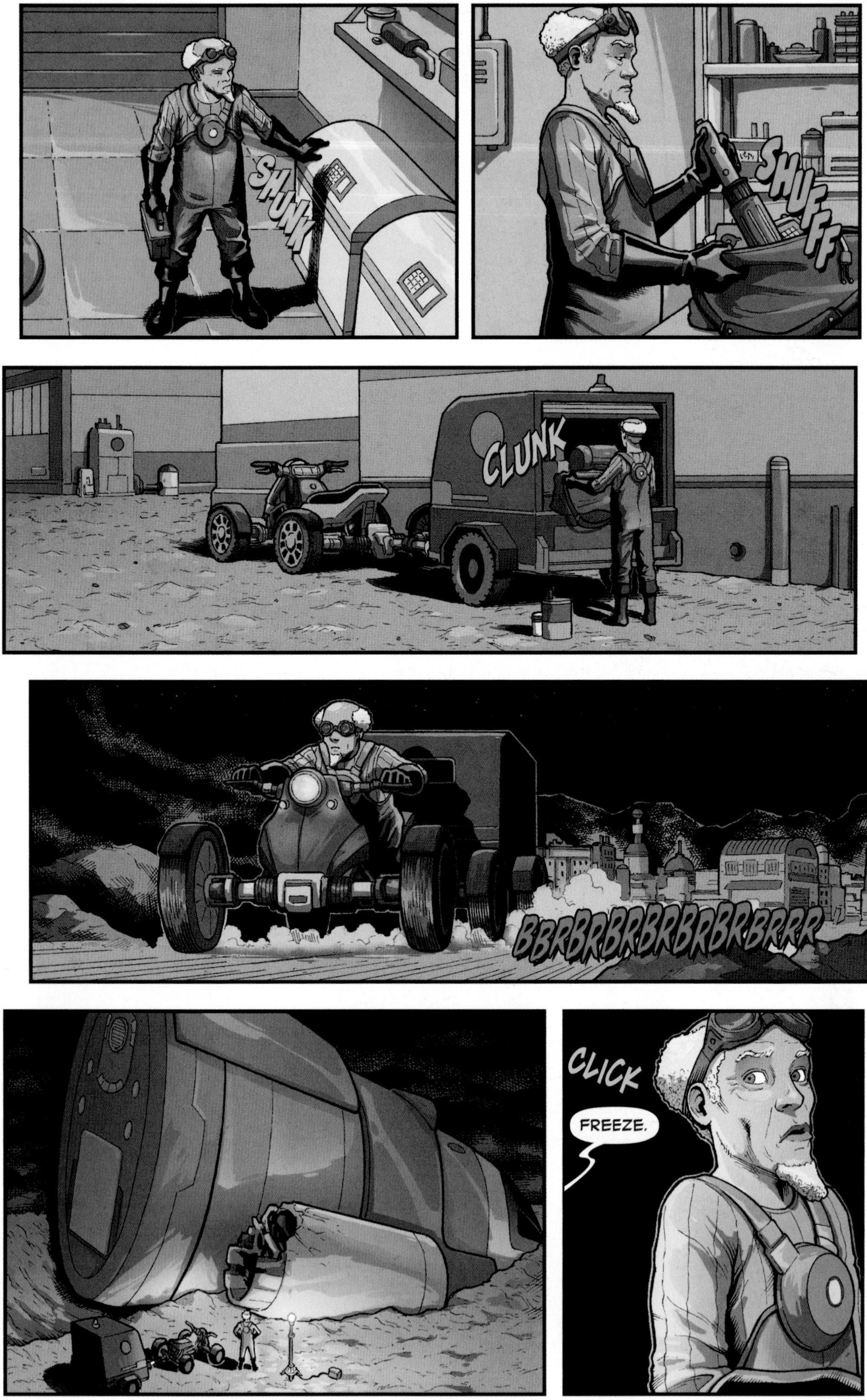
SHUNK
SHUFFF
CLUNK
BBRBRBRBRBRBRBRBRRR
CLICK
FREEZE.

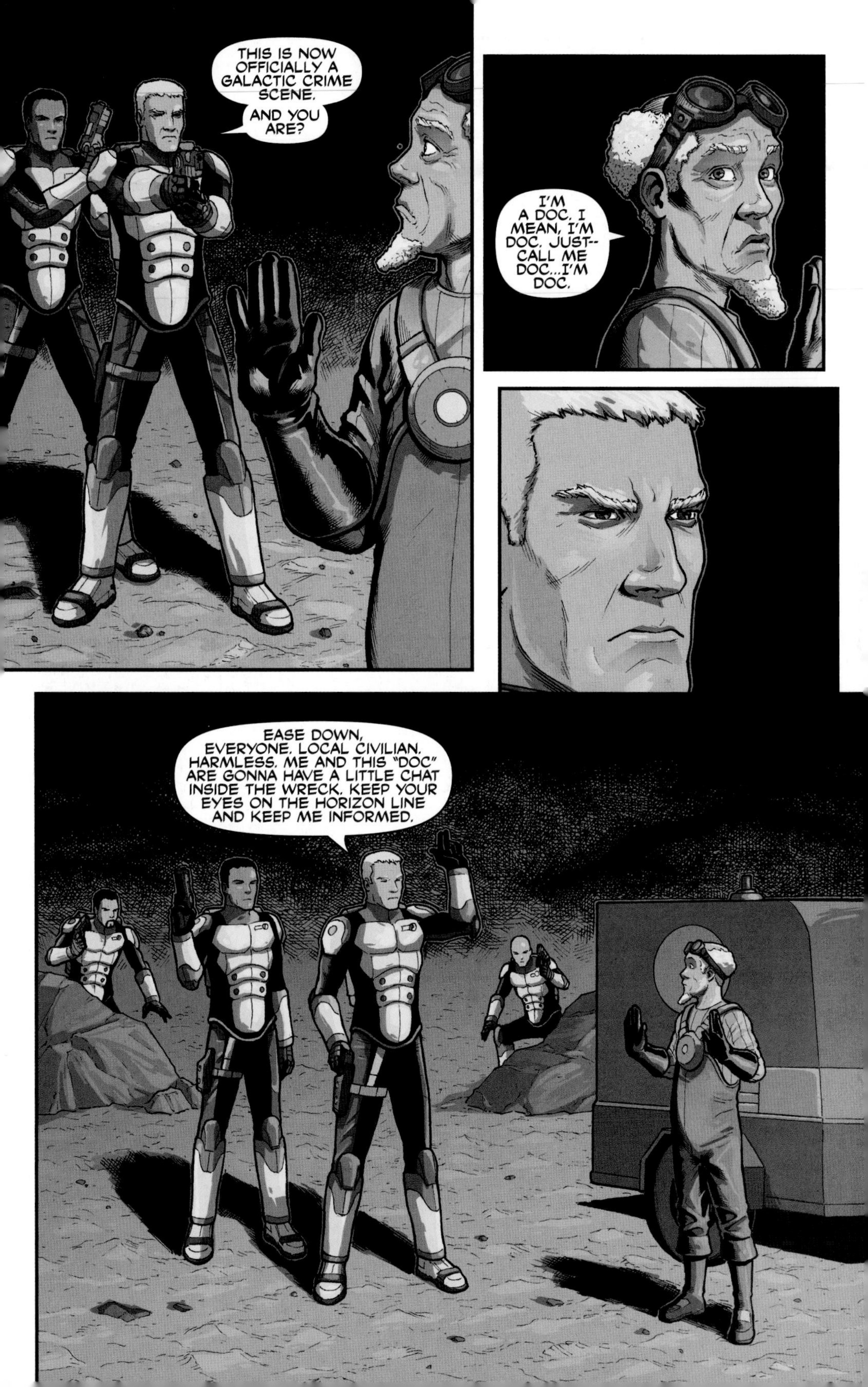
THIS IS NOW OFFICIALLY A GALACTIC CRIME SCENE.
AND YOU ARE?
I'M A DOC. I MEAN, I'M DOC. JUST-- CALL ME DOC...I'M DOC.
EASE DOWN, EVERYONE. LOCAL CIVILIAN. HARMLESS. ME AND THIS "DOC" ARE GONNA HAVE A LITTLE CHAT INSIDE THE WRECK. KEEP YOUR EYES ON THE HORIZON LINE AND KEEP ME INFORMED.

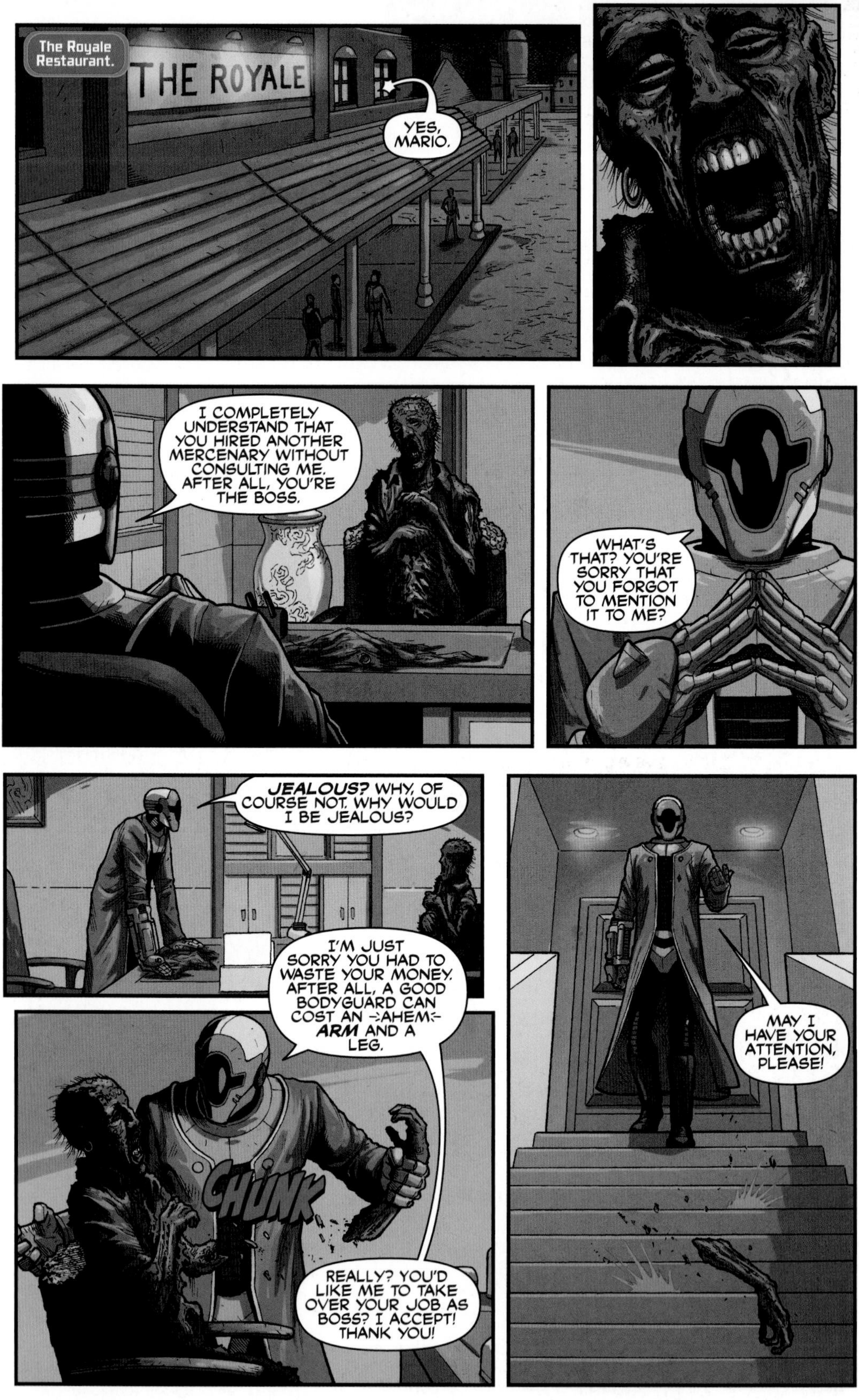
The Royale Restaurant.
THE ROYALE
YES, MARIO.
I COMPLETELY UNDERSTAND THAT YOU HIRED ANOTHER MERCENARY WITHOUT CONSULTING ME. AFTER ALL, YOU'RE THE BOSS.
WHAT'S THAT? YOU'RE SORRY THAT YOU FORGOT TO MENTION IT TO ME?
JEALOUS? WHY, OF COURSE NOT. WHY WOULD I BE JEALOUS?
I'M JUST SORRY YOU HAD TO WASTE YOUR MONEY. AFTER ALL, A GOOD BODYGUARD CAN COST AN -AHEM- ARM AND A LEG.
CHUNK
REALLY? YOU'D LIKE ME TO TAKE OVER YOUR JOB AS BOSS? I ACCEPT! THANK YOU!
MAY I HAVE YOUR ATTENTION, PLEASE!

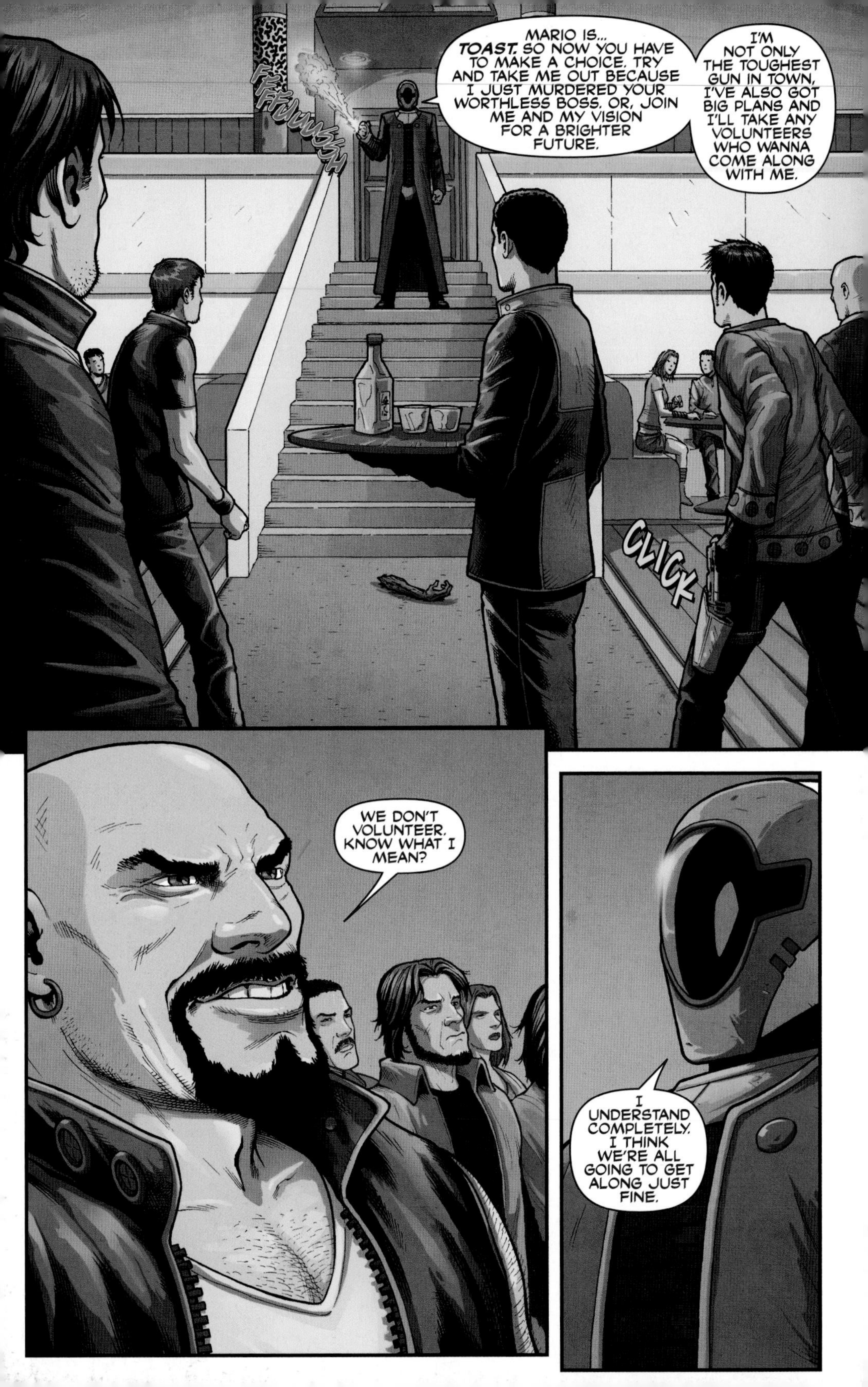
FFFFUUUUSSSH
MARIO IS... TOAST. SO NOW YOU HAVE TO MAKE A CHOICE. TRY AND TAKE ME OUT BECAUSE I JUST MURDERED YOUR WORTHLESS BOSS. OR, JOIN ME AND MY VISION FOR A BRIGHTER FUTURE.
I'M NOT ONLY THE TOUGHEST GUN IN TOWN, I'VE ALSO GOT BIG PLANS AND I'LL TAKE ANY VOLUNTEERS WHO WANNA COME ALONG WITH ME.
CLICK
WE DON'T VOLUNTEER. KNOW WHAT I MEAN?
I UNDERSTAND COMPLETELY. I THINK WE'RE ALL GOING TO GET ALONG JUST FINE.

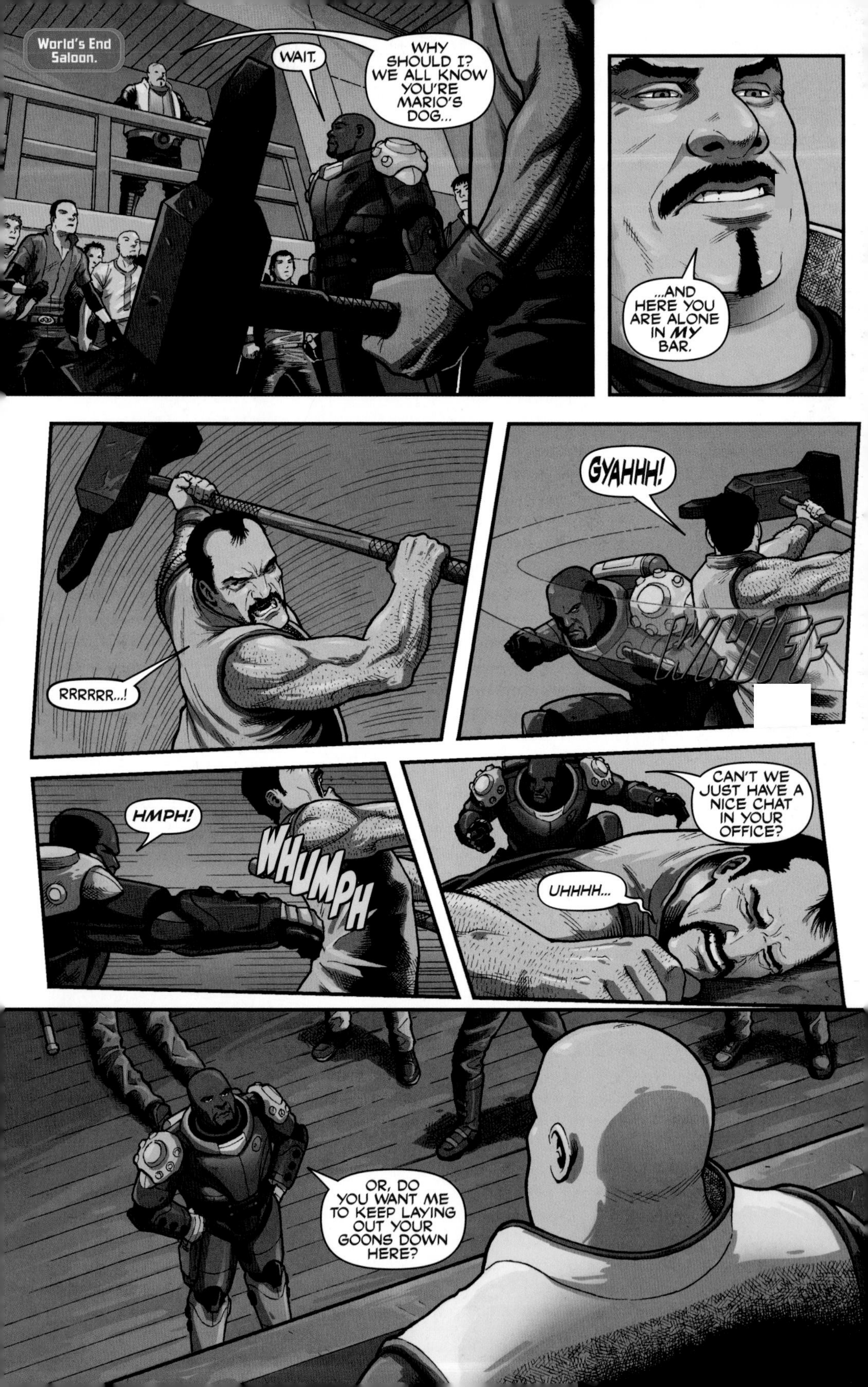

World's End Saloon.
WAIT.
WHY SHOULD I? WE ALL KNOW YOU'RE MARIO'S DOG...
...AND HERE YOU ARE ALONE IN MY BAR.
RRRRRR...!
GYAHHH!
HMPH!
WHUMPH
CAN'T WE JUST HAVE A NICE CHAT IN YOUR OFFICE?
UHHHH...
OR, DO YOU WANT ME TO KEEP LAYING OUT YOUR GOONS DOWN HERE?

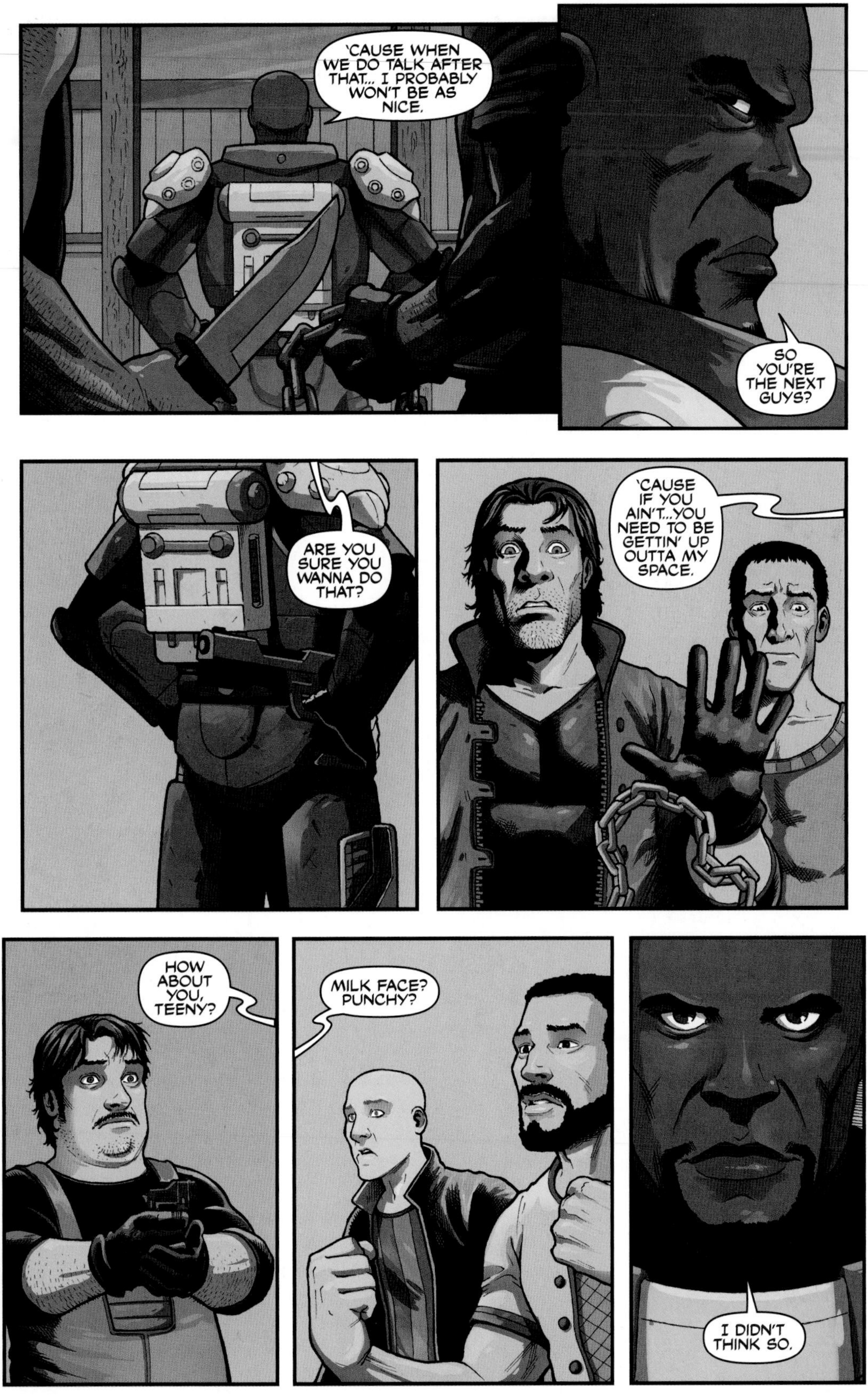
'CAUSE WHEN WE DO TALK AFTER THAT... I PROBABLY WON'T BE AS NICE.
SO YOU'RE THE NEXT GUYS?
ARE YOU SURE YOU WANNA DO THAT?
'CAUSE IF YOU AIN'T...YOU NEED TO BE GETTIN' UP OUTTA MY SPACE.
HOW ABOUT YOU, TEENY?
MILK FACE? PUNCHY?
I DIDN'T THINK SO.

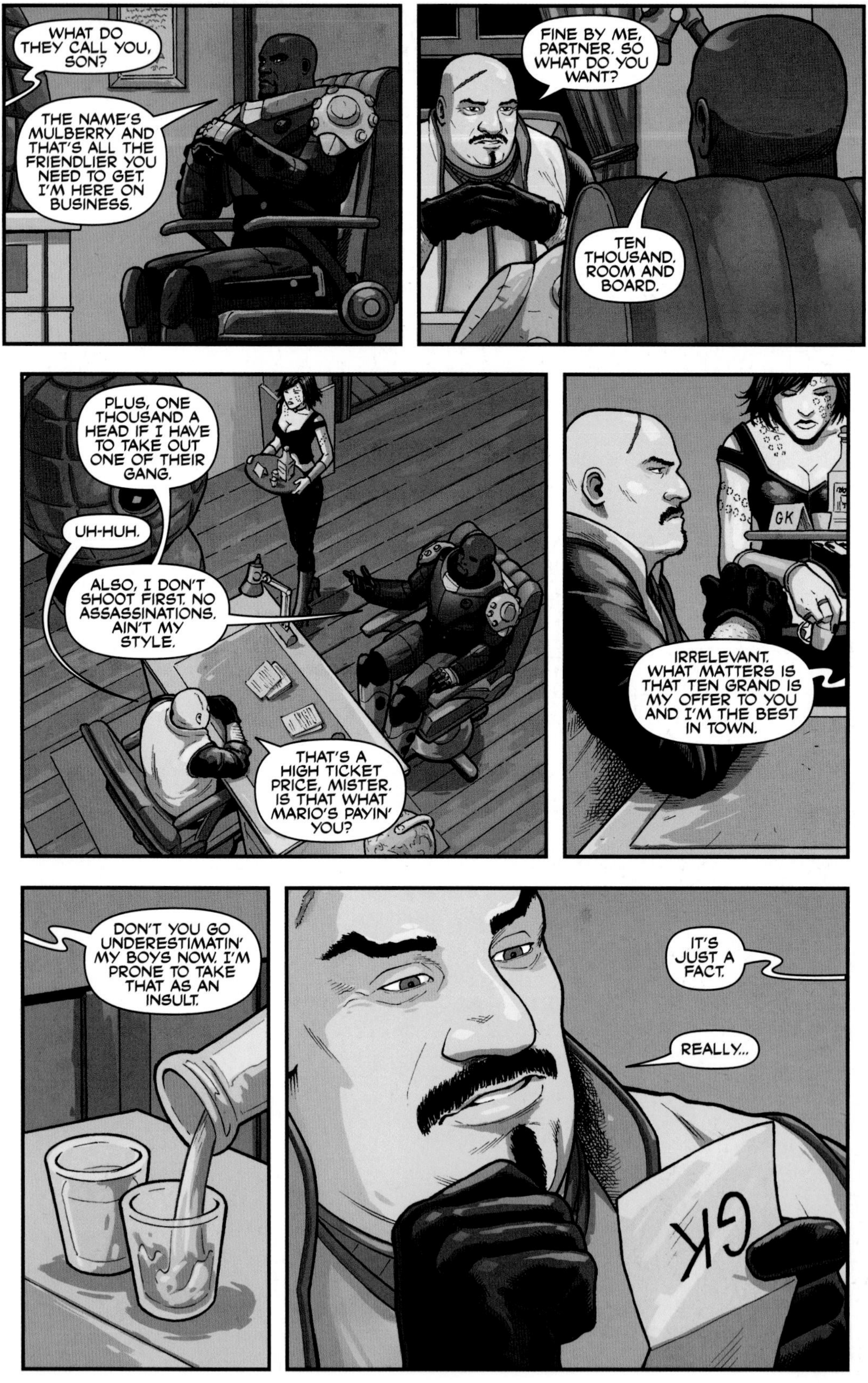
WHAT DO THEY CALL YOU, SON?
THE NAME'S MULBERRY AND THAT'S ALL THE FRIENDLIER YOU NEED TO GET. I'M HERE ON BUSINESS.
FINE BY ME, PARTNER. SO WHAT DO YOU WANT?
TEN THOUSAND. ROOM AND BOARD.
PLUS, ONE THOUSAND A HEAD IF I HAVE TO TAKE OUT ONE OF THEIR GANG.
UH-HUH.
ALSO, I DON'T SHOOT FIRST. NO ASSASSINATIONS. AIN'T MY STYLE.
THAT'S A HIGH TICKET PRICE, MISTER. IS THAT WHAT MARIO'S PAYIN' YOU?
GK
IRRELEVANT. WHAT MATTERS IS THAT TEN GRAND IS MY OFFER TO YOU AND I'M THE BEST IN TOWN.
DON'T YOU GO UNDERESTIMATIN' MY BOYS NOW. I'M PRONE TO TAKE THAT AS AN INSULT.
IT'S JUST A FACT.
REALLY...
GK

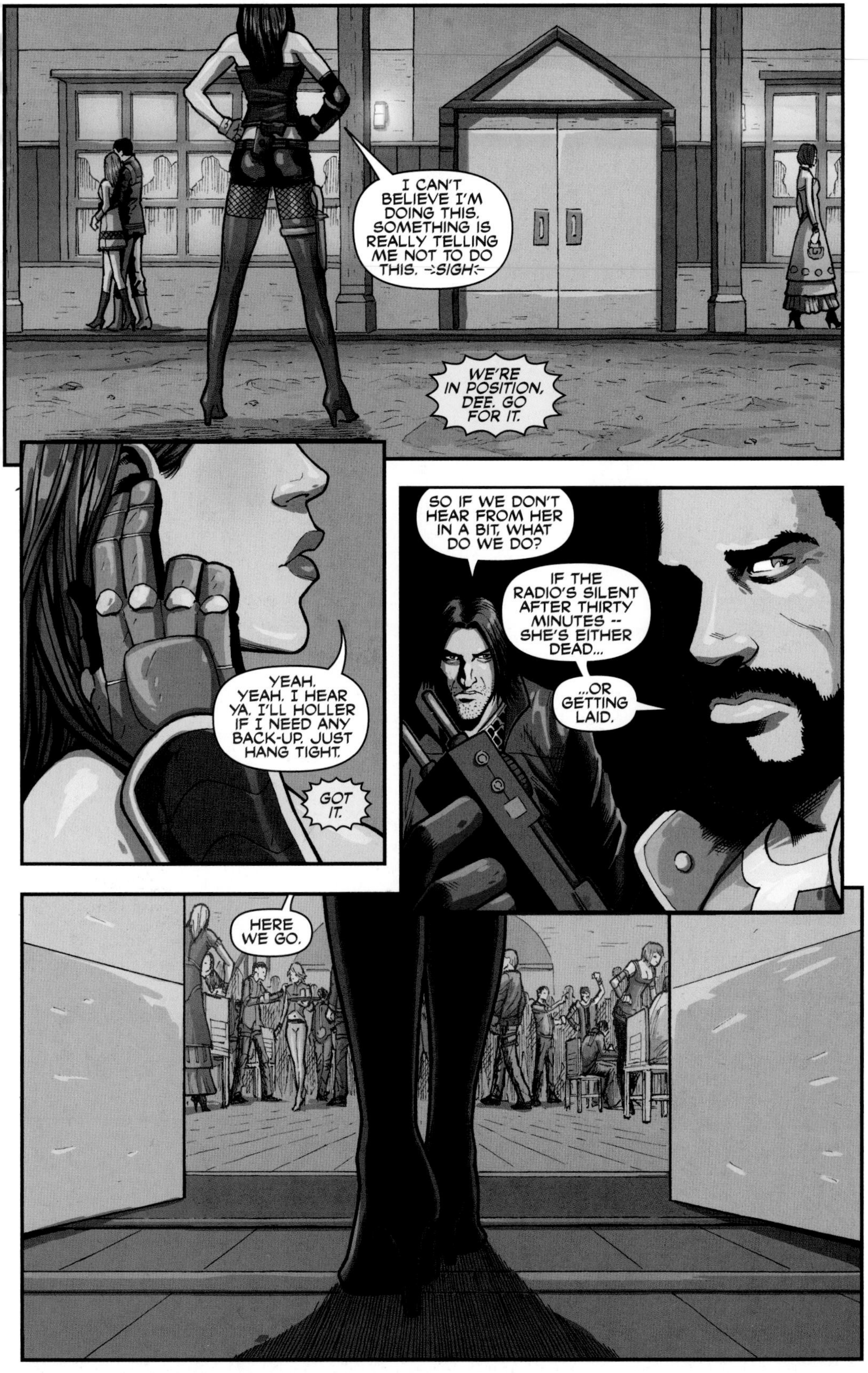
I CAN'T BELIEVE I'M DOING THIS. SOMETHING IS REALLY TELLING ME NOT TO DO THIS. ~SIGH~
WE'RE IN POSITION, DEE. GO FOR IT.
YEAH. YEAH. I HEAR YA. I'LL HOLLER IF I NEED ANY BACK-UP. JUST HANG TIGHT.
GOT IT.
SO IF WE DON'T HEAR FROM HER IN A BIT, WHAT DO WE DO?
IF THE RADIO'S SILENT AFTER THIRTY MINUTES -- SHE'S EITHER DEAD...
...OR GETTING LAID.
HERE WE GO.

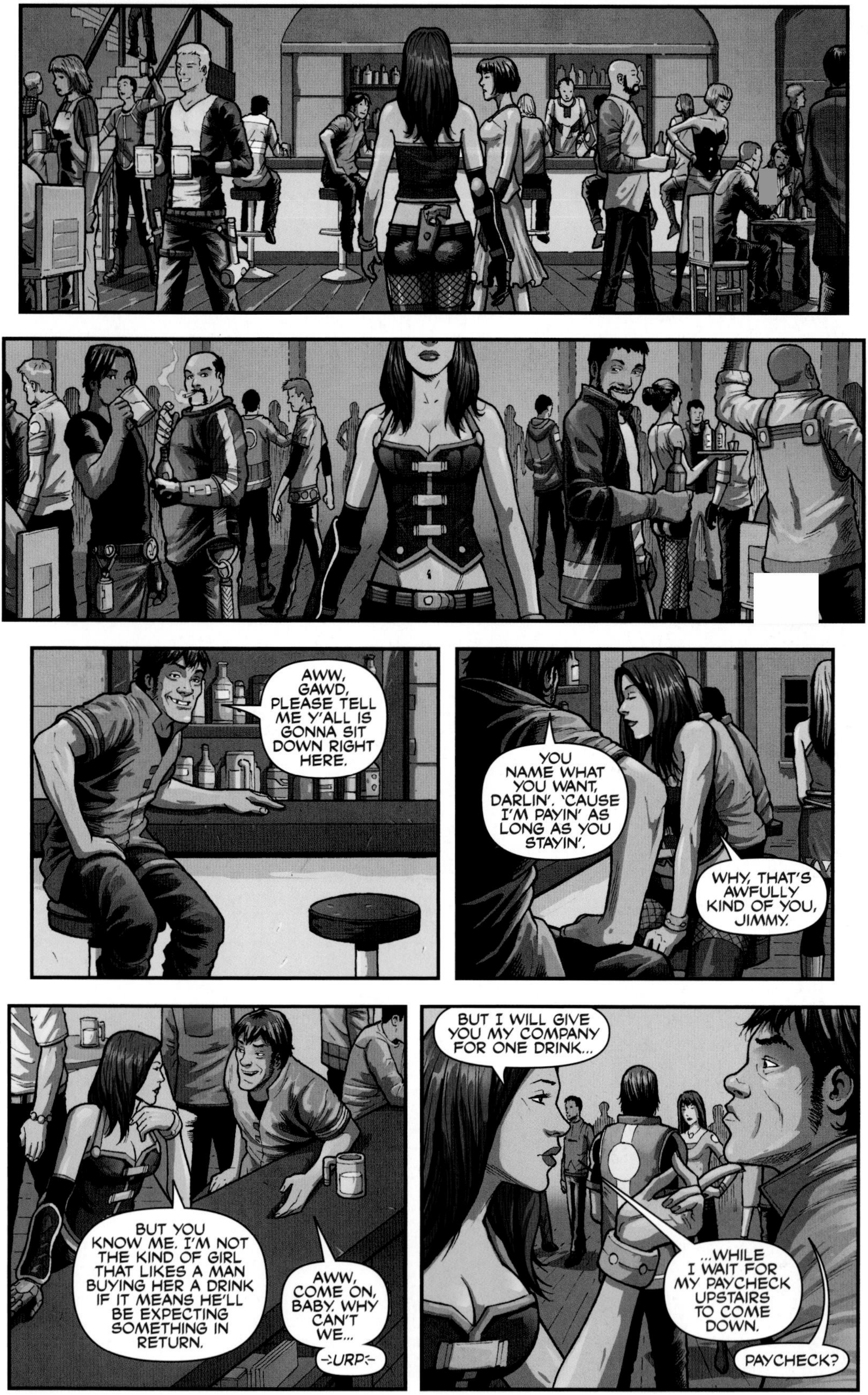
AWW, GAWD, PLEASE TELL ME Y'ALL IS GONNA SIT DOWN RIGHT HERE.
YOU NAME WHAT YOU WANT, DARLIN'. 'CAUSE I'M PAYIN' AS LONG AS YOU STAYIN'.
WHY, THAT'S AWFULLY KIND OF YOU, JIMMY.
BUT YOU KNOW ME. I'M NOT THE KIND OF GIRL THAT LIKES A MAN BUYING HER A DRINK IF IT MEANS HE'LL BE EXPECTING SOMETHING IN RETURN.
AWW, COME ON, BABY. WHY CAN'T WE...
-URP-
BUT I WILL GIVE YOU MY COMPANY FOR ONE DRINK...
...WHILE I WAIT FOR MY PAYCHECK UPSTAIRS TO COME DOWN.
PAYCHECK?

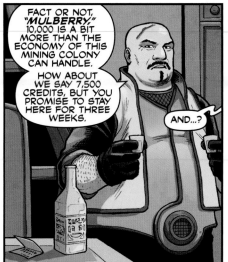

FACT OR NOT, *"MULBERRY,"* 10,000 IS A BIT MORE THAN THE ECONOMY OF THIS MINING COLONY CAN HANDLE.

HOW ABOUT WE SAY 7,500 CREDITS, BUT YOU PROMISE TO STAY HERE FOR THREE WEEKS.

AND...?

DON'T PUSH IT, PARTNER. HAVE YOUR DRINK AND LET'S CALL IT A DEAL BEFORE I GET MOODY.

MARIO WAID IS DEAD.

—B. CARLSON.

CHANGED MY MIND. I'LL THINK ABOUT YOUR COUNTER OFFER AND COME BACK TOMORROW. IN THE MEANTIME, REMEMBER I'M STILL ON MARIO'S BOOKS, SO DON'T LET YOUR MEN...

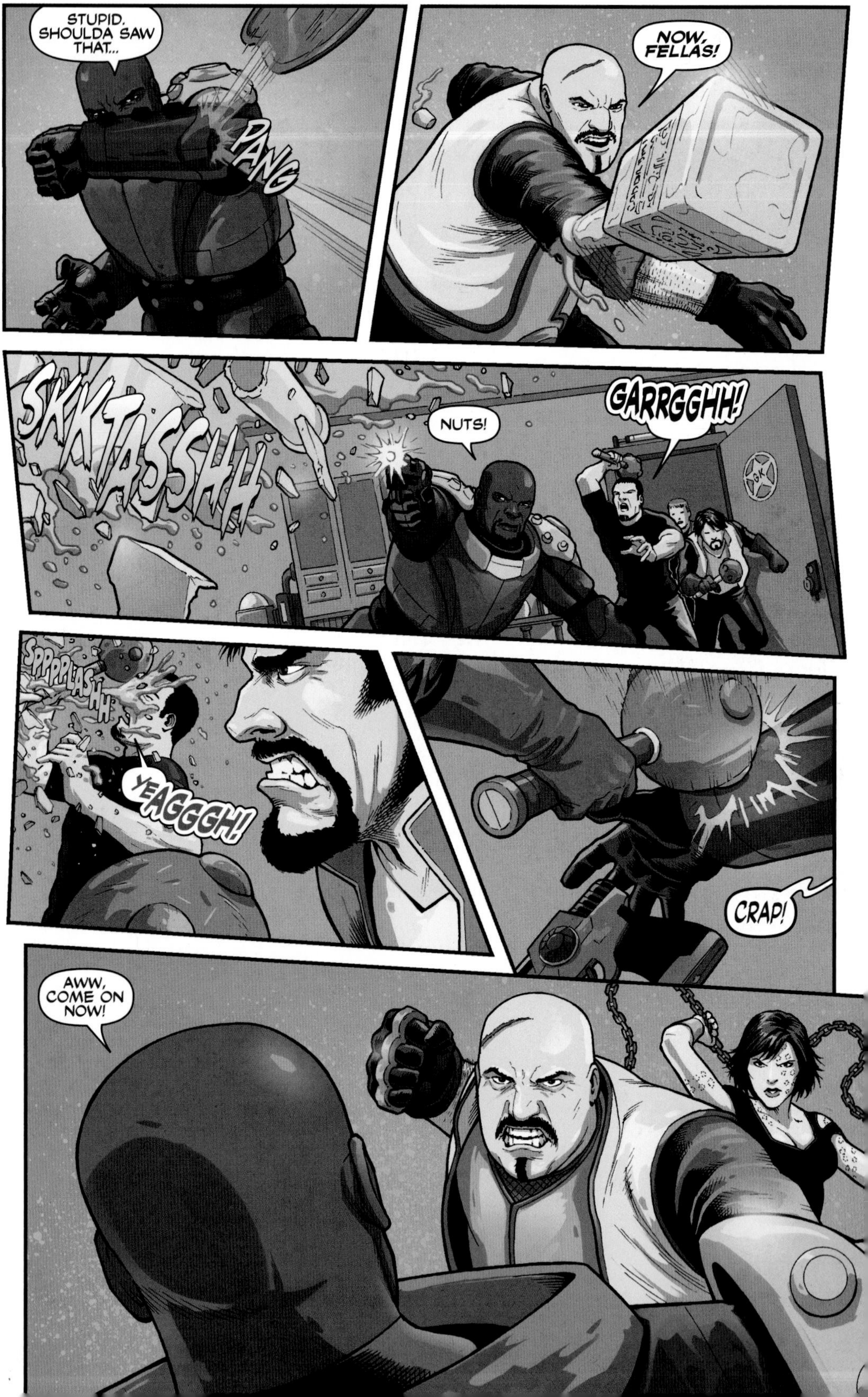
STUPID. SHOULDA SAW THAT...
PANG
NOW, FELLAS!
SKKTASSHH
NUTS!
GARRGGHH!
SPPPPLASHH
YEAGGGH!
CRAP!
AWW, COME ON NOW!

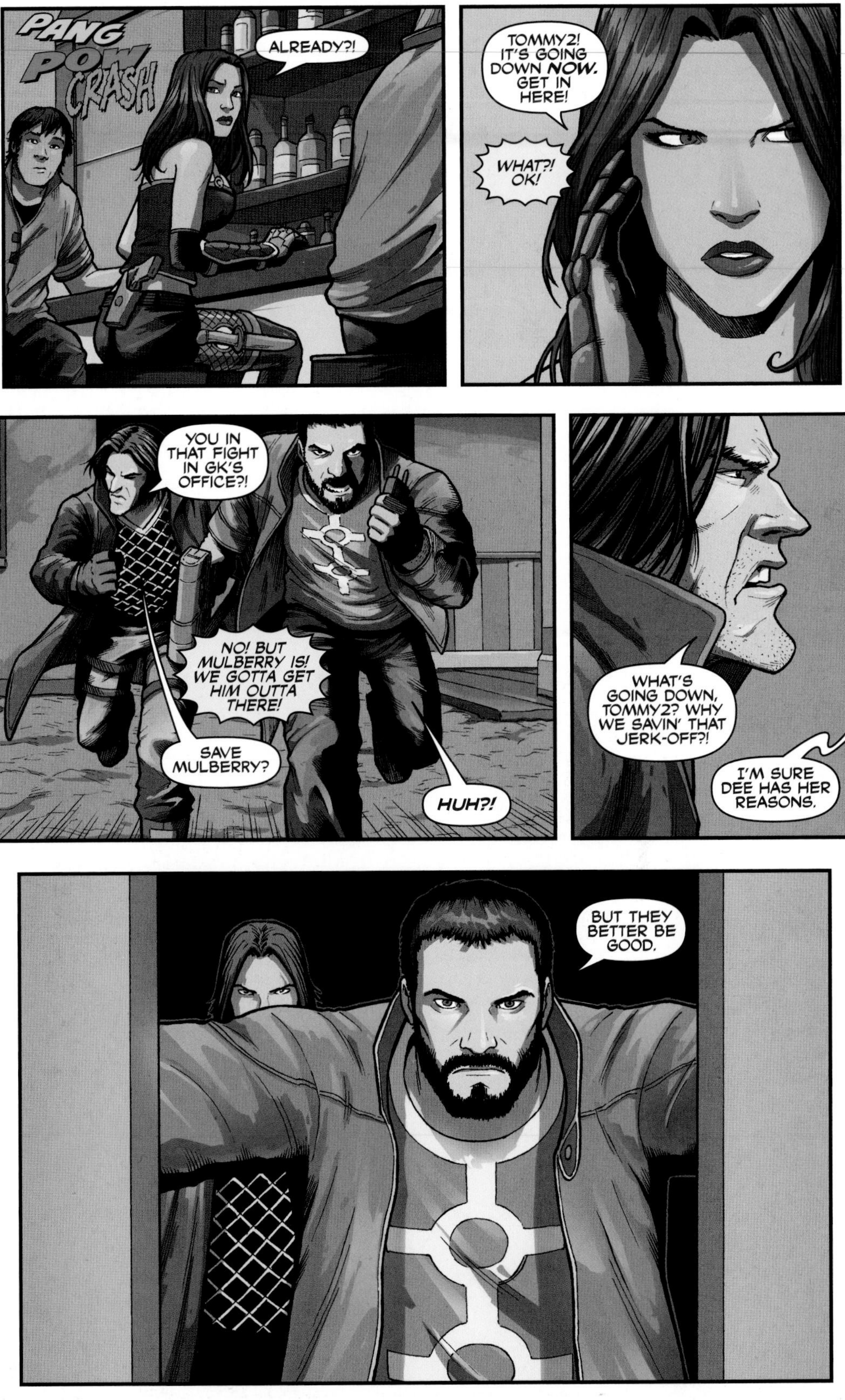
PANG
POW
CRASH
ALREADY?!
TOMMY2! IT'S GOING DOWN NOW. GET IN HERE!
WHAT?! OK!
YOU IN THAT FIGHT IN GK'S OFFICE?!
NO! BUT MULBERRY IS! WE GOTTA GET HIM OUTTA THERE!
SAVE MULBERRY?
HUH?!
WHAT'S GOING DOWN, TOMMY2? WHY WE SAVIN' THAT JERK-OFF?!
I'M SURE DEE HAS HER REASONS.
BUT THEY BETTER BE GOOD.

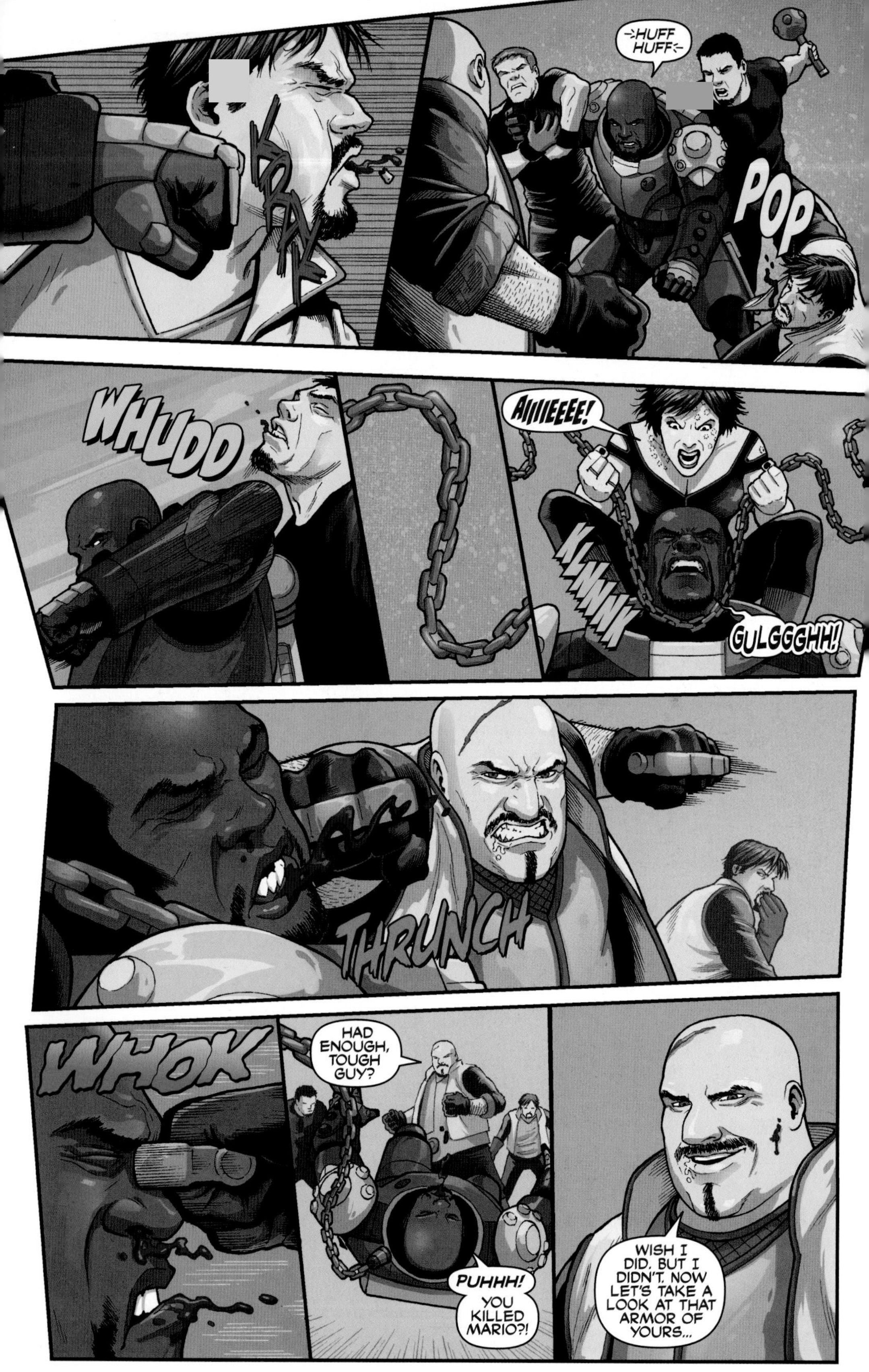

HUFF HUFF
POP
WHUDD
AIIIEEEE!
KLNNNK
GULGGGHH!
THRUNCH
WHOK
HAD ENOUGH, TOUGH GUY?
PUHHH!
YOU KILLED MARIO?!
WISH I DID. BUT I DIDN'T. NOW LET'S TAKE A LOOK AT THAT ARMOR OF YOURS...

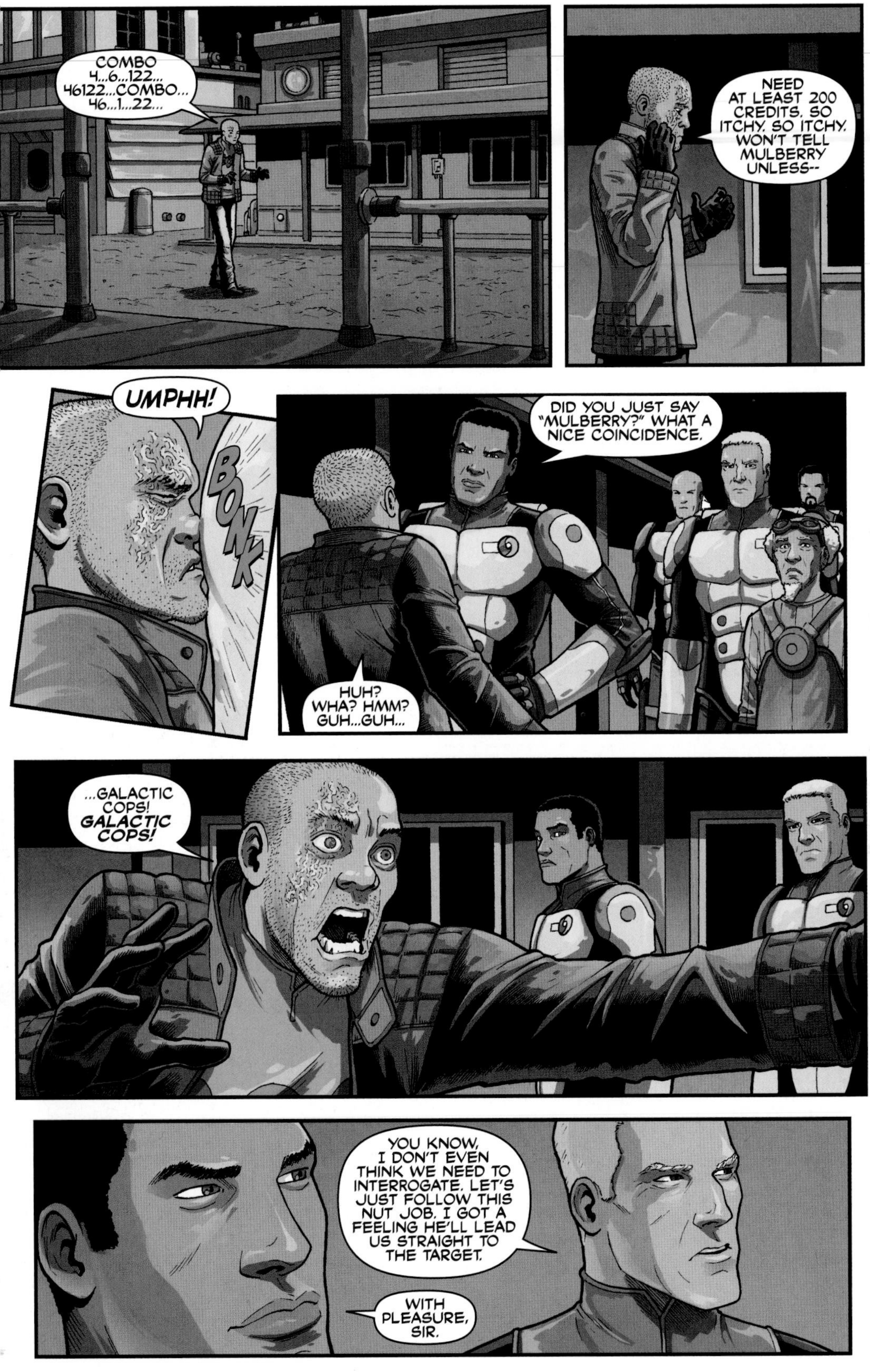
COMBO 4...6...122... 46122...COMBO... 46...1...22...
NEED AT LEAST 200 CREDITS. SO ITCHY. SO ITCHY. WON'T TELL MULBERRY UNLESS--
UMPHH!
BONK
DID YOU JUST SAY "MULBERRY?" WHAT A NICE COINCIDENCE.
HUH? WHA? HMM? GUH...GUH...
...GALACTIC COPS! GALACTIC COPS!
YOU KNOW, I DON'T EVEN THINK WE NEED TO INTERROGATE. LET'S JUST FOLLOW THIS NUT JOB. I GOT A FEELING HE'LL LEAD US STRAIGHT TO THE TARGET.
WITH PLEASURE, SIR.

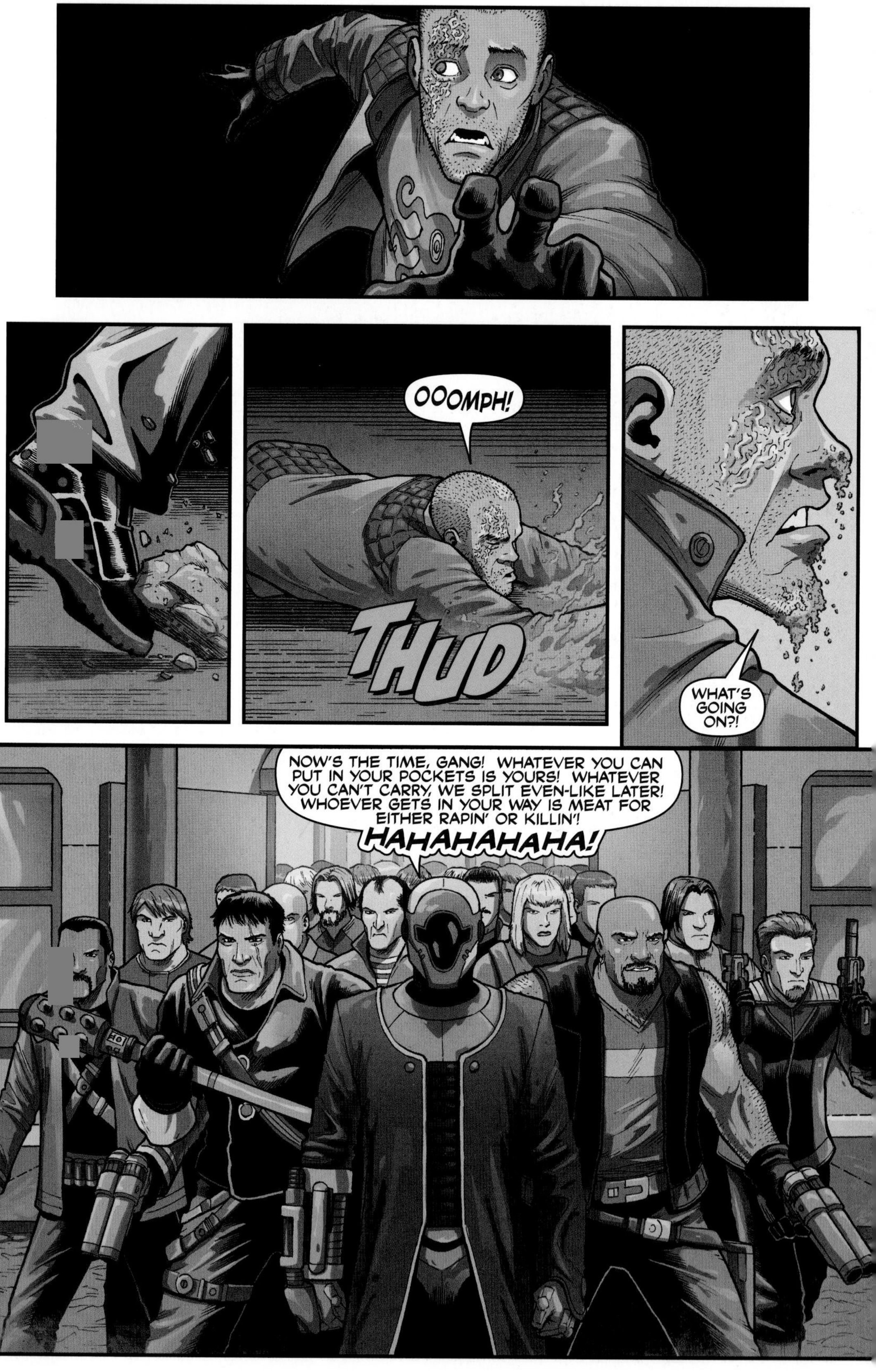
OOOMPH!
THUD
WHAT'S GOING ON?!
NOW'S THE TIME, GANG! WHATEVER YOU CAN PUT IN YOUR POCKETS IS YOURS! WHATEVER YOU CAN'T CARRY, WE SPLIT EVEN-LIKE LATER! WHOEVER GETS IN YOUR WAY IS MEAT FOR EITHER RAPIN' OR KILLIN'!
HAHAHAHAHA!

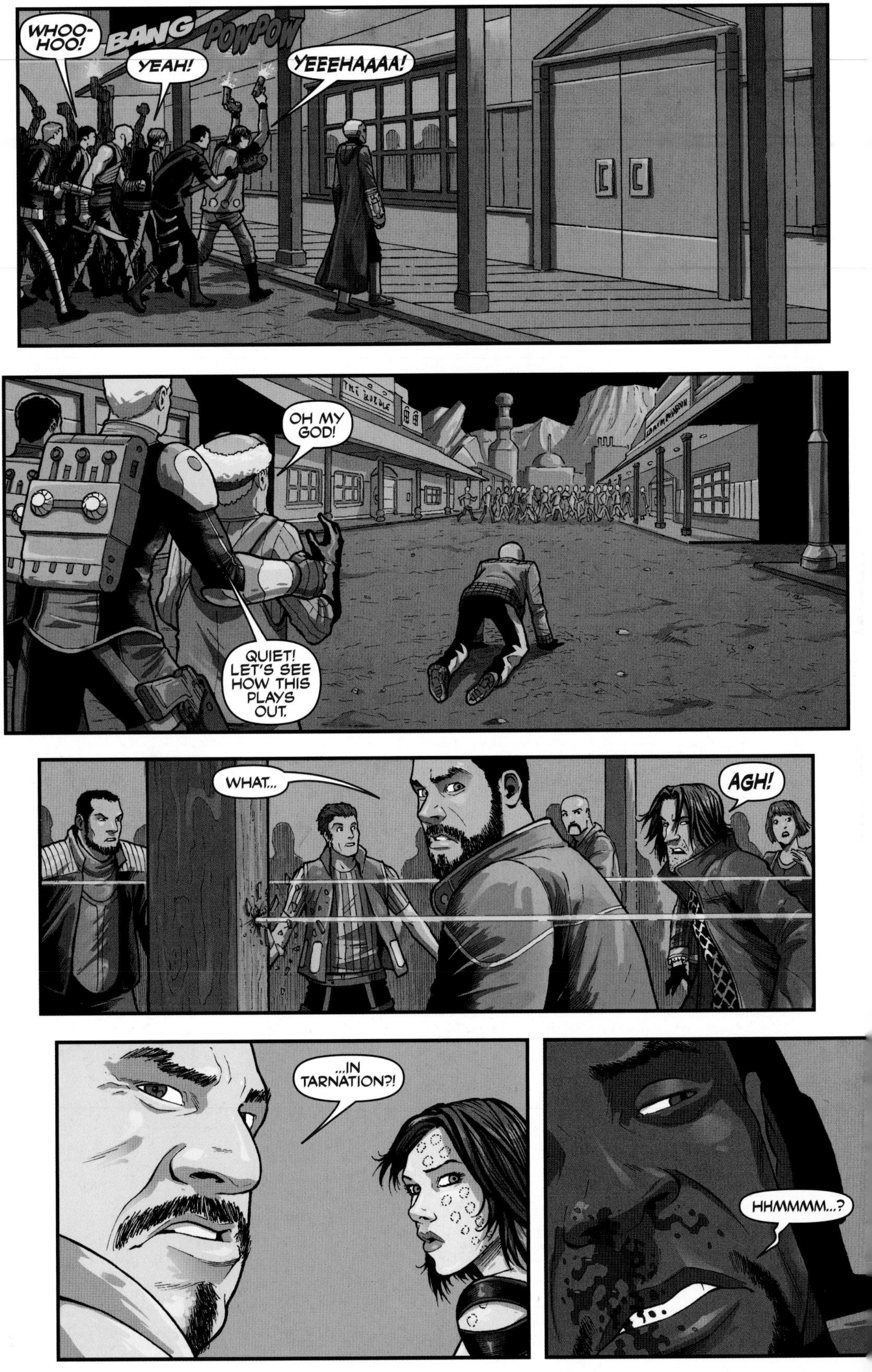
WHOO-HOO!
BANG
POWPOW
YEAH!
YEEEHAAAA!
OH MY GOD!
QUIET! LET'S SEE HOW THIS PLAYS OUT.
WHAT...
AGH!
...IN TARNATION?!
HHMMMM...?

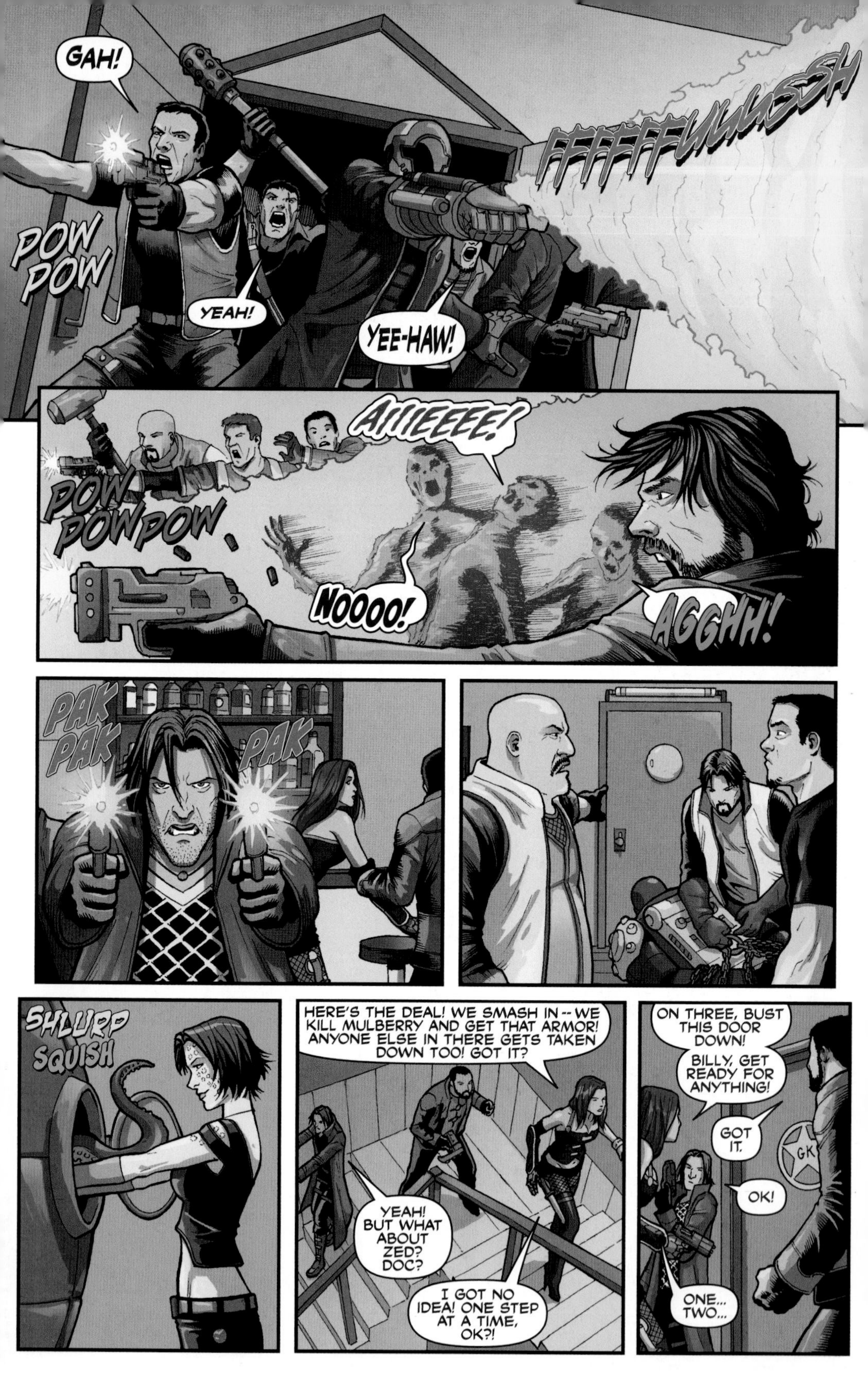
GAH!
POW POW
YEAH!
YEE-HAW!
FFFFFFFUUUUSSSH
AIIIEEEEE!
POW POWPOW
NOOOO!
AGGHH!
PAK PAK
PAK
SHLURP
SQUISH
HERE'S THE DEAL! WE SMASH IN -- WE KILL MULBERRY AND GET THAT ARMOR! ANYONE ELSE IN THERE GETS TAKEN DOWN TOO! GOT IT?
YEAH! BUT WHAT ABOUT ZED? DOC?
I GOT NO IDEA! ONE STEP AT A TIME, OK?!
ON THREE, BUST THIS DOOR DOWN!
BILLY, GET READY FOR ANYTHING!
GOT IT.
OK!
ONE... TWO...

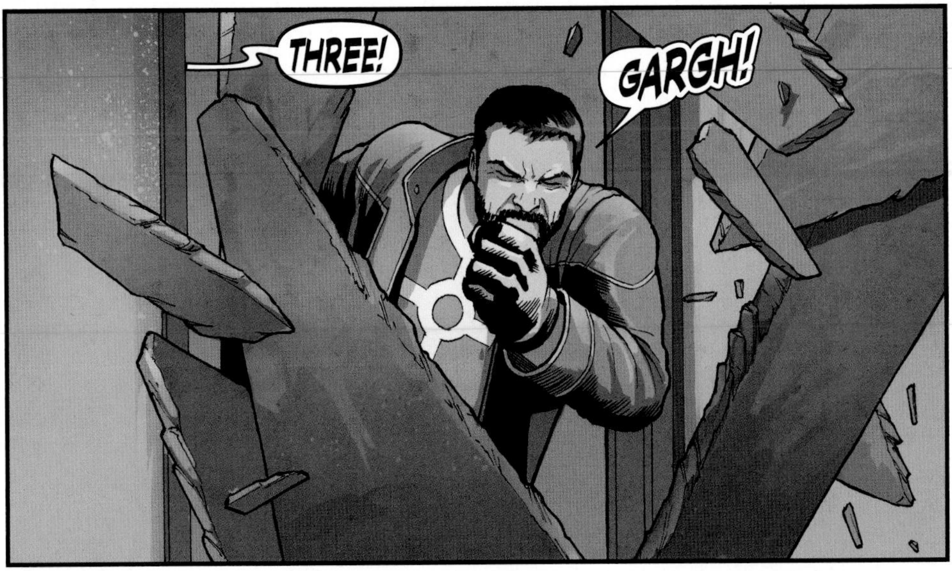
THREE!
GARGH!

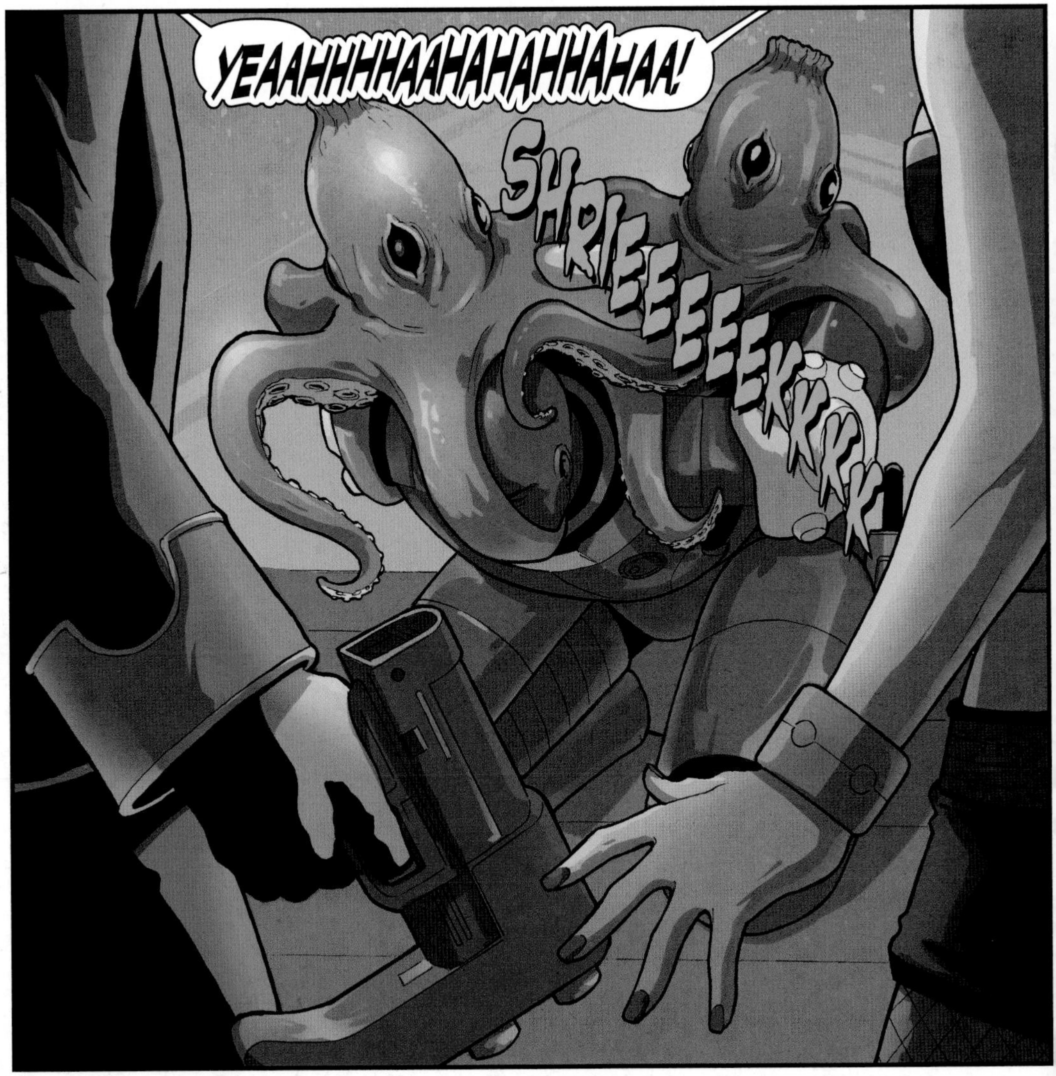
YEAAHHHHAAHAHAHHAHAA!
SHRIEEEEEEKKKKK

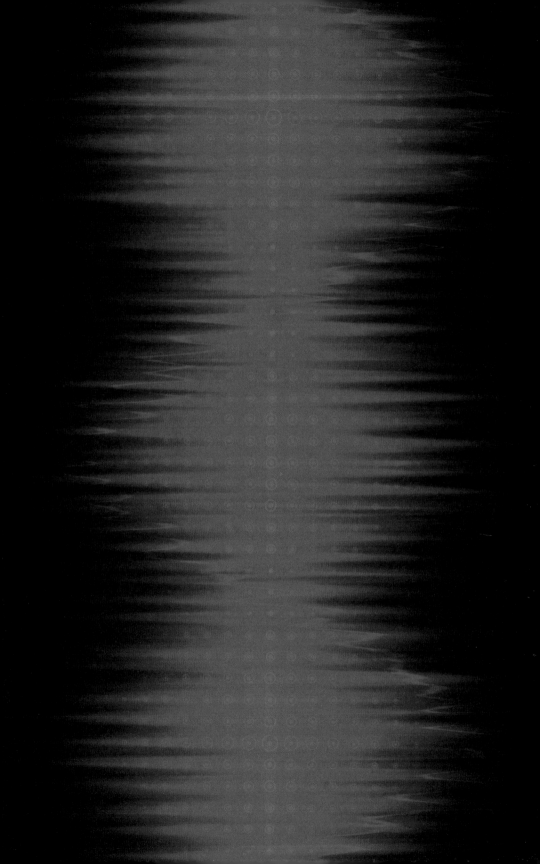

COLD
SPACE

CHAPTER 4

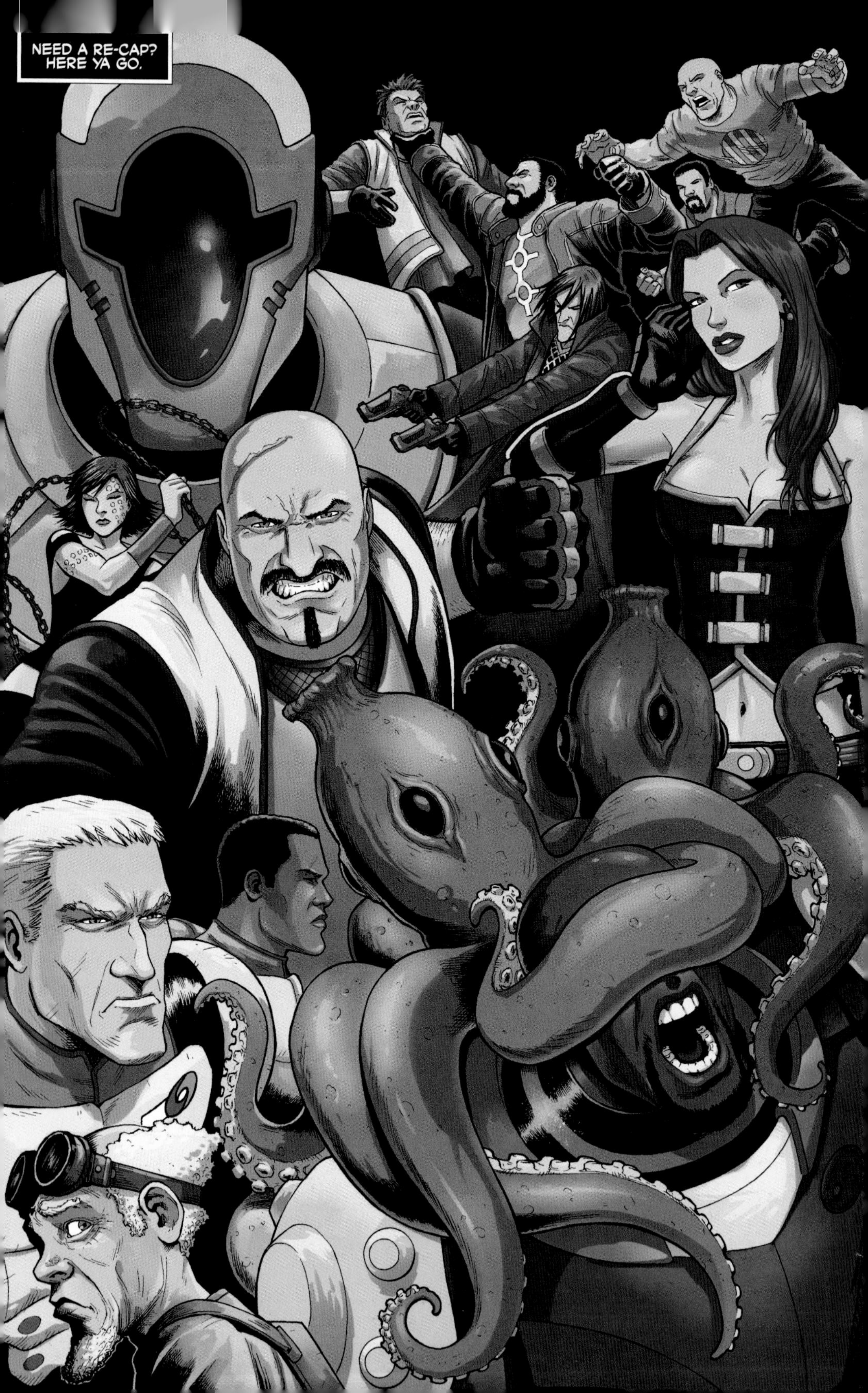
NEED A RE-CAP? HERE YA GO.

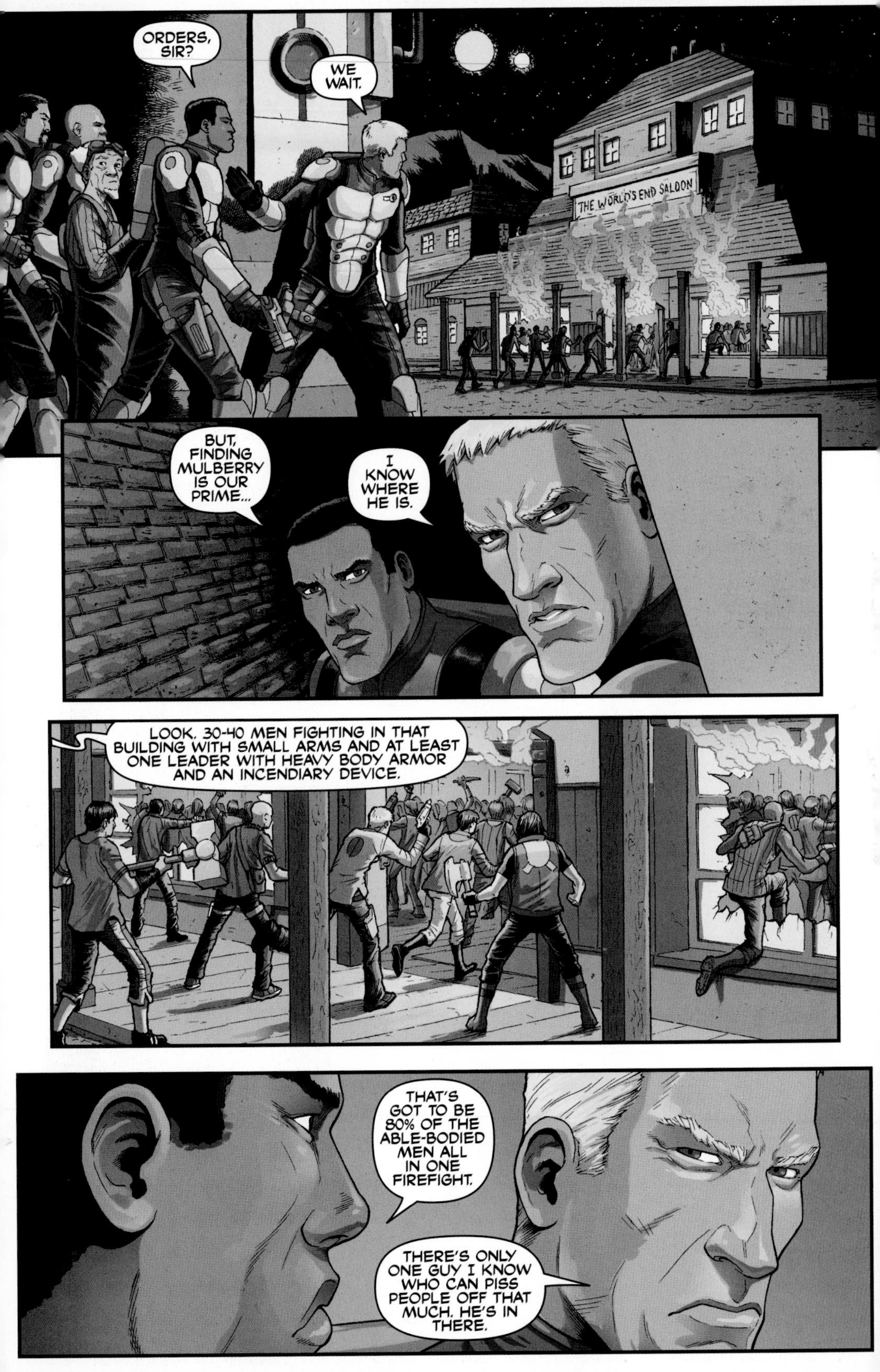
ORDERS, SIR?
WE WAIT.
THE WORLD'S END SALOON
BUT, FINDING MULBERRY IS OUR PRIME...
I KNOW WHERE HE IS.
LOOK. 30-40 MEN FIGHTING IN THAT BUILDING WITH SMALL ARMS AND AT LEAST ONE LEADER WITH HEAVY BODY ARMOR AND AN INCENDIARY DEVICE.
THAT'S GOT TO BE 80% OF THE ABLE-BODIED MEN ALL IN ONE FIREFIGHT.
THERE'S ONLY ONE GUY I KNOW WHO CAN PISS PEOPLE OFF THAT MUCH. HE'S IN THERE.

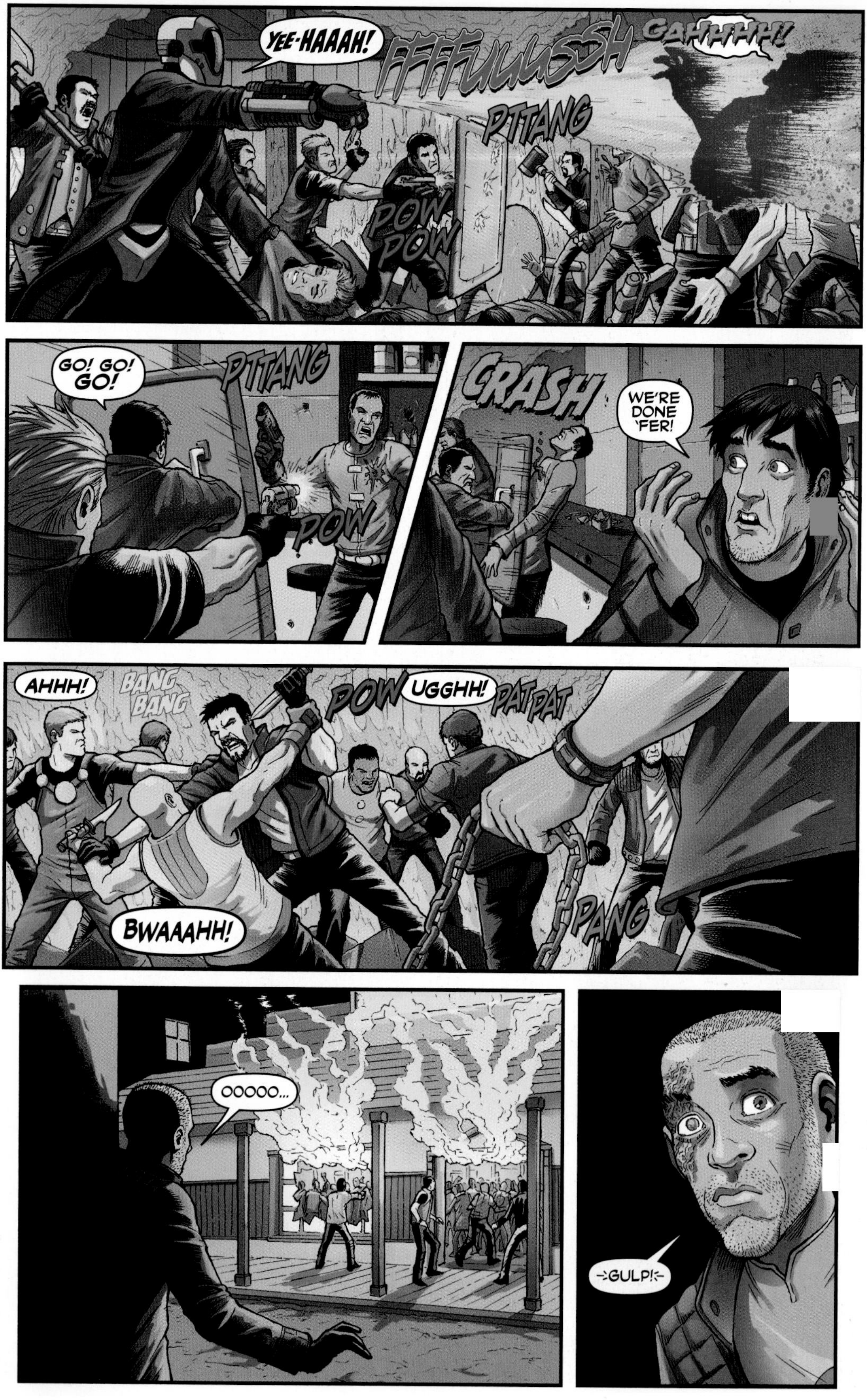
YEE-HAAAH!
FFFFUUUUSSH
GAHHHH!
PTTANG
POW POW
GO! GO! GO!
PTTANG
POW
CRASH
WE'RE DONE 'FER!
AHHH!
BANG BANG
POW
UGGHH!
PAT PAT
BWAAAHH!
PANG
OOOOO...
-GULP!-

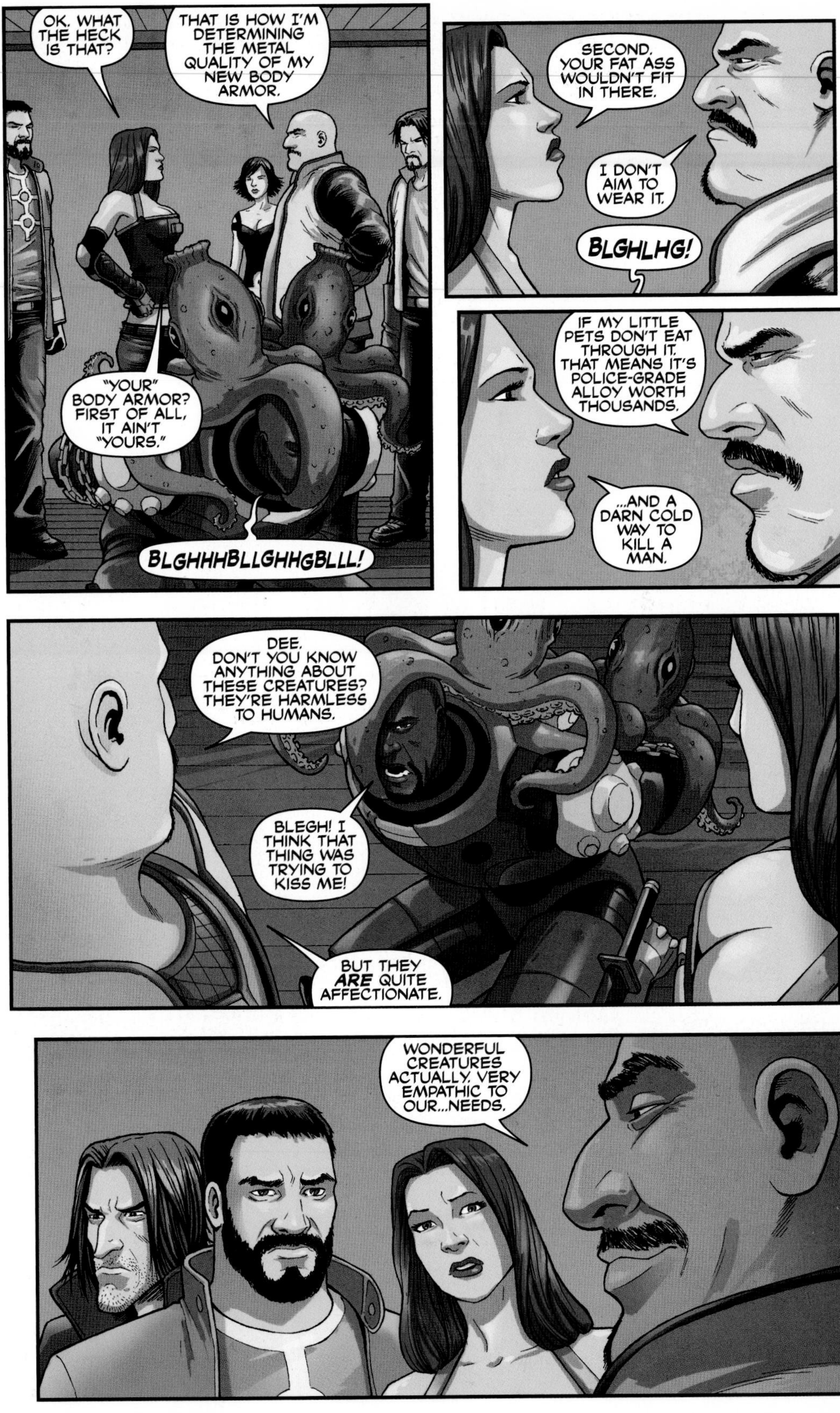
OK. WHAT THE HECK IS THAT?
THAT IS HOW I'M DETERMINING THE METAL QUALITY OF MY NEW BODY ARMOR.
"YOUR" BODY ARMOR? FIRST OF ALL, IT AIN'T "YOURS."
BLGHHHBLLGHHGBLLL!
SECOND, YOUR FAT ASS WOULDN'T FIT IN THERE.
I DON'T AIM TO WEAR IT.
BLGHLHG!
IF MY LITTLE PETS DON'T EAT THROUGH IT, THAT MEANS IT'S POLICE-GRADE ALLOY WORTH THOUSANDS.
...AND A DARN COLD WAY TO KILL A MAN.
DEE, DON'T YOU KNOW ANYTHING ABOUT THESE CREATURES? THEY'RE HARMLESS TO HUMANS.
BLEGH! I THINK THAT THING WAS TRYING TO KISS ME!
BUT THEY ARE QUITE AFFECTIONATE.
WONDERFUL CREATURES ACTUALLY. VERY EMPATHIC TO OUR...NEEDS.

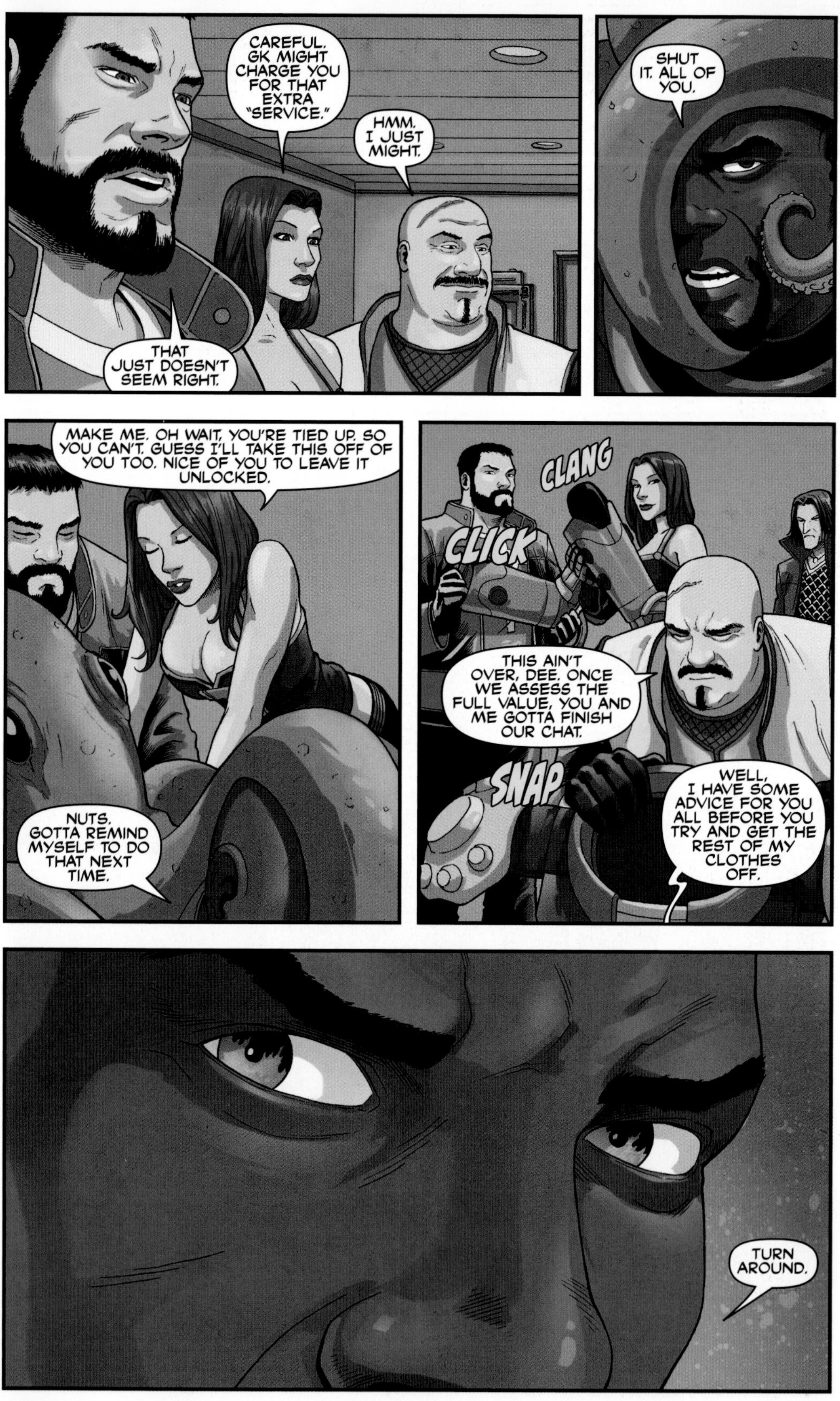
CAREFUL. GK MIGHT CHARGE YOU FOR THAT EXTRA "SERVICE."
HMM. I JUST MIGHT.
THAT JUST DOESN'T SEEM RIGHT.
SHUT IT. ALL OF YOU.
MAKE ME. OH WAIT, YOU'RE TIED UP. SO YOU CAN'T. GUESS I'LL TAKE THIS OFF OF YOU TOO. NICE OF YOU TO LEAVE IT UNLOCKED.
NUTS. GOTTA REMIND MYSELF TO DO THAT NEXT TIME.
CLANG
CLICK
THIS AIN'T OVER, DEE. ONCE WE ASSESS THE FULL VALUE, YOU AND ME GOTTA FINISH OUR CHAT.
SNAP
WELL, I HAVE SOME ADVICE FOR YOU ALL BEFORE YOU TRY AND GET THE REST OF MY CLOTHES OFF.
TURN AROUND.

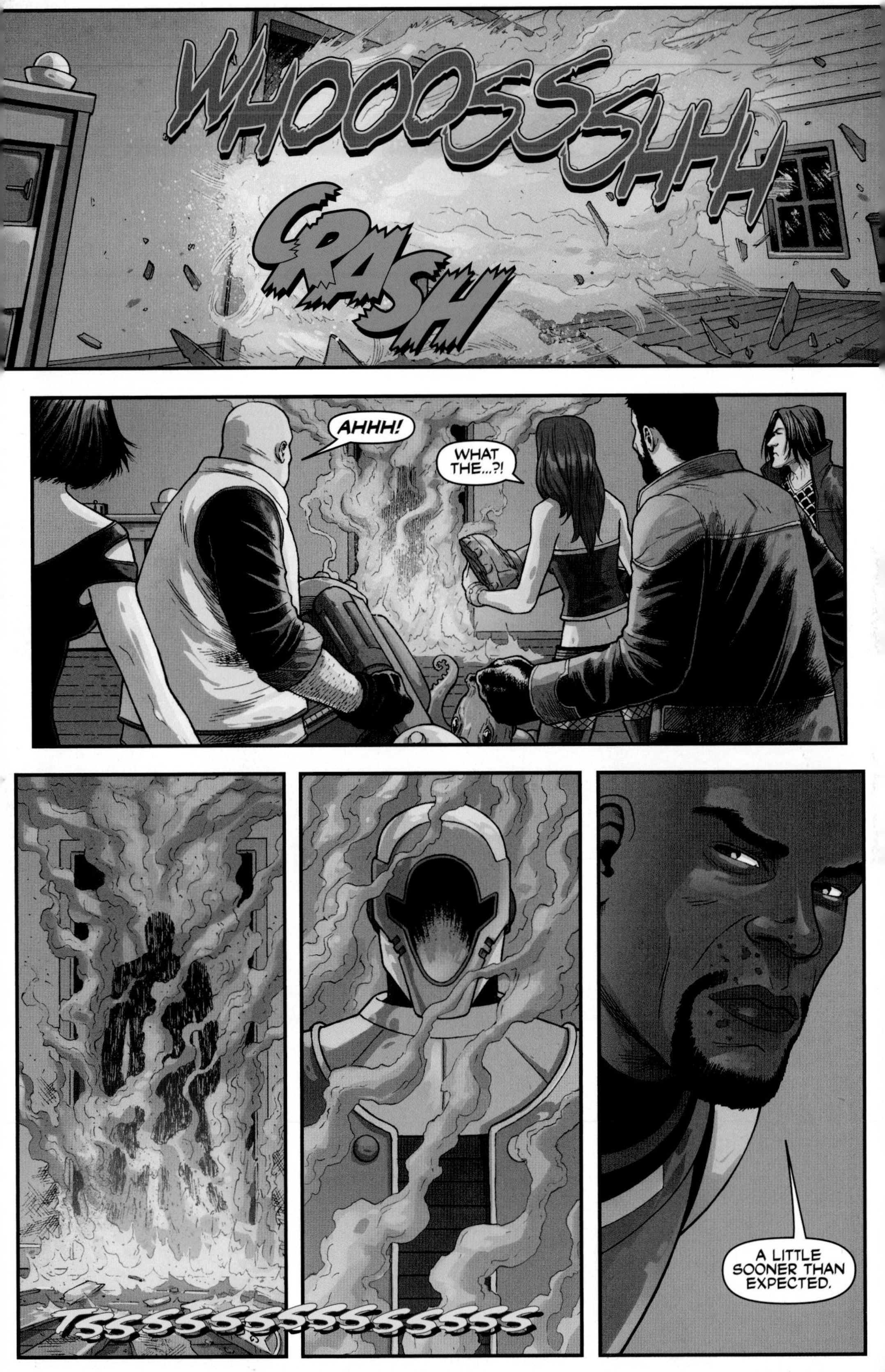
WHOOOSSSHHH
CRASH
AHHH!
WHAT THE...?!
TSSSSSSSSSSSSSSSSS
A LITTLE SOONER THAN EXPECTED.

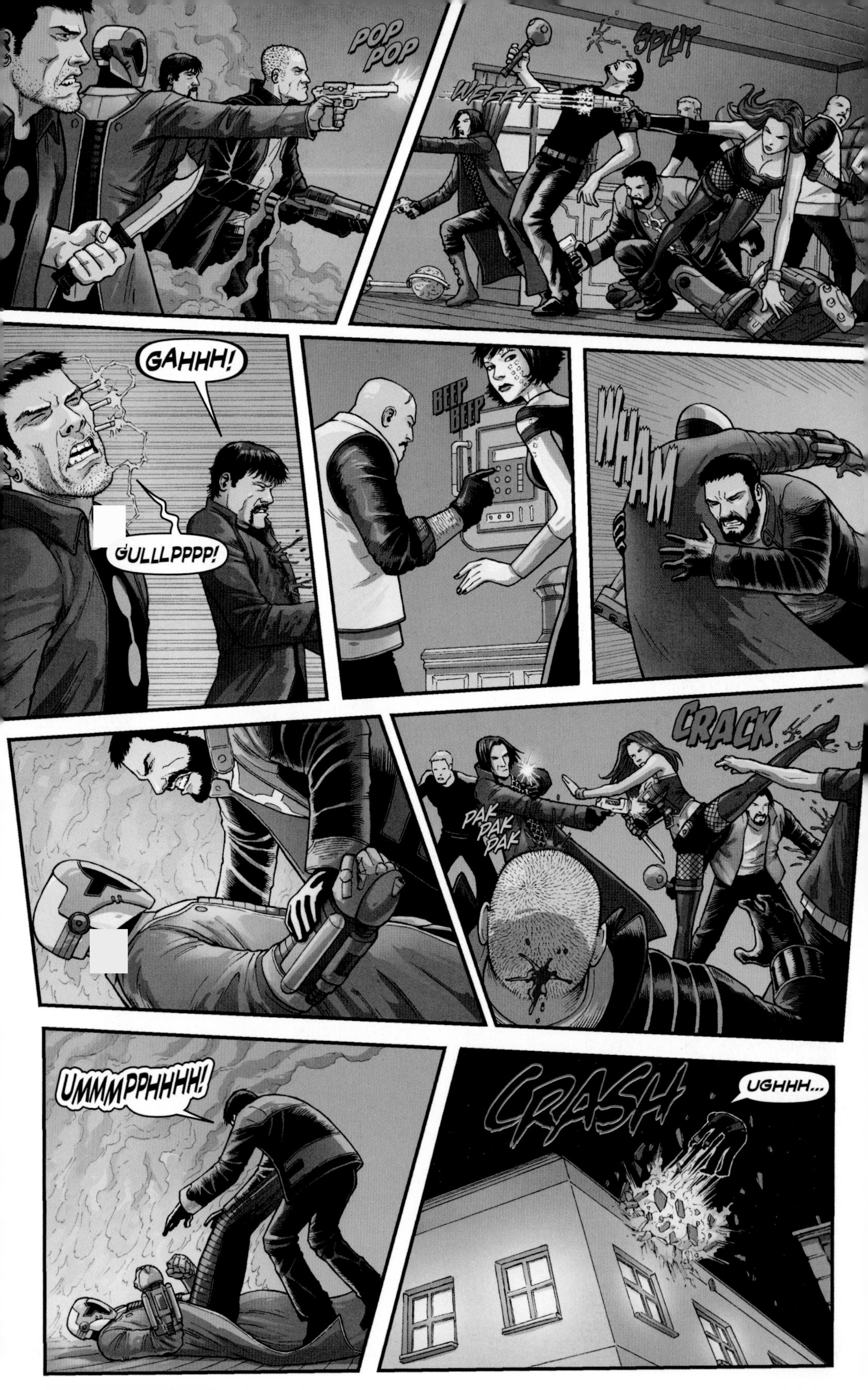
POP POP
WFFFT
SPLUT
GAHHH!
GULLLPPPP!
BEEP BEEP
WHAM
CRACK
PAK PAK PAK
UMMMPPHHHH!
CRASH
UGHHH...

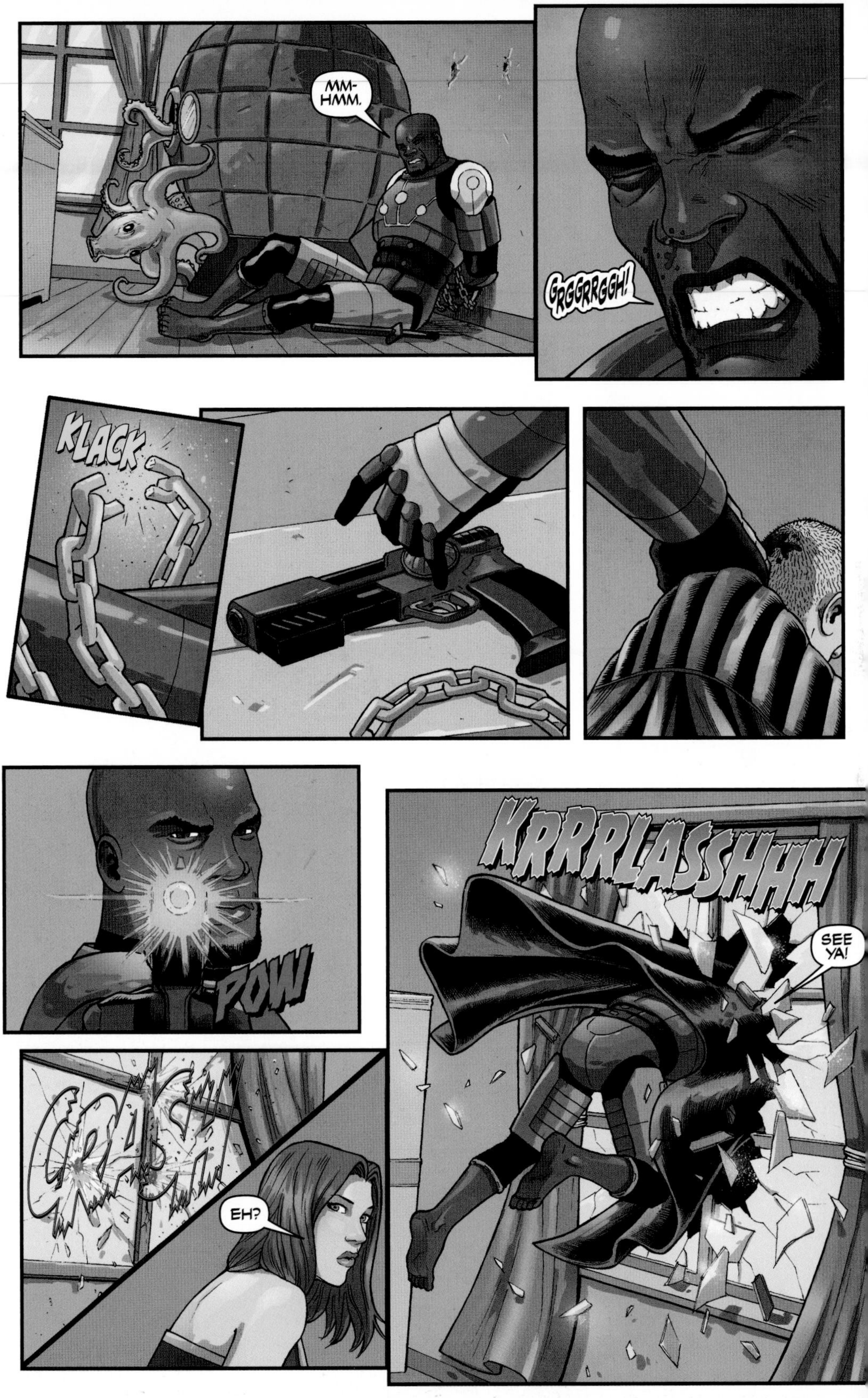
MM-HMM.
GRGGRRGGH!
KLACK
KRRRLASSHHH
SEE YA!
POW
EH?

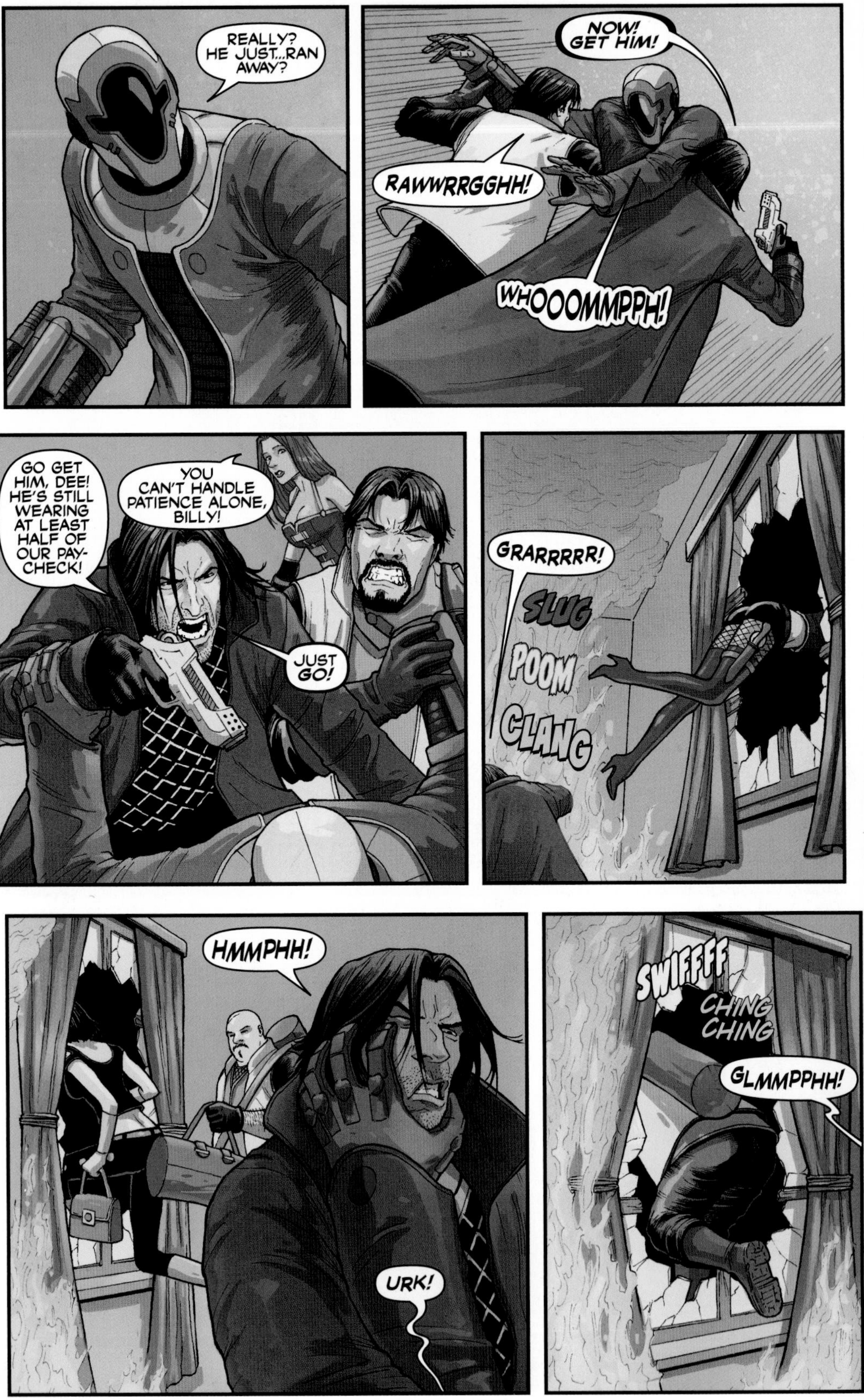
REALLY? HE JUST...RAN AWAY?
NOW! GET HIM!
RAWWRRGGHH!
WHOOOMMPPH!
GO GET HIM, DEE! HE'S STILL WEARING AT LEAST HALF OF OUR PAY-CHECK!
YOU CAN'T HANDLE PATIENCE ALONE, BILLY!
JUST GO!
GRARRRRR!
SLUG
POOM
CLANG
HMMPHH!
URK!
SWIFFFF
CHING CHING
GLMMPPHH!

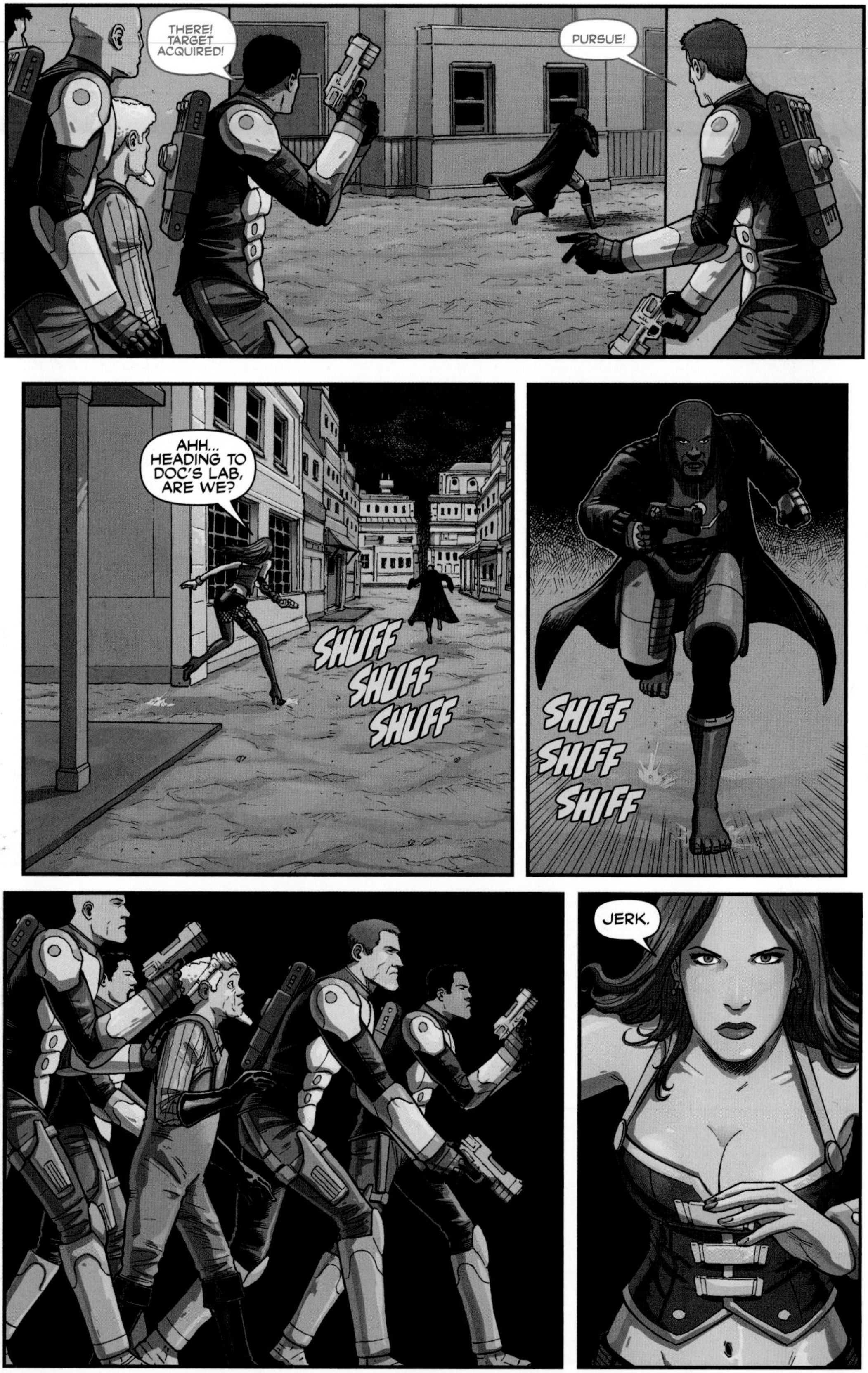
THERE! TARGET ACQUIRED!
PURSUE!
AHH... HEADING TO DOC'S LAB, ARE WE?
SHUFF SHUFF SHUFF
SHIFF SHIFF SHIFF
JERK.

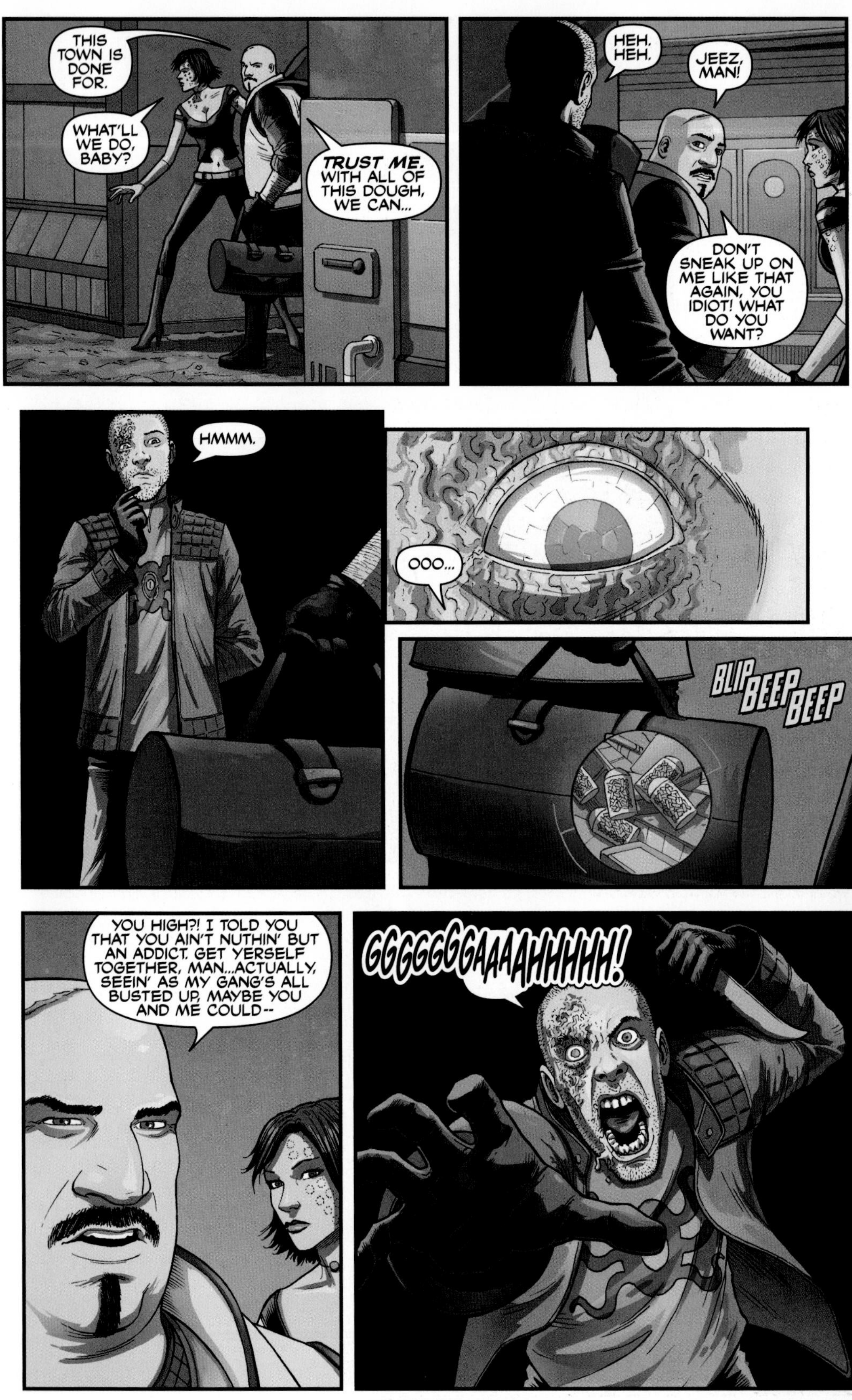
THIS TOWN IS DONE FOR.
WHAT'LL WE DO, BABY?
TRUST ME. WITH ALL OF THIS DOUGH, WE CAN...
HEH, HEH.
JEEZ, MAN!
DON'T SNEAK UP ON ME LIKE THAT AGAIN, YOU IDIOT! WHAT DO YOU WANT?
HMMM.
OOO...
BLIP BEEP BEEP
YOU HIGH?! I TOLD YOU THAT YOU AIN'T NUTHIN' BUT AN ADDICT. GET YERSELF TOGETHER, MAN...ACTUALLY, SEEIN' AS MY GANG'S ALL BUSTED UP, MAYBE YOU AND ME COULD--
GGGGGGAAAAHHHHH!

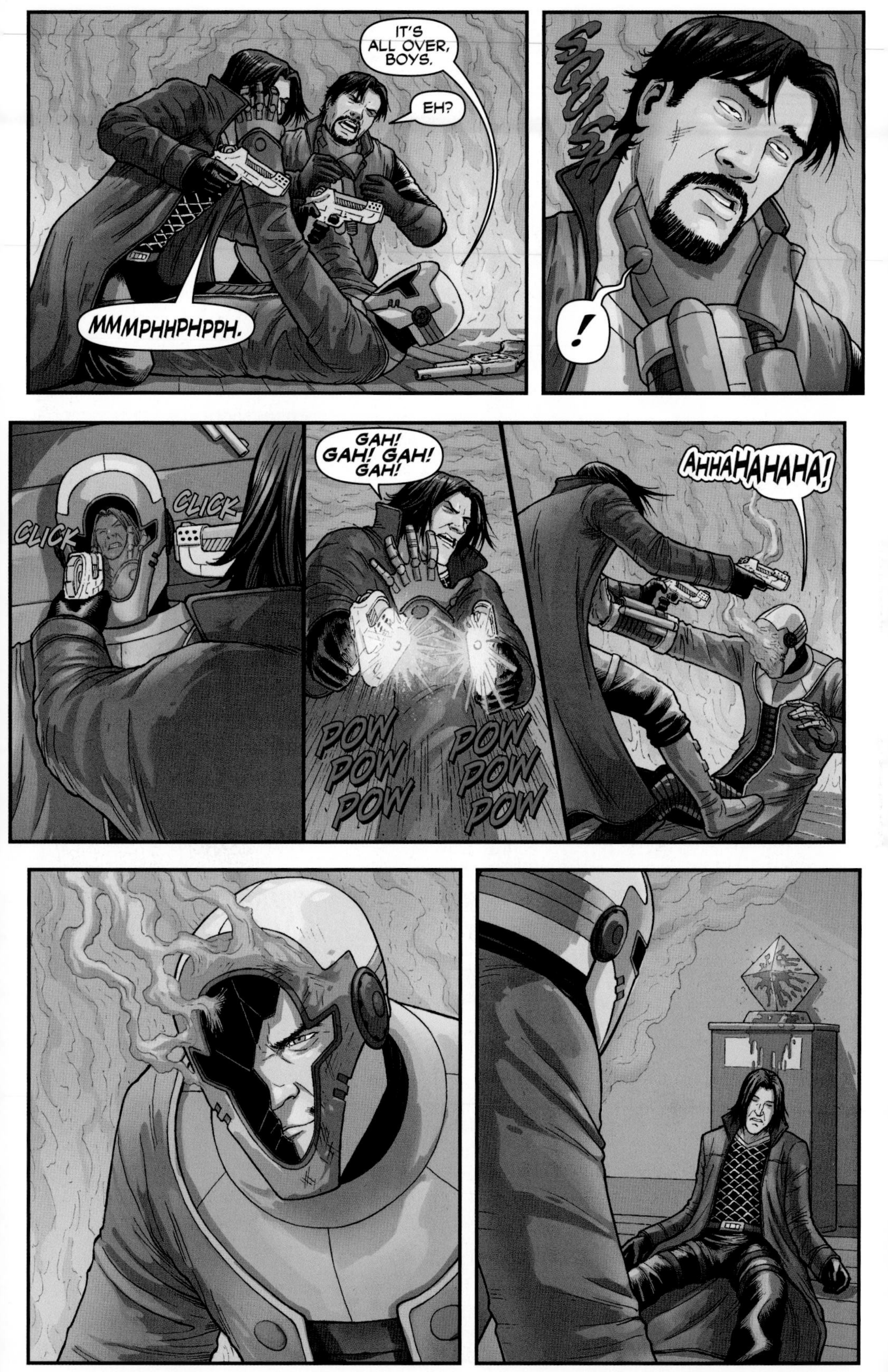
IT'S ALL OVER, BOYS.
EH?
MMMPHHPHPPH.
SQUISH
!
CLICK
CLICK
GAH! GAH! GAH! GAH!
POW POW POW
POW POW POW
AHHAHAHAHA!

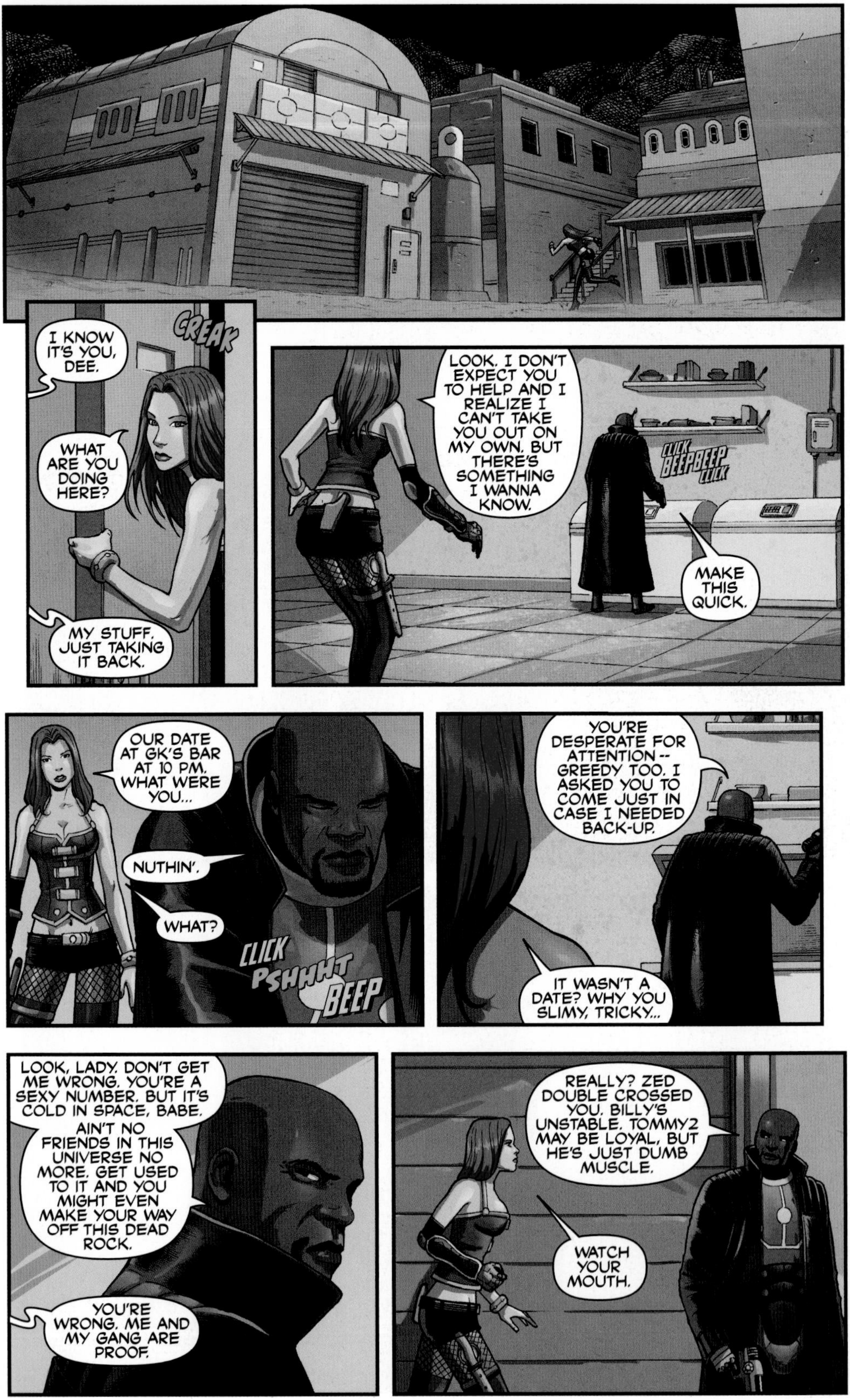
CREAK
I KNOW IT'S YOU, DEE.
WHAT ARE YOU DOING HERE?
MY STUFF. JUST TAKING IT BACK.
LOOK, I DON'T EXPECT YOU TO HELP AND I REALIZE I CAN'T TAKE YOU OUT ON MY OWN. BUT THERE'S SOMETHING I WANNA KNOW.
CLICK BEEPBEEP CLICK
MAKE THIS QUICK.
OUR DATE AT GK'S BAR AT 10 PM. WHAT WERE YOU...
NUTHIN'.
WHAT?
CLICK PSHHHT BEEP
YOU'RE DESPERATE FOR ATTENTION -- GREEDY TOO. I ASKED YOU TO COME JUST IN CASE I NEEDED BACK-UP.
IT WASN'T A DATE? WHY YOU SLIMY, TRICKY...
LOOK, LADY. DON'T GET ME WRONG. YOU'RE A SEXY NUMBER. BUT IT'S COLD IN SPACE, BABE.
AIN'T NO FRIENDS IN THIS UNIVERSE NO MORE. GET USED TO IT AND YOU MIGHT EVEN MAKE YOUR WAY OFF THIS DEAD ROCK.
YOU'RE WRONG. ME AND MY GANG ARE PROOF.
REALLY? ZED DOUBLE CROSSED YOU. BILLY'S UNSTABLE. TOMMY2 MAY BE LOYAL, BUT HE'S JUST DUMB MUSCLE.
WATCH YOUR MOUTH.

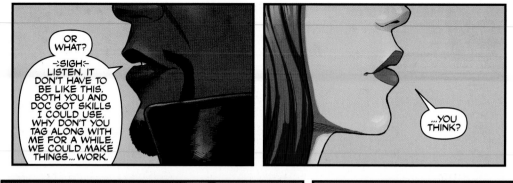

OR WHAT?

~SIGH~ LISTEN. IT DON'T HAVE TO BE LIKE THIS. BOTH YOU AND DOC GOT SKILLS I COULD USE. WHY DON'T YOU TAG ALONG WITH ME FOR A WHILE. WE COULD MAKE THINGS... WORK.

...YOU THINK?

SLAP

NICE PULL. DIDN'T EVEN FEEL YOU TAKE MY GUN. NOW BE A GOOD GIRL AND --

I'M GOING TO SAVE MY FRIENDS FIRST. IF YOU'RE STILL HERE WHEN I GET BACK, I'LL CONSIDER YOUR OFFER.

BY THE WAY, THE GALACTIC COPS ARE HERE. GOOD LUCK WITH THAT.

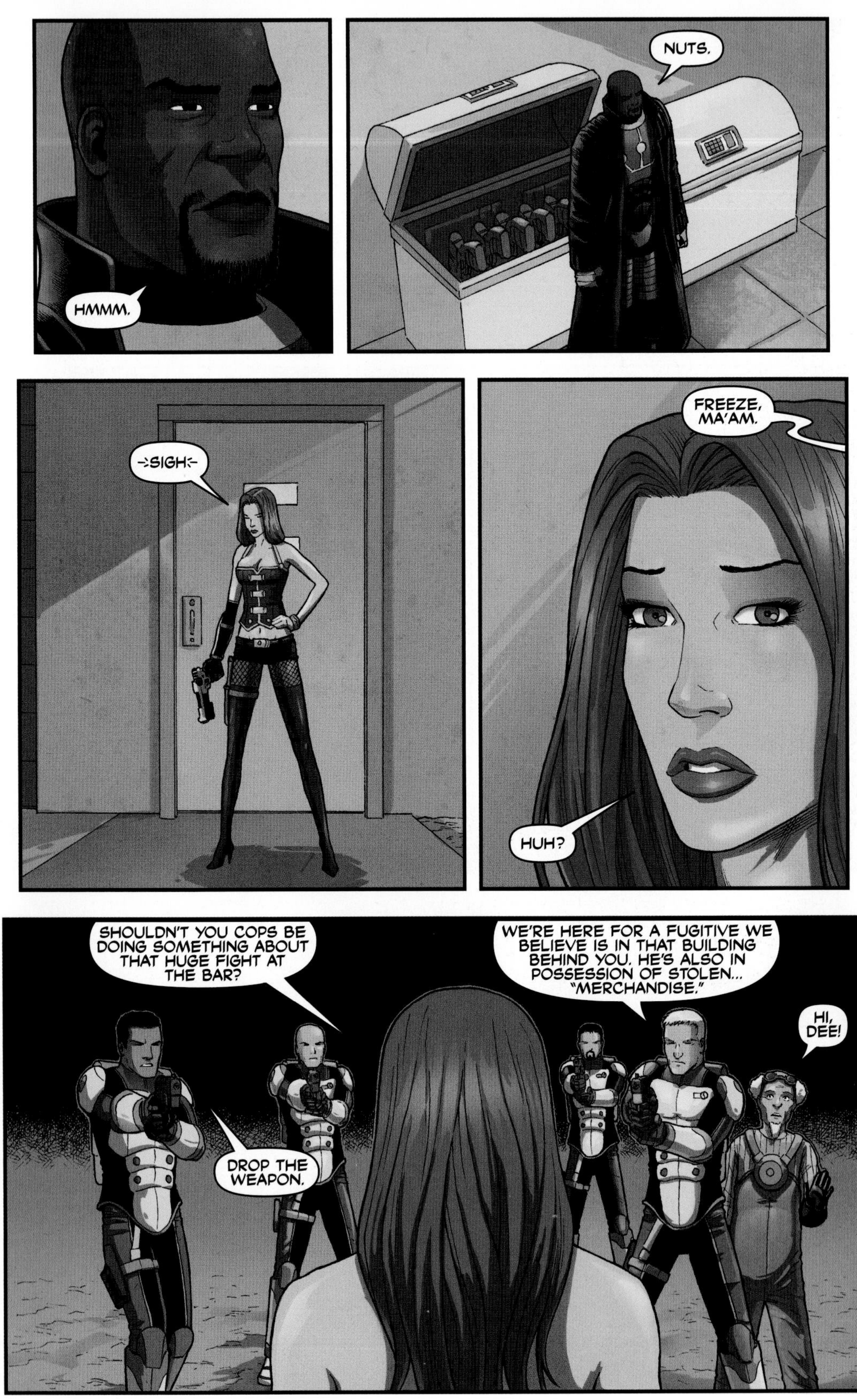
HMMM.
NUTS.
-:SIGH:-
FREEZE, MA'AM.
HUH?
SHOULDN'T YOU COPS BE DOING SOMETHING ABOUT THAT HUGE FIGHT AT THE BAR?
DROP THE WEAPON.
WE'RE HERE FOR A FUGITIVE WE BELIEVE IS IN THAT BUILDING BEHIND YOU. HE'S ALSO IN POSSESSION OF STOLEN... "MERCHANDISE."
HI, DEE!

MA'AM, I REPEAT. DROP THE WEAPON.
HE'S IN THERE, ISN'T HE?
YOU COPS SUCK. PEOPLE ARE DYING OVER THERE AND YOU'VE GOT THE FIREPOWER TO STOP IT!
FIND OUT YOURSELF, SOLDIER BOY.
YOU HAVE HIS GUN. IS HE ARMED?
THIS IS YOUR LAST WARNING. DROP THE WEAPON.
SCREW YOU, PIG!
YOU SHOULDN'T HAVE SAID THAT. I'M ENDING THIS.
CLICK
CLACK
WHHHOOOOSSHH
YEAGGGHHHH!
SMITHSON!

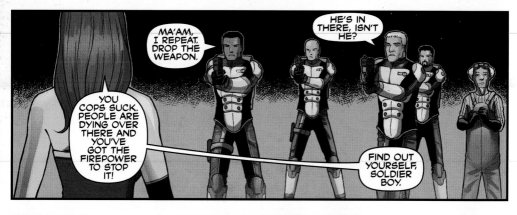

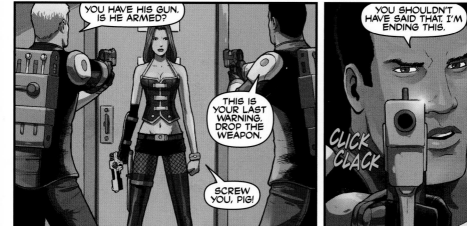

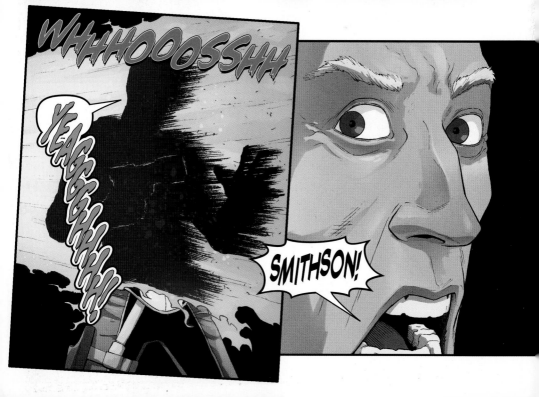

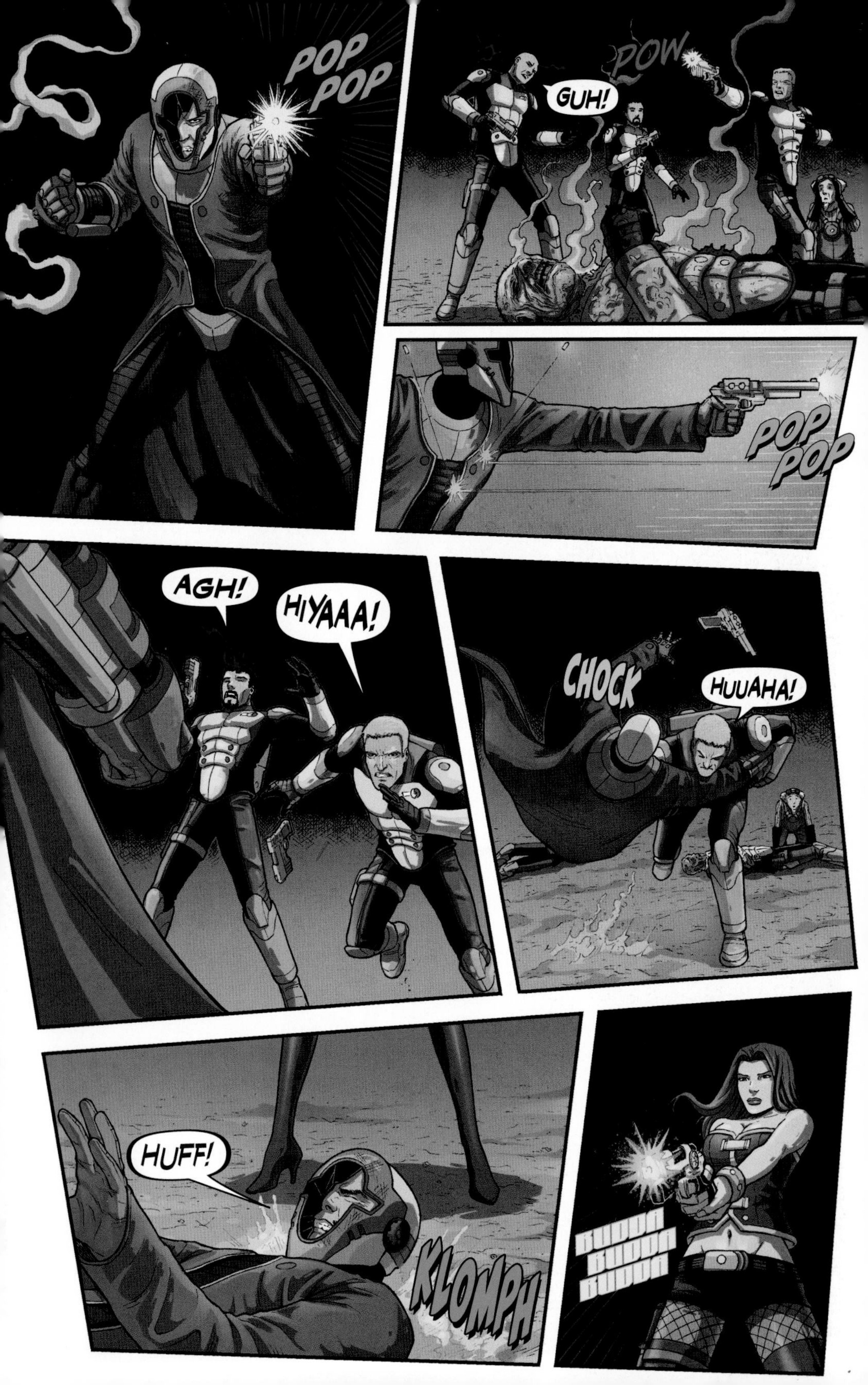
POP
POP
POW
GUH!
POP
POP
AGH!
HIYAAA!
CHOCK
HUUAHA!
HUFF!
KLOMPH
BUDDA
BUDDA
BUDDA

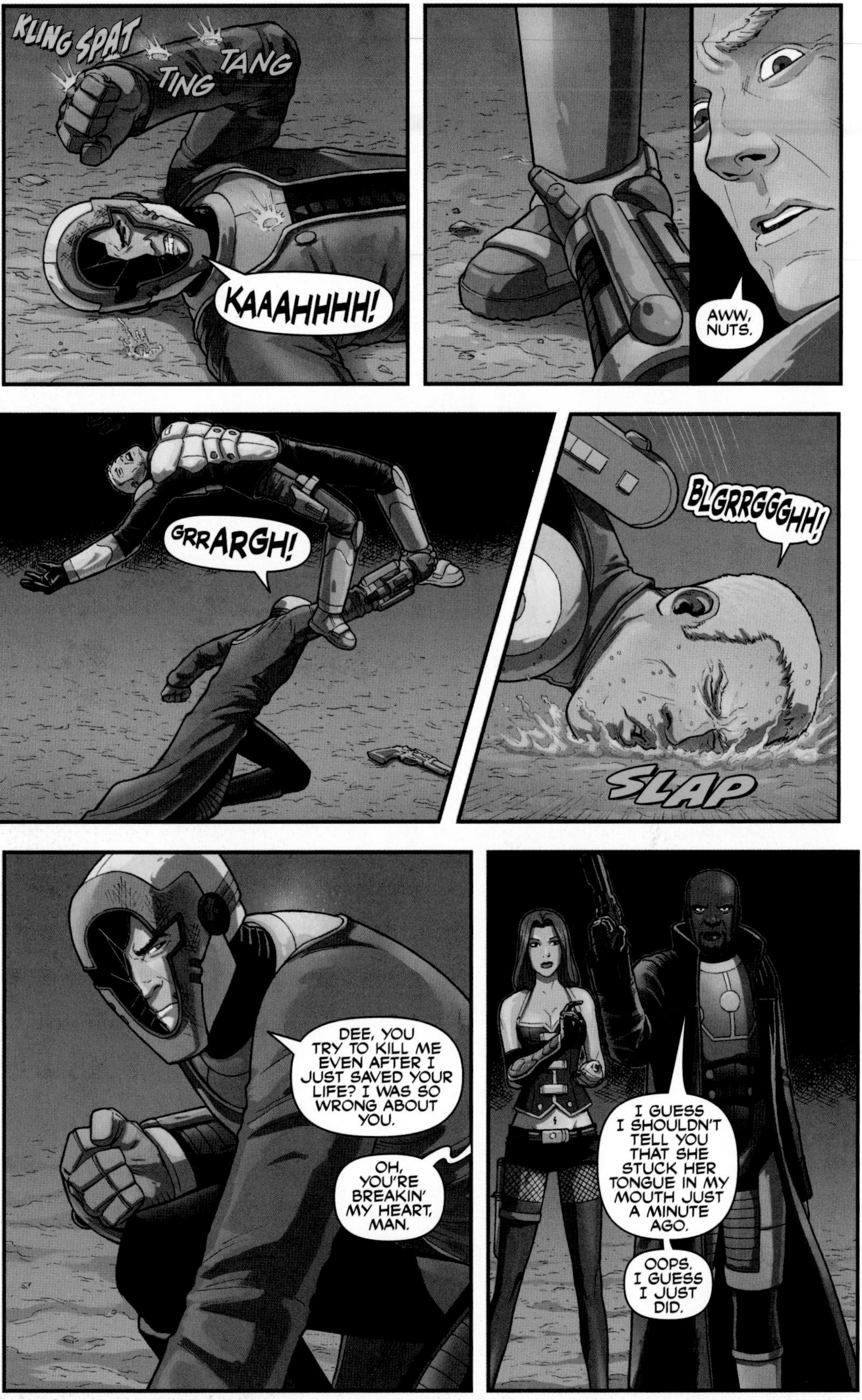
KLING SPAT
TING
TANG
KAAAHHHH!
AWW, NUTS.
GRRARGH!
BLGRRGGGHH!
SLAP
DEE, YOU TRY TO KILL ME EVEN AFTER I JUST SAVED YOUR LIFE? I WAS SO WRONG ABOUT YOU.
OH, YOU'RE BREAKIN' MY HEART, MAN.
I GUESS I SHOULDN'T TELL YOU THAT SHE STUCK HER TONGUE IN MY MOUTH JUST A MINUTE AGO.
OOPS. I GUESS I JUST DID.

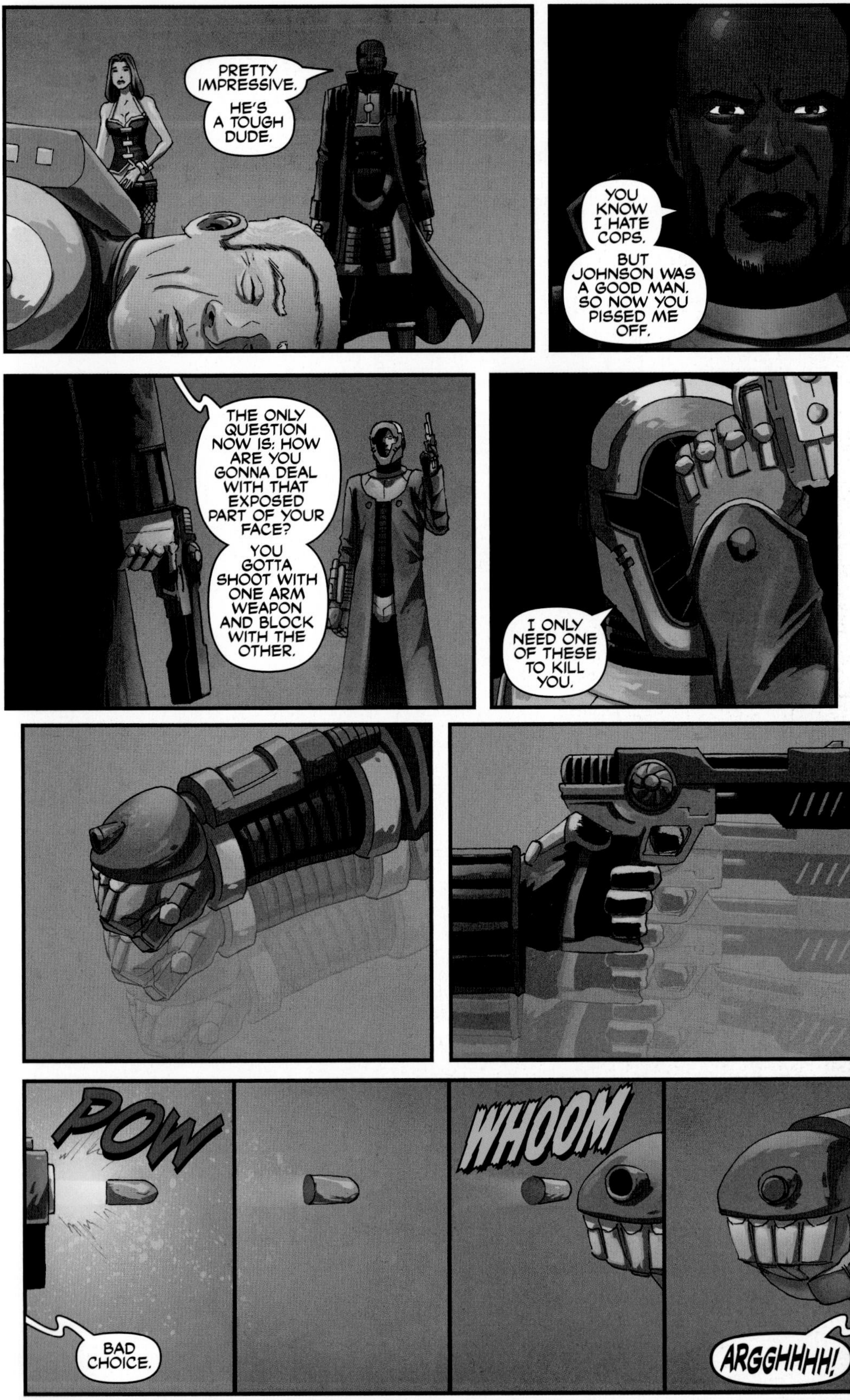
PRETTY IMPRESSIVE.
HE'S A TOUGH DUDE.
YOU KNOW I HATE COPS.
BUT JOHNSON WAS A GOOD MAN. SO NOW YOU PISSED ME OFF.
THE ONLY QUESTION NOW IS: HOW ARE YOU GONNA DEAL WITH THAT EXPOSED PART OF YOUR FACE?
YOU GOTTA SHOOT WITH ONE ARM WEAPON AND BLOCK WITH THE OTHER.
I ONLY NEED ONE OF THESE TO KILL YOU.
POW
BAD CHOICE.
WHOOM
ARGGHHHH!

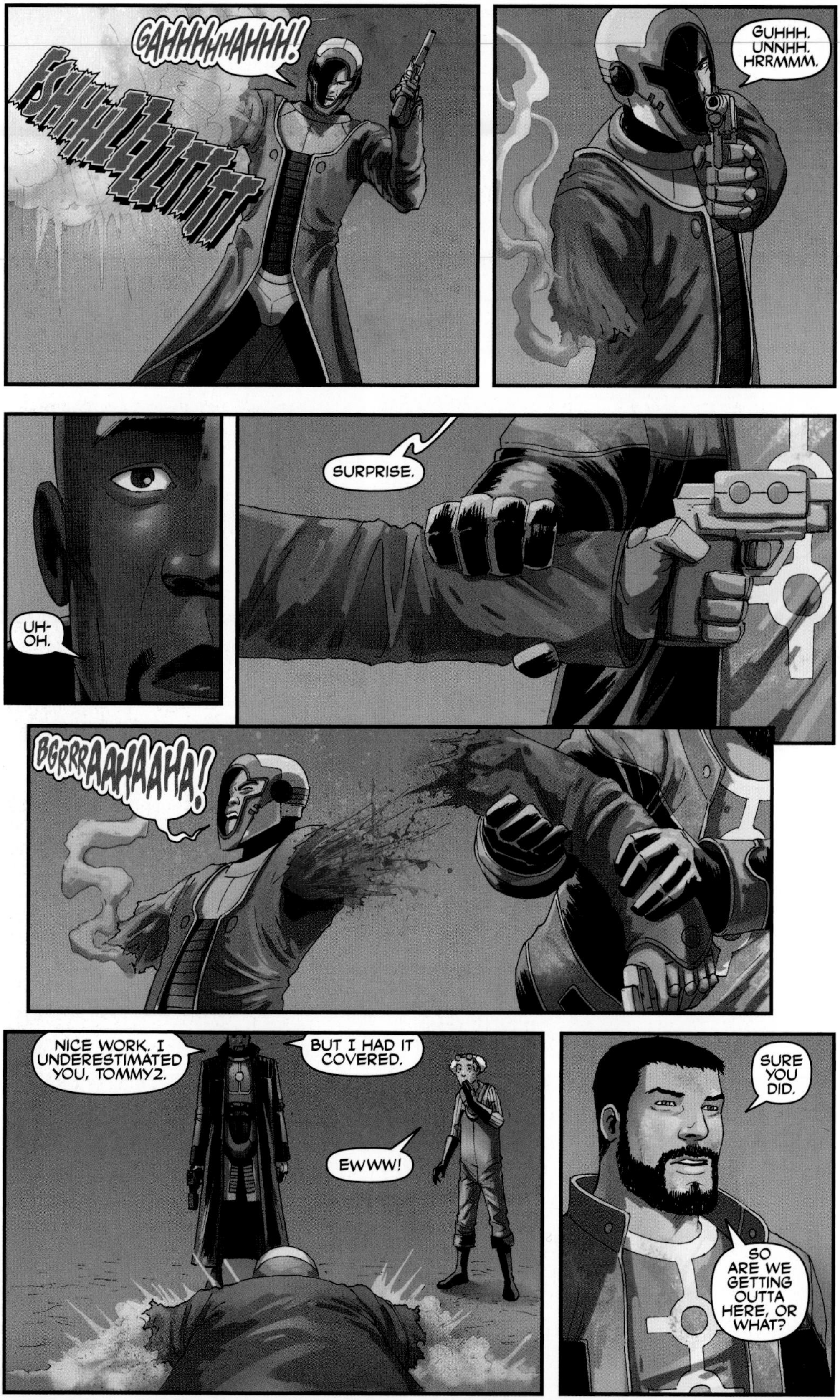
GAHHHHAHHH!
FSHHHZZZTTTT
GUHHH. UNNH. HRRMMM.
UH-OH.
SURPRISE.
BGRRRAAHAAHA!
NICE WORK. I UNDERESTIMATED YOU, TOMMY2.
BUT I HAD IT COVERED.
EWWW!
SURE YOU DID.
SO ARE WE GETTING OUTTA HERE, OR WHAT?

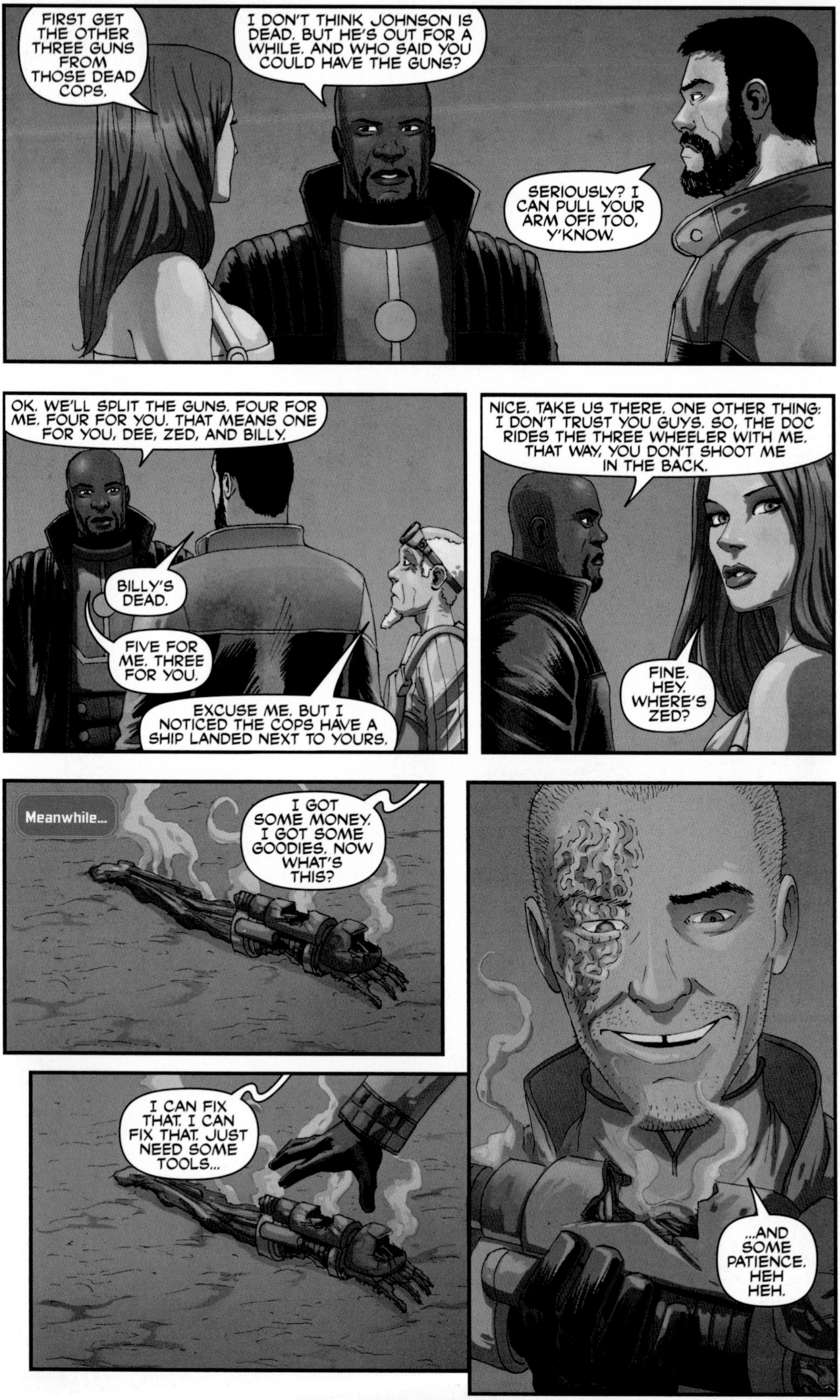
FIRST GET THE OTHER THREE GUNS FROM THOSE DEAD COPS.
I DON'T THINK JOHNSON IS DEAD. BUT HE'S OUT FOR A WHILE. AND WHO SAID YOU COULD HAVE THE GUNS?
SERIOUSLY? I CAN PULL YOUR ARM OFF TOO, Y'KNOW.
OK. WE'LL SPLIT THE GUNS. FOUR FOR ME. FOUR FOR YOU. THAT MEANS ONE FOR YOU, DEE, ZED, AND BILLY.
BILLY'S DEAD.
FIVE FOR ME. THREE FOR YOU.
EXCUSE ME. BUT I NOTICED THE COPS HAVE A SHIP LANDED NEXT TO YOURS.
NICE. TAKE US THERE. ONE OTHER THING: I DON'T TRUST YOU GUYS. SO, THE DOC RIDES THE THREE WHEELER WITH ME. THAT WAY, YOU DON'T SHOOT ME IN THE BACK.
FINE. HEY. WHERE'S ZED?
Meanwhile...
I GOT SOME MONEY. I GOT SOME GOODIES. NOW WHAT'S THIS?
I CAN FIX THAT. I CAN FIX THAT. JUST NEED SOME TOOLS...
...AND SOME PATIENCE. HEH HEH.

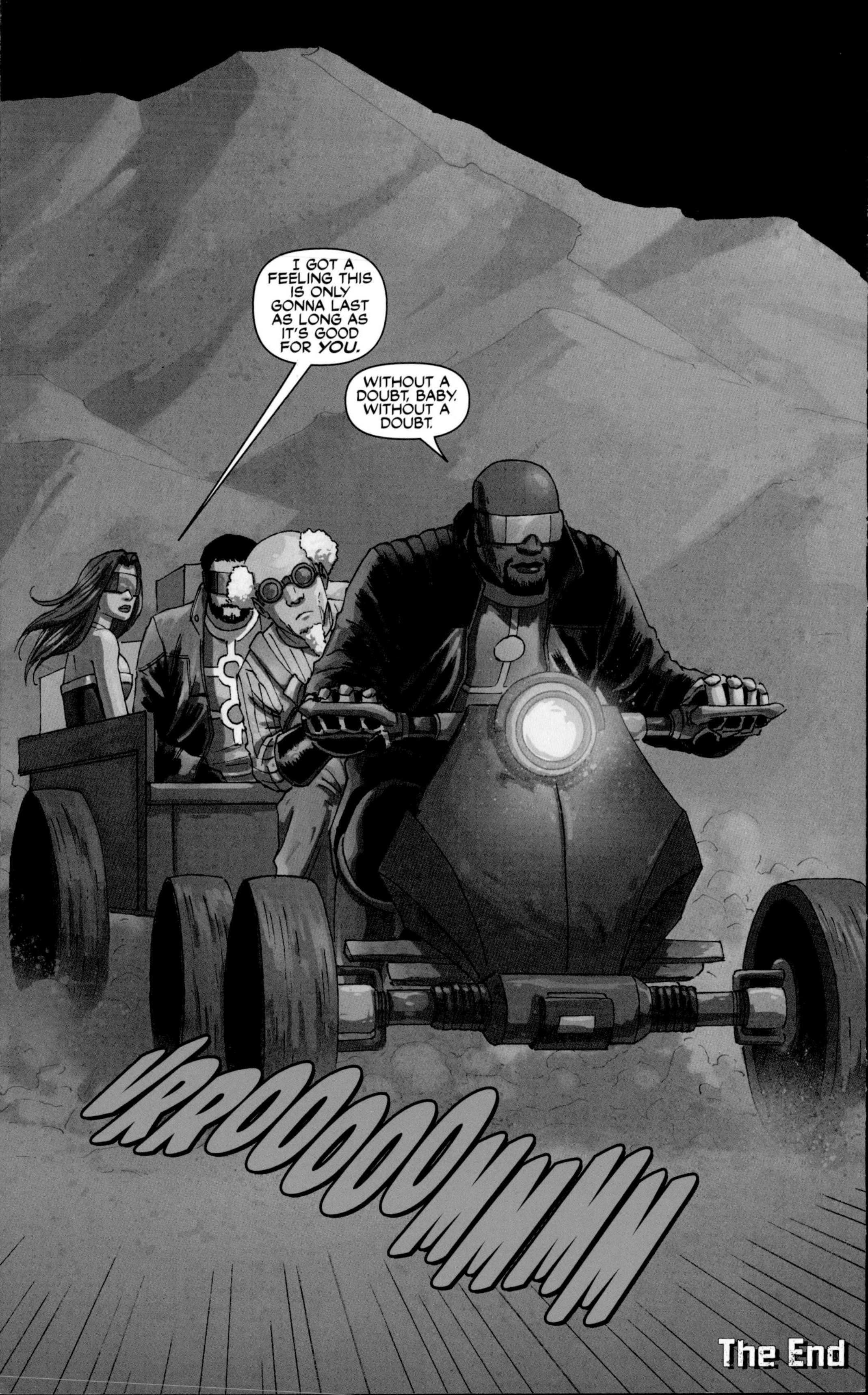
I GOT A FEELING THIS IS ONLY GONNA LAST AS LONG AS IT'S GOOD FOR **YOU.**
WITHOUT A DOUBT, BABY. WITHOUT A DOUBT.
VROOOOOOMMMMN

The End

COVER GALLERY

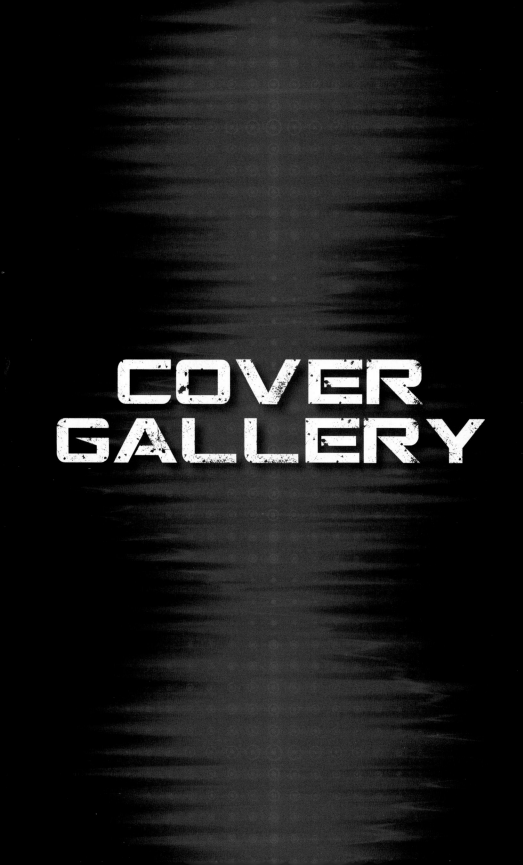

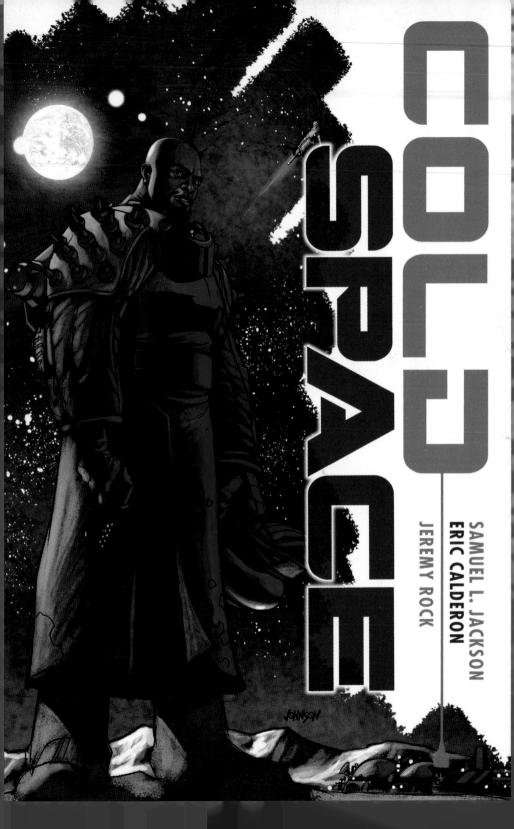

COLD SPACE

SAMUEL L. JACKSON
ERIC CALDERON

JEREMY ROCK

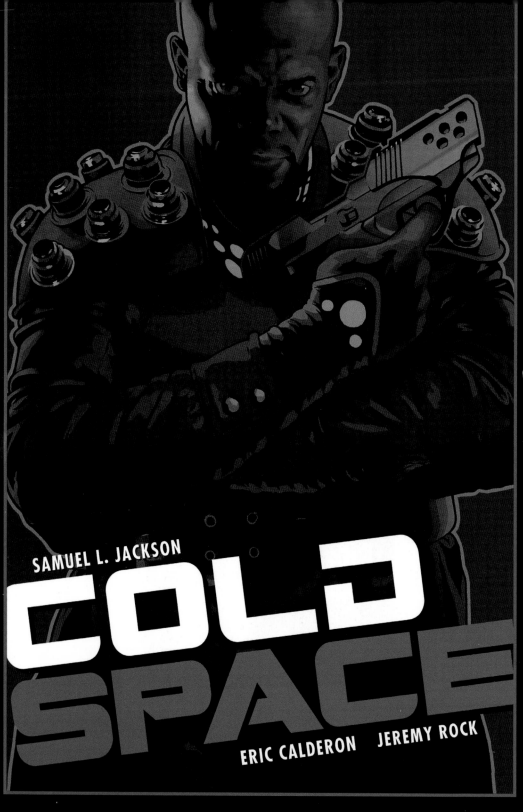

SAMUEL L. JACKSON

COLD SPACE

ERIC CALDERON   JEREMY ROCK

COVER 1B: JEFFREY SPOKES

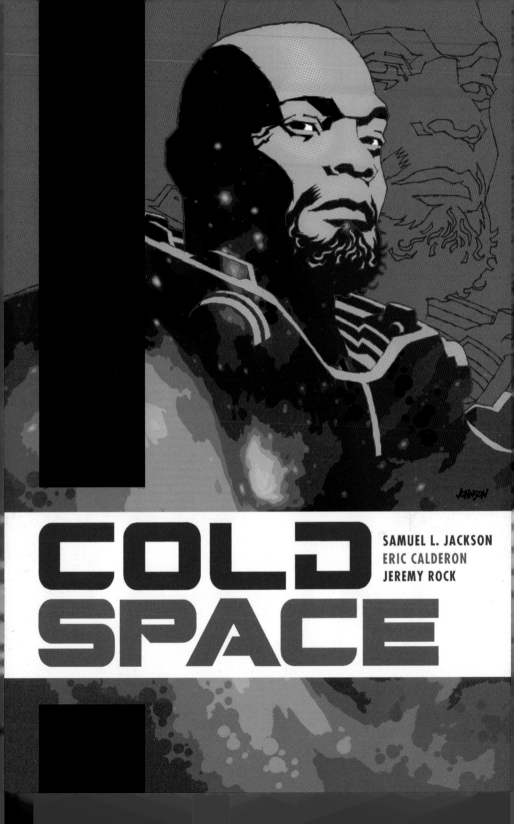

COLD
SPACE

SAMUEL L. JACKSON
ERIC CALDERON
JEREMY ROCK

Ross Richie - Chief Executive Officer

Mark Waid - Chief Creative Officer

Matt Gagnon - Editor-in-Chief

Adam Fortier - VP-New Business

Wes Harris - VP-Publishing

Lance Kreiter - VP-Licensing & Merchandising

Chip Mosher - Marketing Director

Bryce Carlson - Managing Editor

Ian Brill - Editor

Dafna Pleban - Editor

Christopher Burns - Editor

Christopher Meyer - Editor

Shannon Watters - Assistant Editor

Neil Loughrie - Publishing Coordinator

Travis Beaty - Traffic Coordinator

Ivan Salazar - Marketing Assistant

Kate Hayden - Executive Assistant

Brian Latimer - Graphic Designer

Erika Terriquez - Graphic Designer

A catalog record for this book is available from OCLC and on our website www.boom-studios.com on the Librarians page.

First Edition: October 2010

10 9 8 7 6 5 4 3 2 1

Printed in U.S.A.

SAMUEL L. JACKSON

COLD
SPACE

ERIC CALDERON JEREMY ROCK